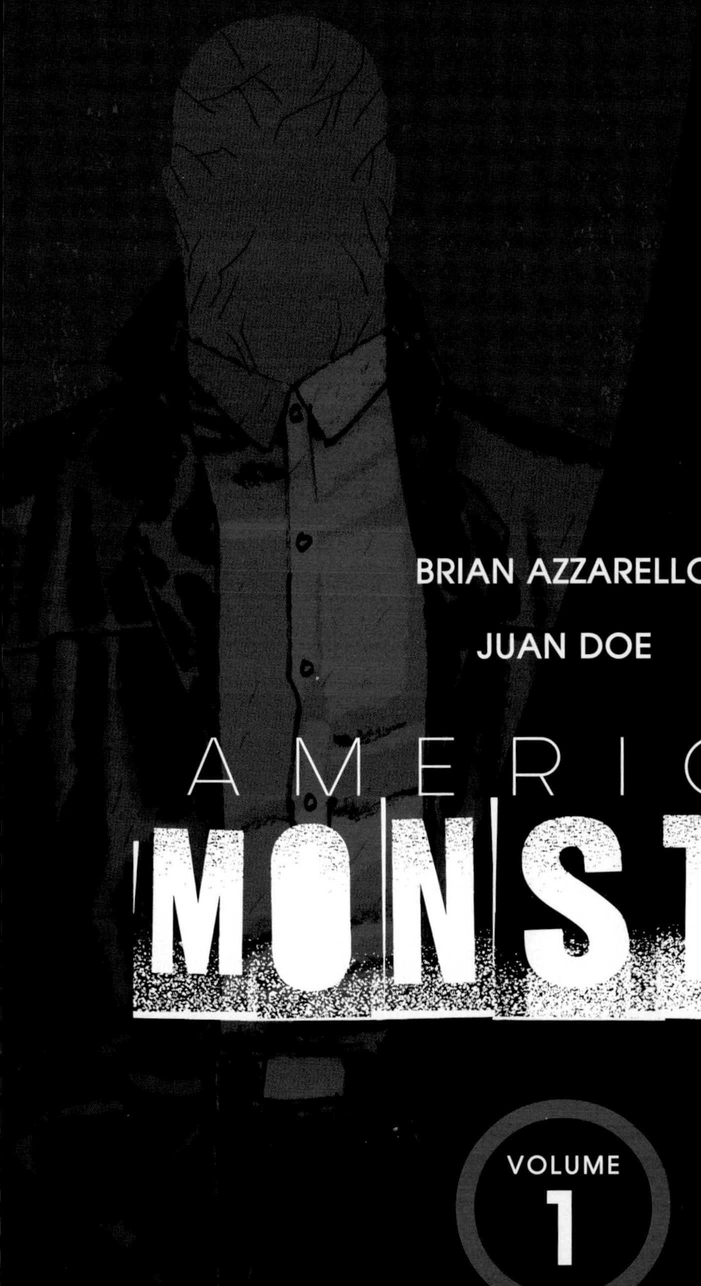

BRIAN AZZARELLO

JUAN DOE

AMERICAN MONSTER

VOLUME
1

SWEETLAND

AFTERSHOCK

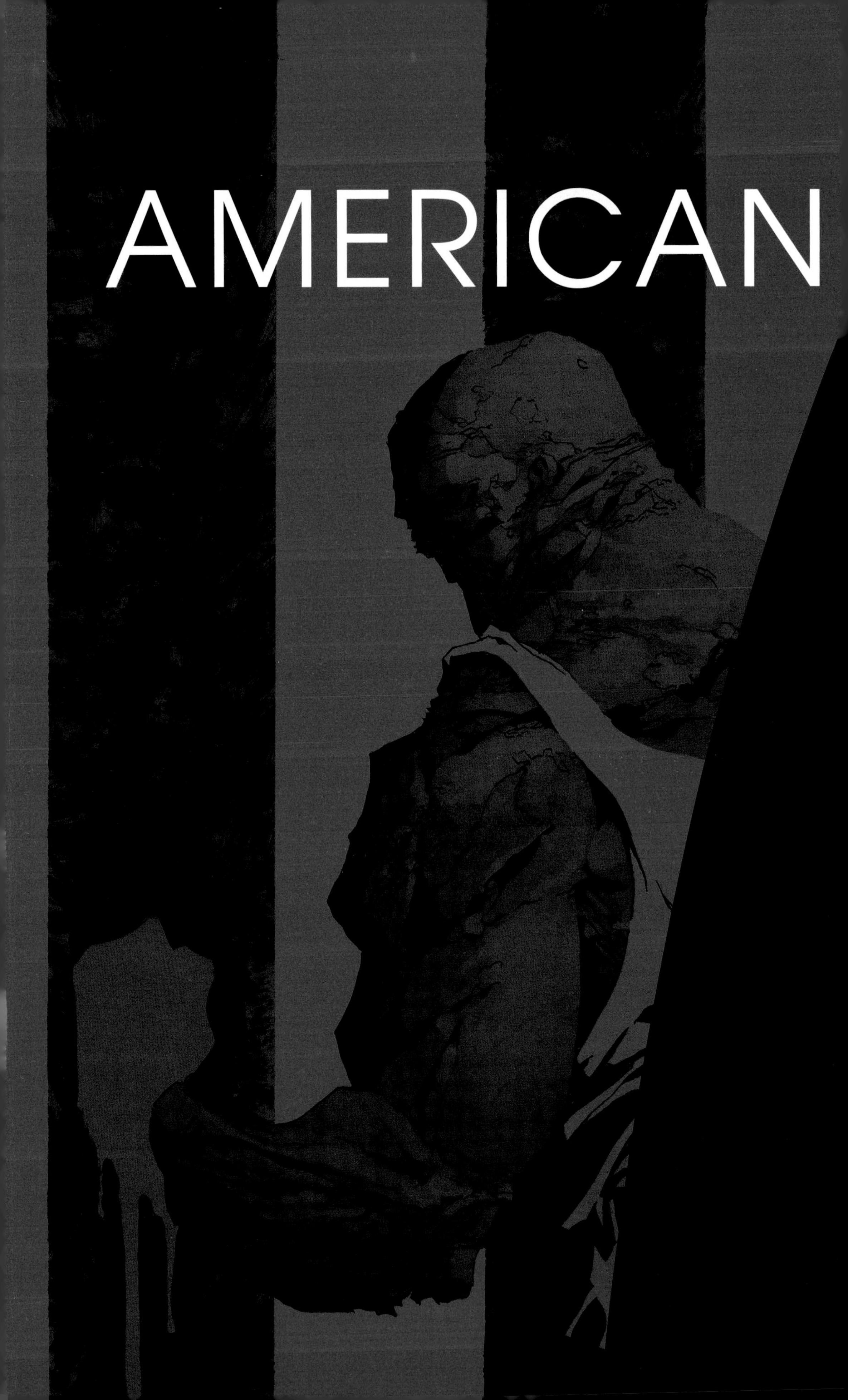
AMERICAN

MONSTER

VOLUME 1

SWEETLAND

BRIAN AZZARELLO creator & writer

JUAN DOE artist, colorist & letterer

JUAN DOE front cover

JUAN DOE original series covers

STEVE EPTING, PHIL HESTER,
DAVE JOHNSON & **ALEXIS ZIRITT** variant covers

JUAN DOE logo designer

JOHN J. HILL book designer

MIKE MARTS editor

AFTERSHOCK™

MIKE MARTS - Editor-in-Chief • JOE PRUETT - Publisher • LEE KRAMER - President
JAWAD QURESHI - SVP, Investor Relations • JON KRAMER - Chief Executive Officer
MIKE ZAGARI - SVP Digital/Creative • JAY BEHLING - Chief Financial Officer • MICHAEL RICHTER - Chief Creative Officer
STEPHAN NILSON - Publishing Operations Manager • LISA Y. WU - Social Media Coordinator

AfterShock Trade Dress and Interior Design by JOHN J. HILL
AfterShock Logo Design by COMICRAFT
Proofreading by J. HARBORE & DOCTOR Z.
Publicity: contact AARON MARION (aaron@fifteenminutes.com) &
RYAN CROY (ryan@fifteenminutes.com) at 15 MINUTES

First Printing: November 2016. 10 9 8 7 6 5 4 3 2 1

AFTERSHOCKCOMICS.COM Follow us on social media

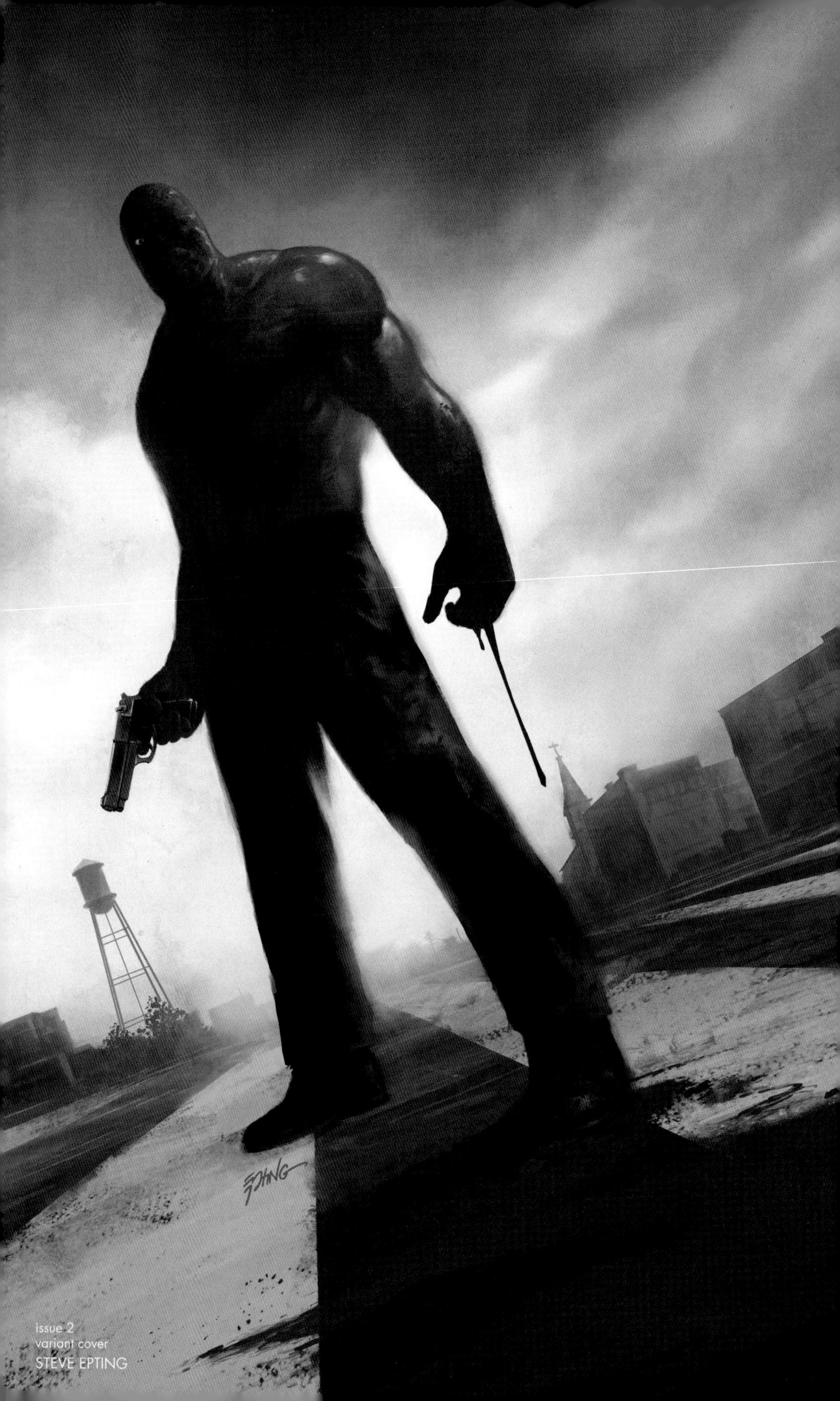

issue 2
variant cover
STEVE EPTING

1

"AMERICAN MONSTER"

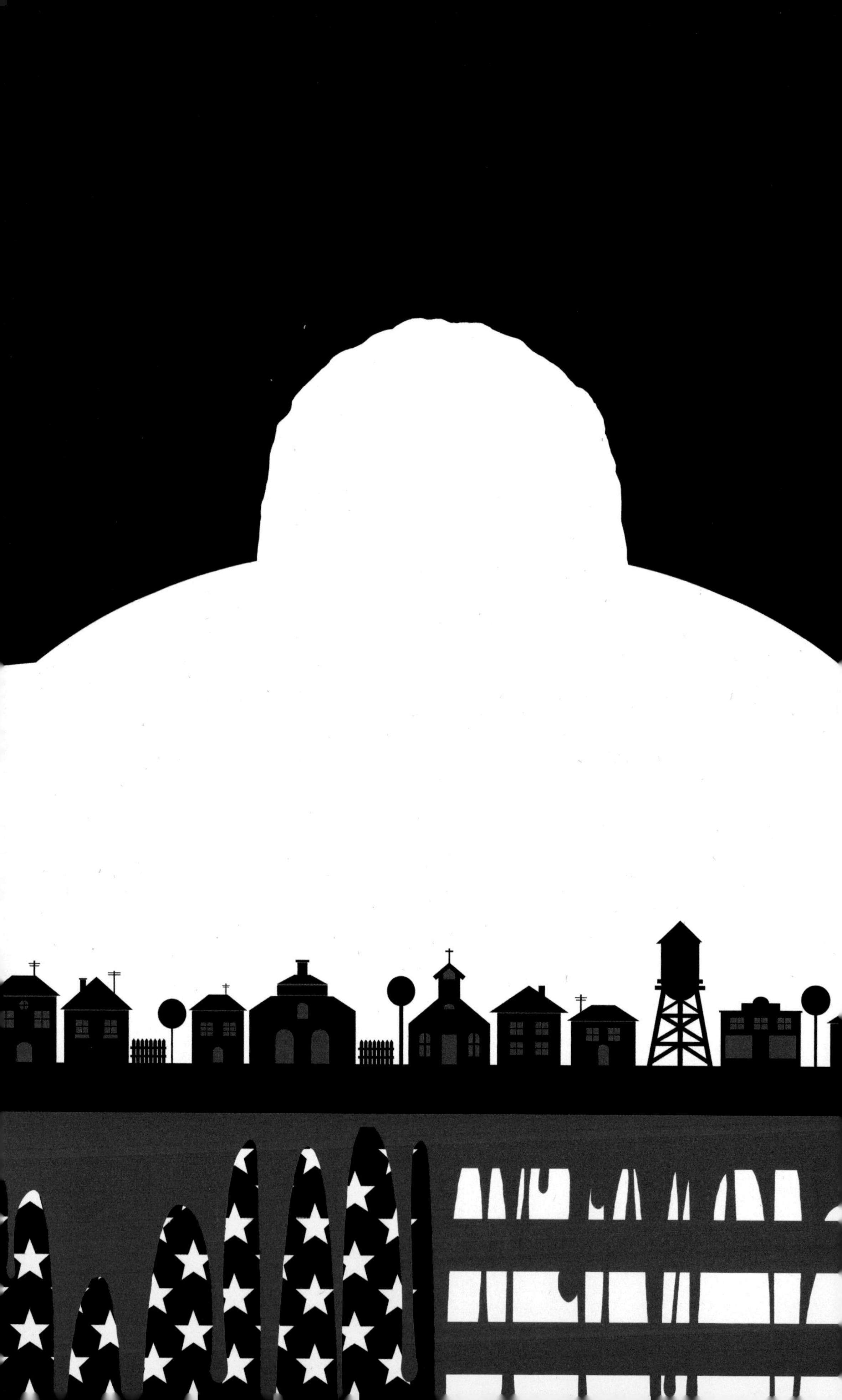

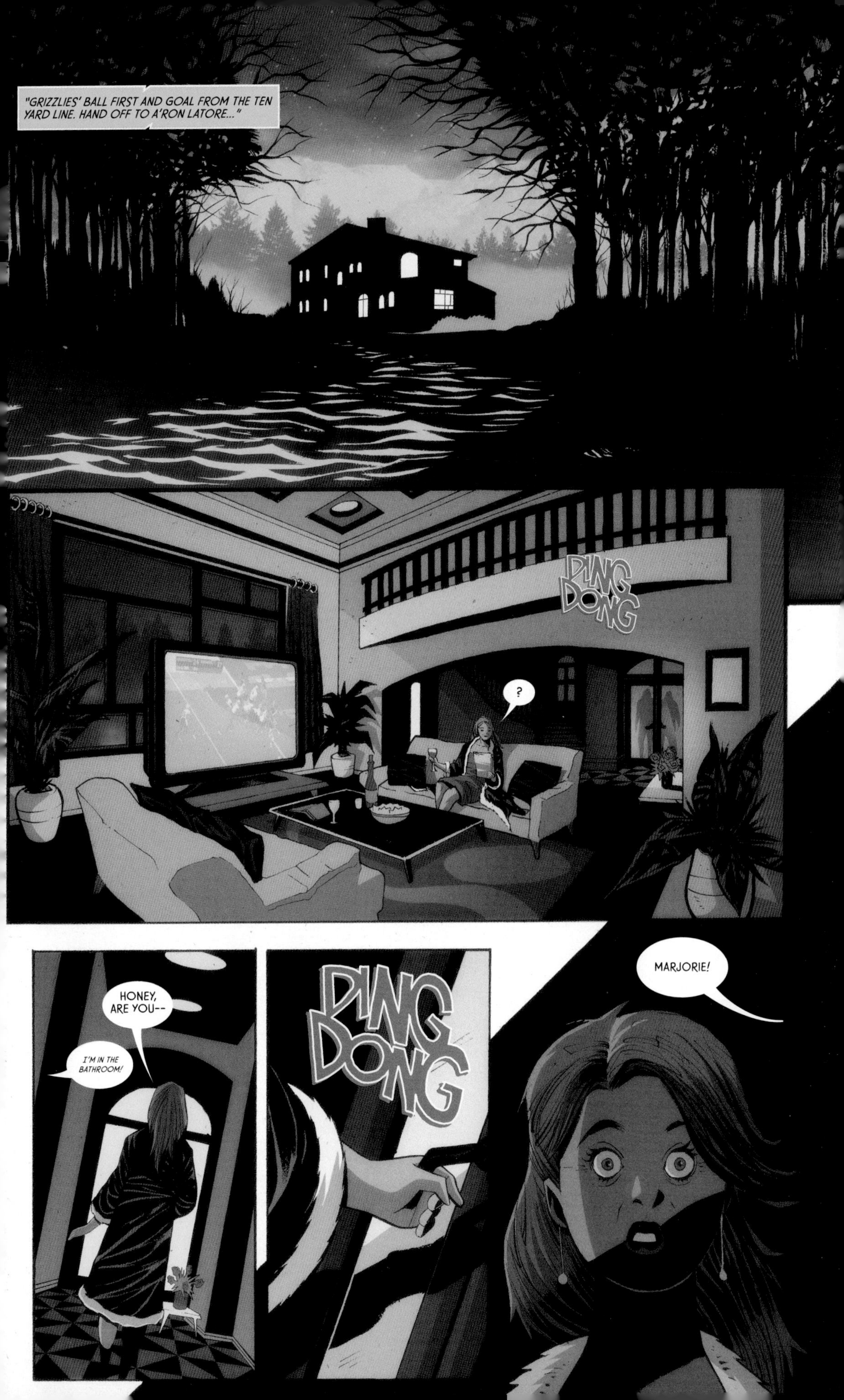
"GRIZZLIES' BALL FIRST AND GOAL FROM THE TEN YARD LINE. HAND OFF TO A'RON LATORE..."
DING DONG
?
HONEY, ARE YOU--
I'M IN THE BATHROOM!
DING DONG
MARJORIE!

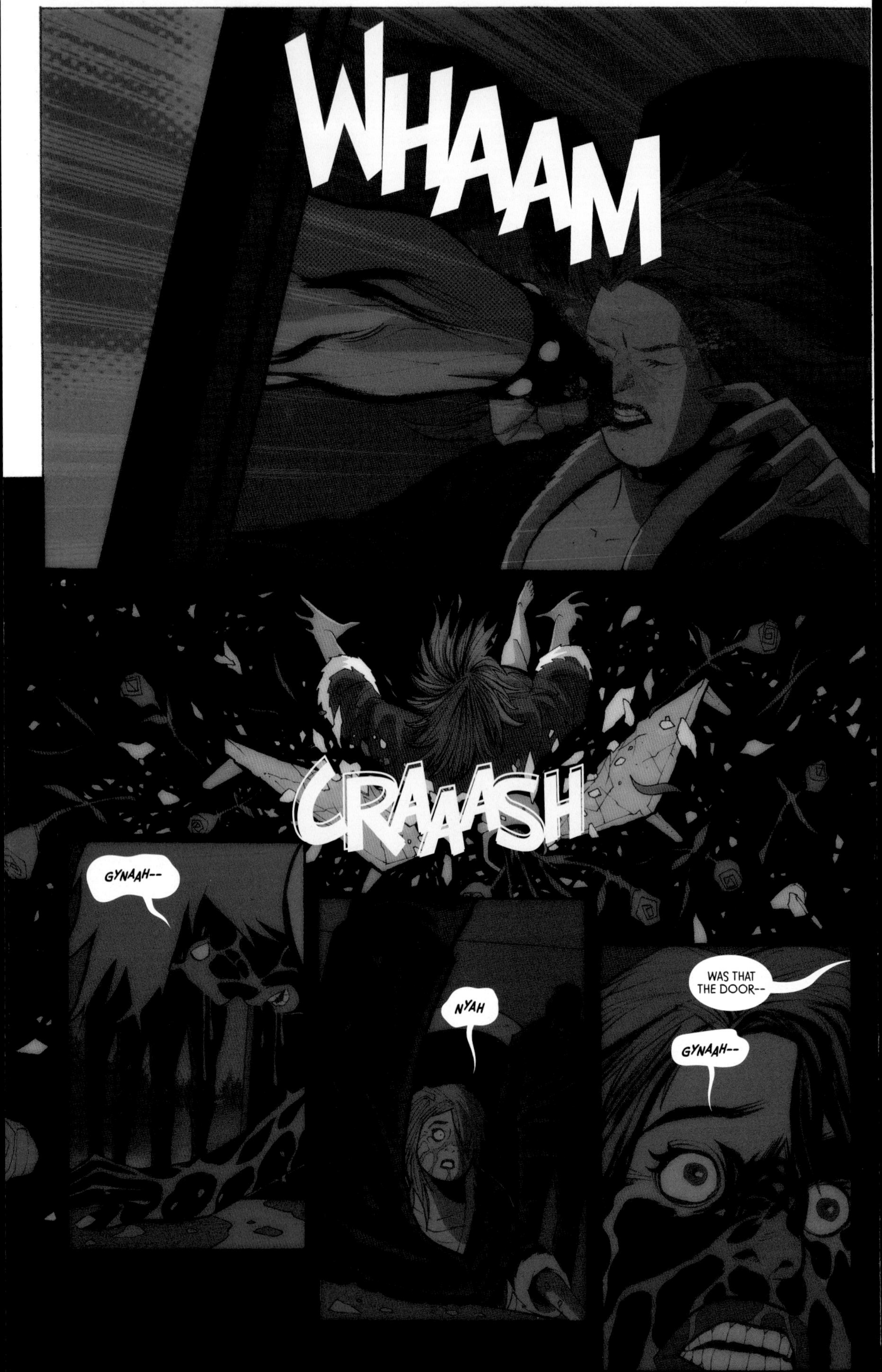
WHAAAM
CRAAASH
GYNAAH--
NYAH
WAS THAT THE DOOR--
GYNAAH--

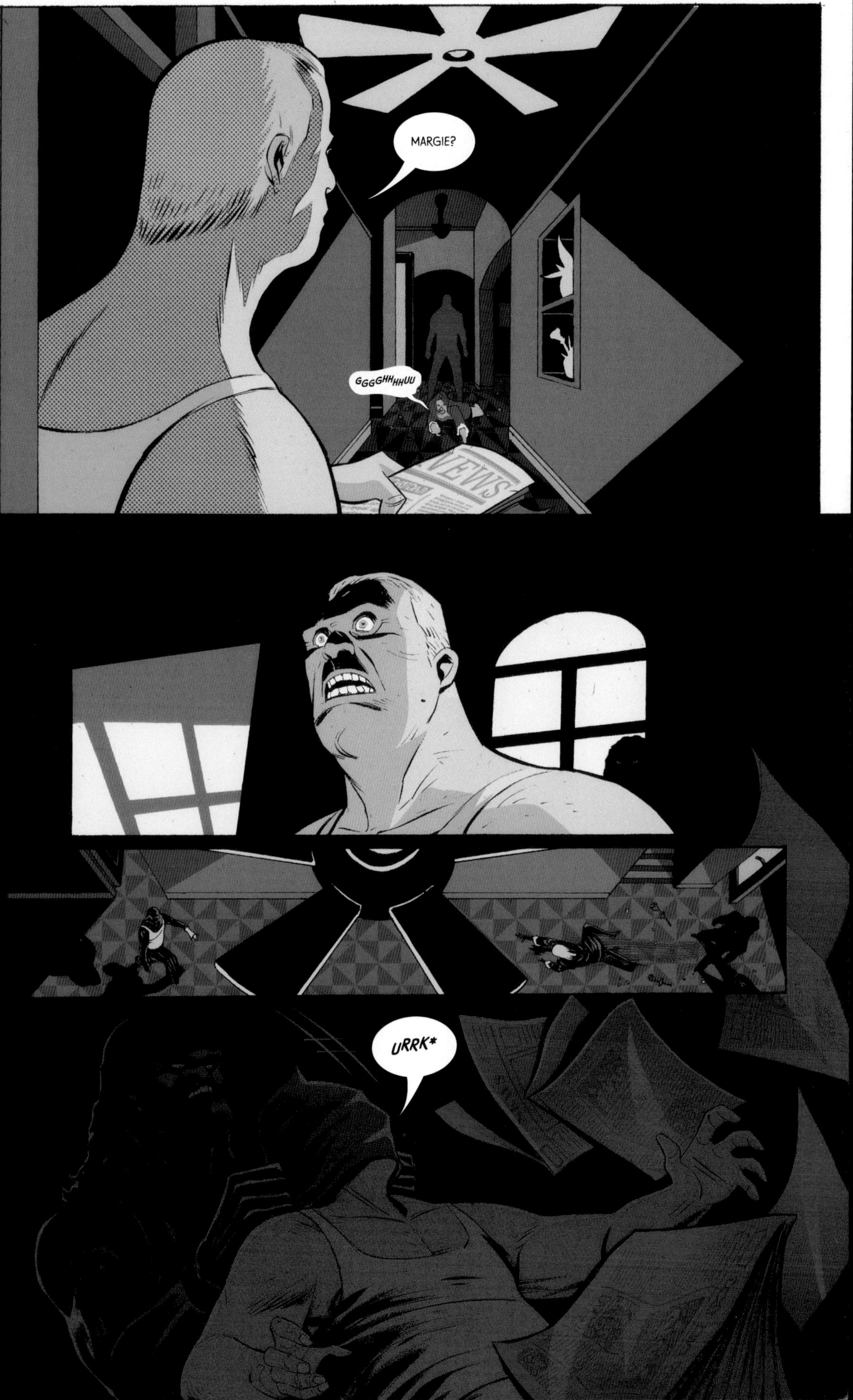
MARGIE?
GGGGHHHHUU
VEWS
URRK*

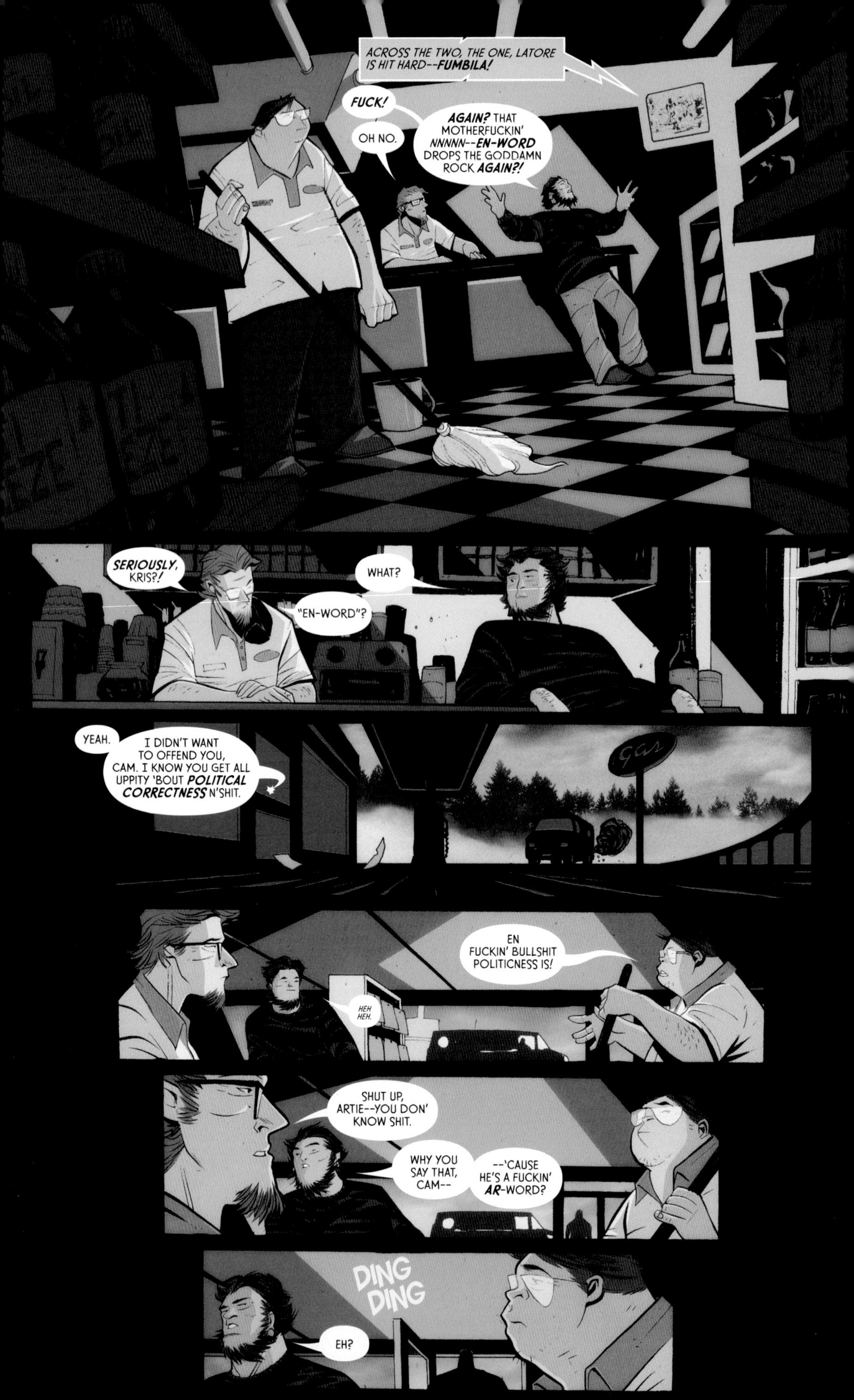

ACROSS THE TWO, THE ONE, LATORE IS HIT HARD--**FUMBILA!**
FUCK!
OH NO.
AGAIN? THAT MOTHERFUCKIN' *NNNNN*--**EN-WORD** DROPS THE GODDAMN ROCK **AGAIN?!**
SERIOUSLY, KRIS?!
WHAT?
"EN-WORD"?
YEAH.
I DIDN'T WANT TO OFFEND YOU, CAM. I KNOW YOU GET ALL UPPITY 'BOUT **POLITICAL CORRECTNESS** N'SHIT.
EN FUCKIN' BULLSHIT POLITICNESS IS!
HEH HEH.
SHUT UP, ARTIE--YOU DON' KNOW SHIT.
WHY YOU SAY THAT, CAM--
--'CAUSE HE'S A FUCKIN' **AR**-WORD?
DING DING
EH?

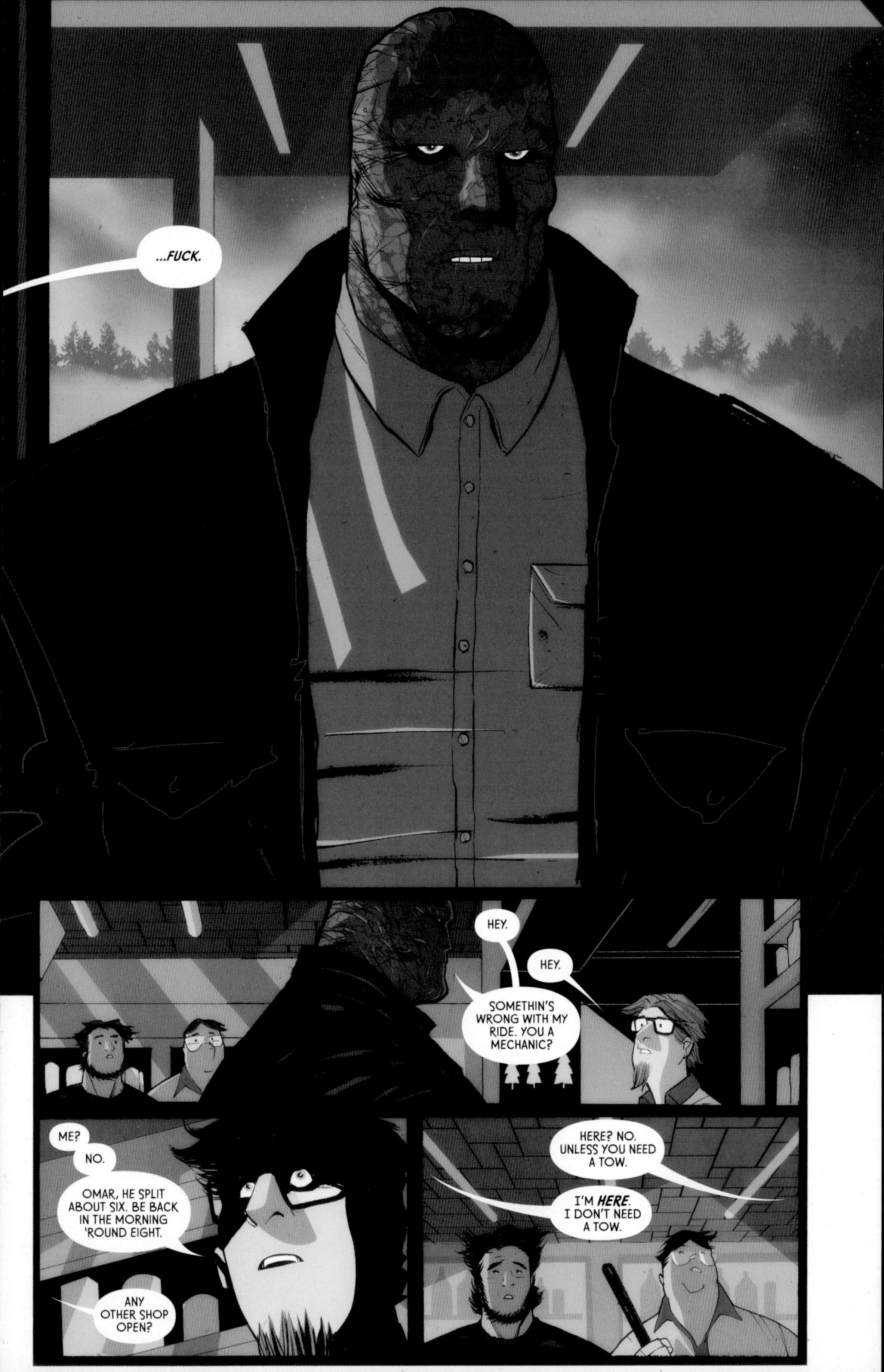
...FUCK.
HEY.
HEY.
SOMETHIN'S WRONG WITH MY RIDE. YOU A MECHANIC?
ME?
NO.
OMAR, HE SPLIT ABOUT SIX. BE BACK IN THE MORNING 'ROUND EIGHT.
ANY OTHER SHOP OPEN?
HERE? NO. UNLESS YOU NEED A TOW.
I'M *HERE*. I DON'T NEED A TOW.

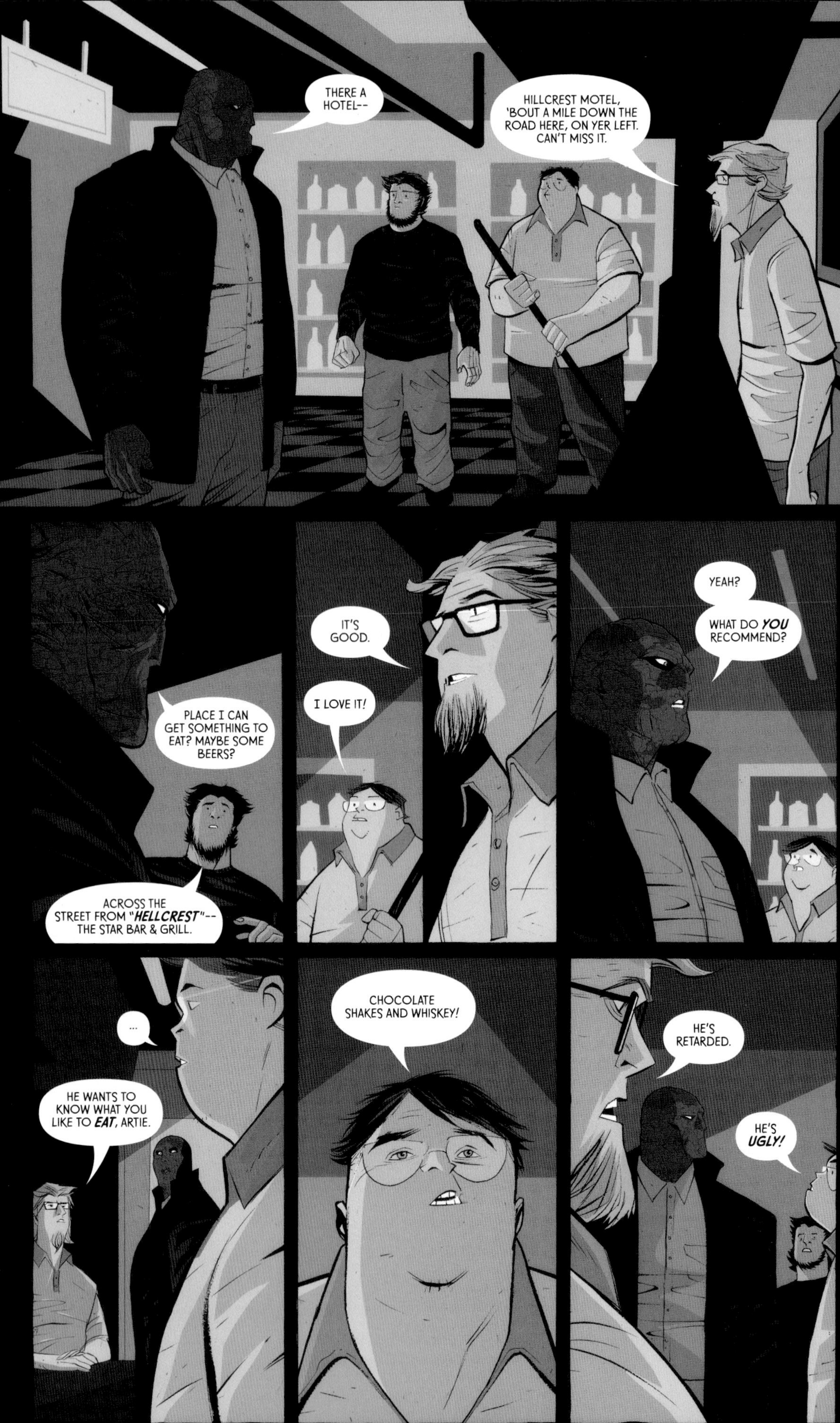
THERE A HOTEL--
HILLCREST MOTEL, 'BOUT A MILE DOWN THE ROAD HERE, ON YER LEFT. CAN'T MISS IT.
PLACE I CAN GET SOMETHING TO EAT? MAYBE SOME BEERS?
ACROSS THE STREET FROM "*HELLCREST*"-- THE STAR BAR & GRILL.
IT'S GOOD.
I LOVE IT!
YEAH?
WHAT DO *YOU* RECOMMEND?
...
HE WANTS TO KNOW WHAT YOU LIKE TO *EAT*, ARTIE.
CHOCOLATE SHAKES AND WHISKEY!
HE'S RETARDED.
HE'S *UGLY!*

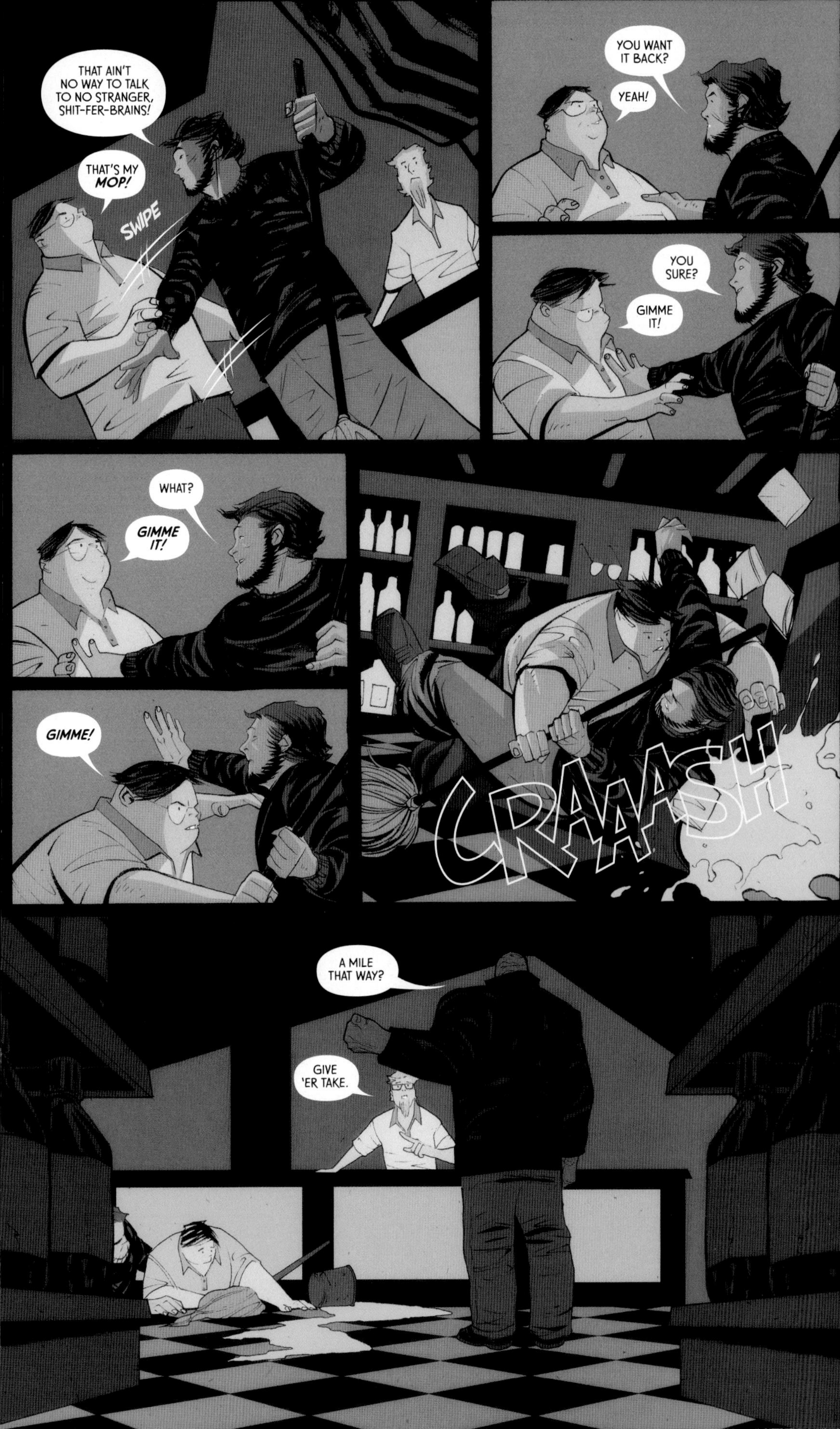

THAT AIN'T NO WAY TO TALK TO NO STRANGER, SHIT-FER-BRAINS!
THAT'S MY *MOP!*
SWIPE
YOU WANT IT BACK?
YEAH!
YOU SURE?
GIMME IT!
WHAT?
GIMME IT!
GIMME!
CRAAASH
A MILE THAT WAY?
GIVE 'ER TAKE.

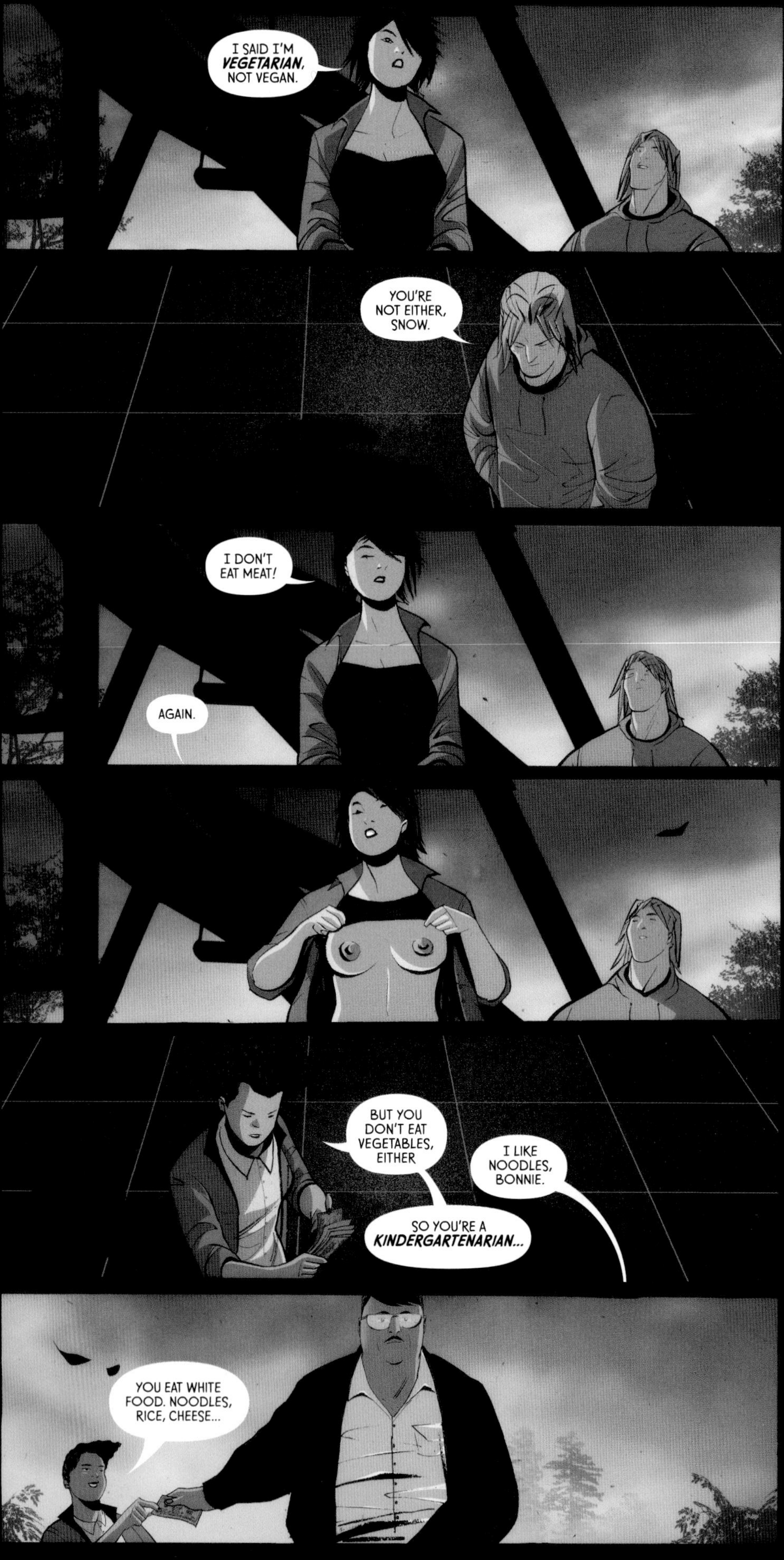
I SAID I'M **VEGETARIAN,** NOT VEGAN.
YOU'RE NOT EITHER, SNOW.
I DON'T EAT MEAT!
AGAIN.
BUT YOU DON'T EAT VEGETABLES, EITHER
SO YOU'RE A **KINDERGARTENARIAN...**
I LIKE NOODLES, BONNIE.
YOU EAT WHITE FOOD. NOODLES, RICE, CHEESE...

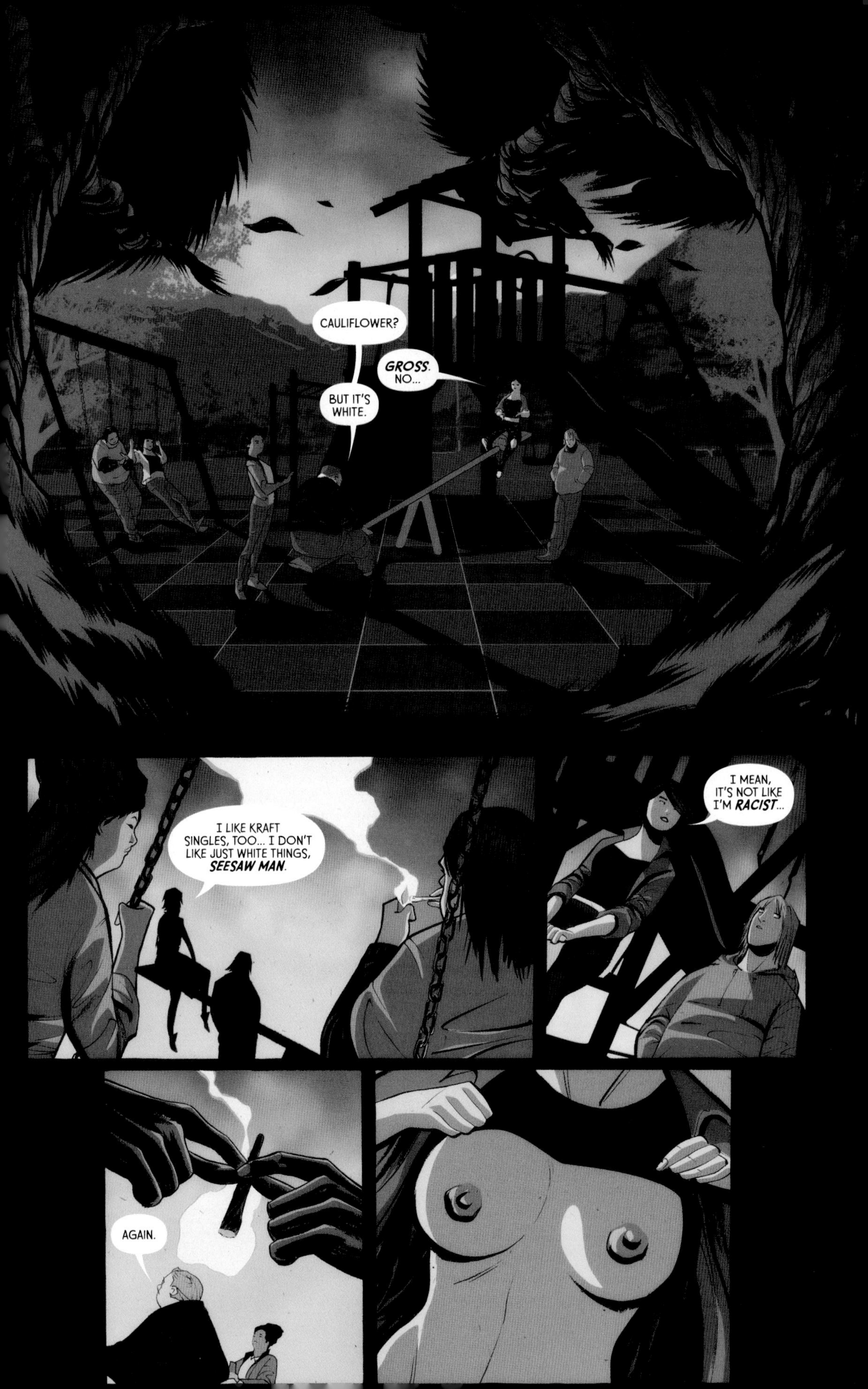
CAULIFLOWER?
GROSS. NO...
BUT IT'S WHITE.
I LIKE KRAFT SINGLES, TOO... I DON'T LIKE JUST WHITE THINGS, *SEESAW MAN*.
I MEAN, IT'S NOT LIKE I'M *RACIST*...
AGAIN.

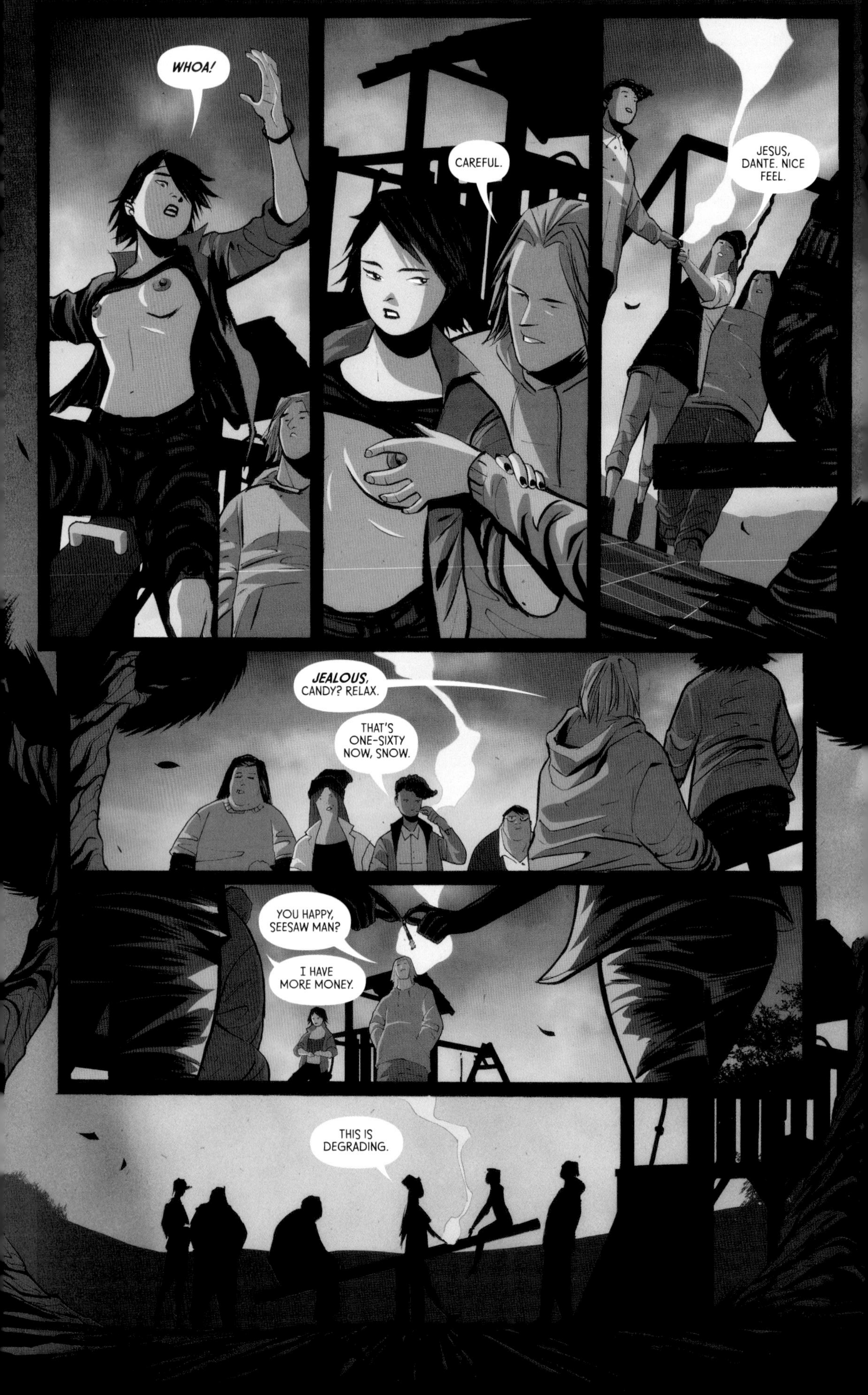
WHOA!
CAREFUL.
JESUS, DANTE. NICE FEEL.
JEALOUS, CANDY? RELAX.
THAT'S ONE-SIXTY NOW, SNOW.
YOU HAPPY, SEESAW MAN?
I HAVE MORE MONEY.
THIS IS DEGRADING.

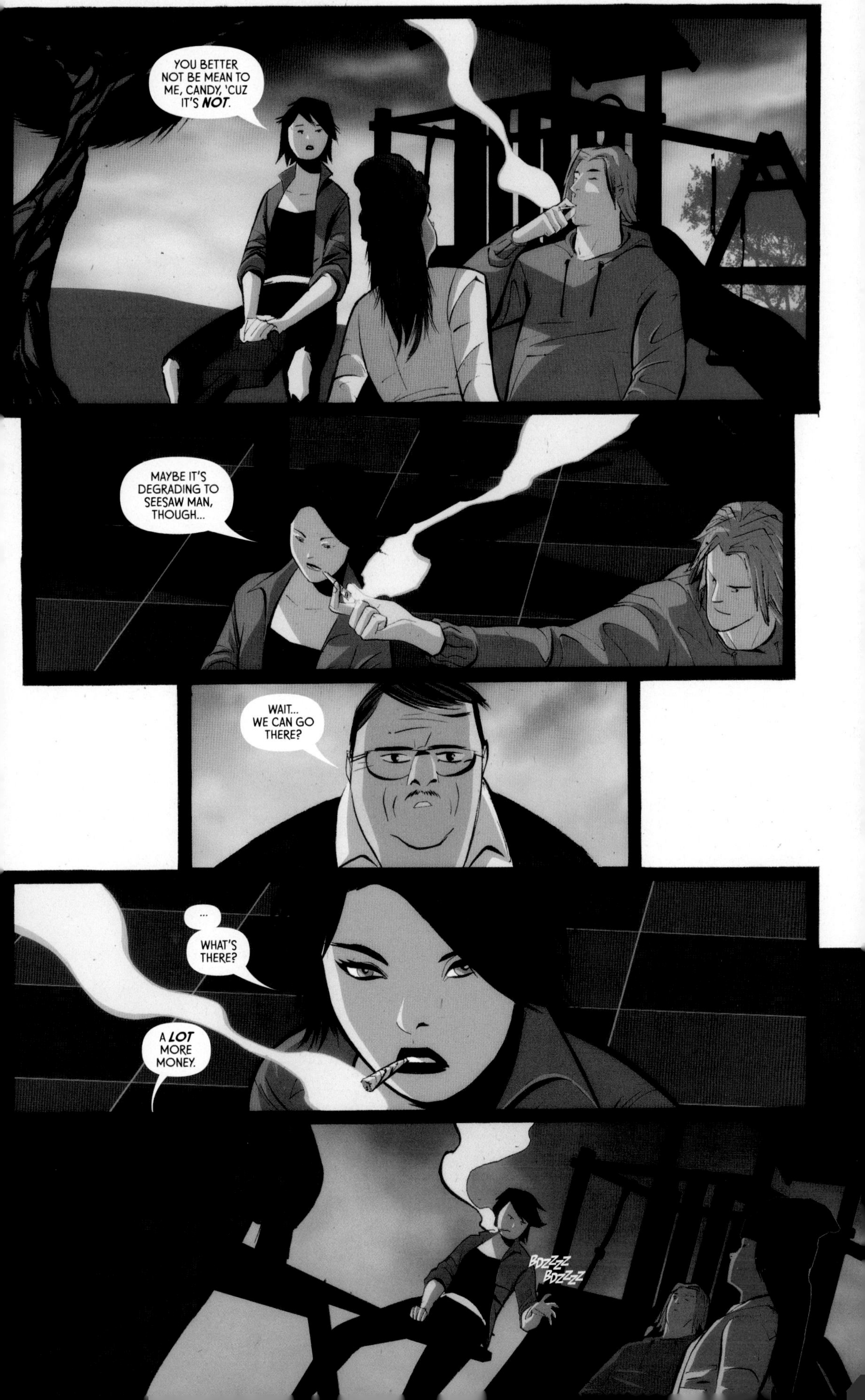
YOU BETTER NOT BE MEAN TO ME, CANDY, 'CUZ IT'S ***NOT***.
MAYBE IT'S DEGRADING TO SEESAW MAN, THOUGH...
WAIT... WE CAN GO THERE?
...
WHAT'S THERE?
A ***LOT*** MORE MONEY.
BDZZZZ BDZZZZ

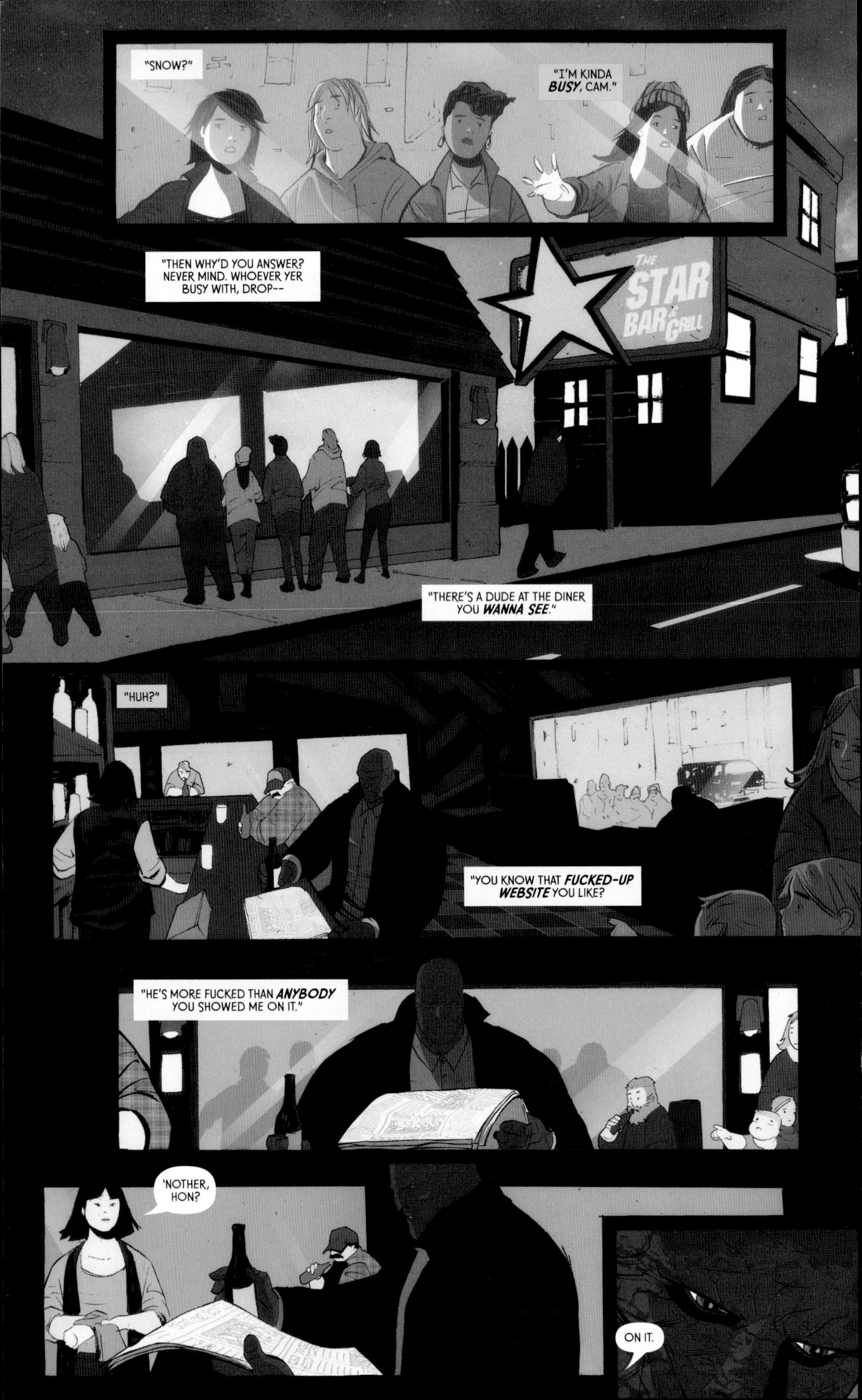
"SNOW?"
"I'M KINDA BUSY, CAM."
"THEN WHY'D YOU ANSWER? NEVER MIND. WHOEVER YER BUSY WITH, DROP--
THE STAR BAR & GRILL
"THERE'S A DUDE AT THE DINER YOU WANNA SEE."
"HUH?"
"YOU KNOW THAT FUCKED-UP WEBSITE YOU LIKE?
"HE'S MORE FUCKED THAN ANYBODY YOU SHOWED ME ON IT."
'NOTHER, HON?
ON IT.

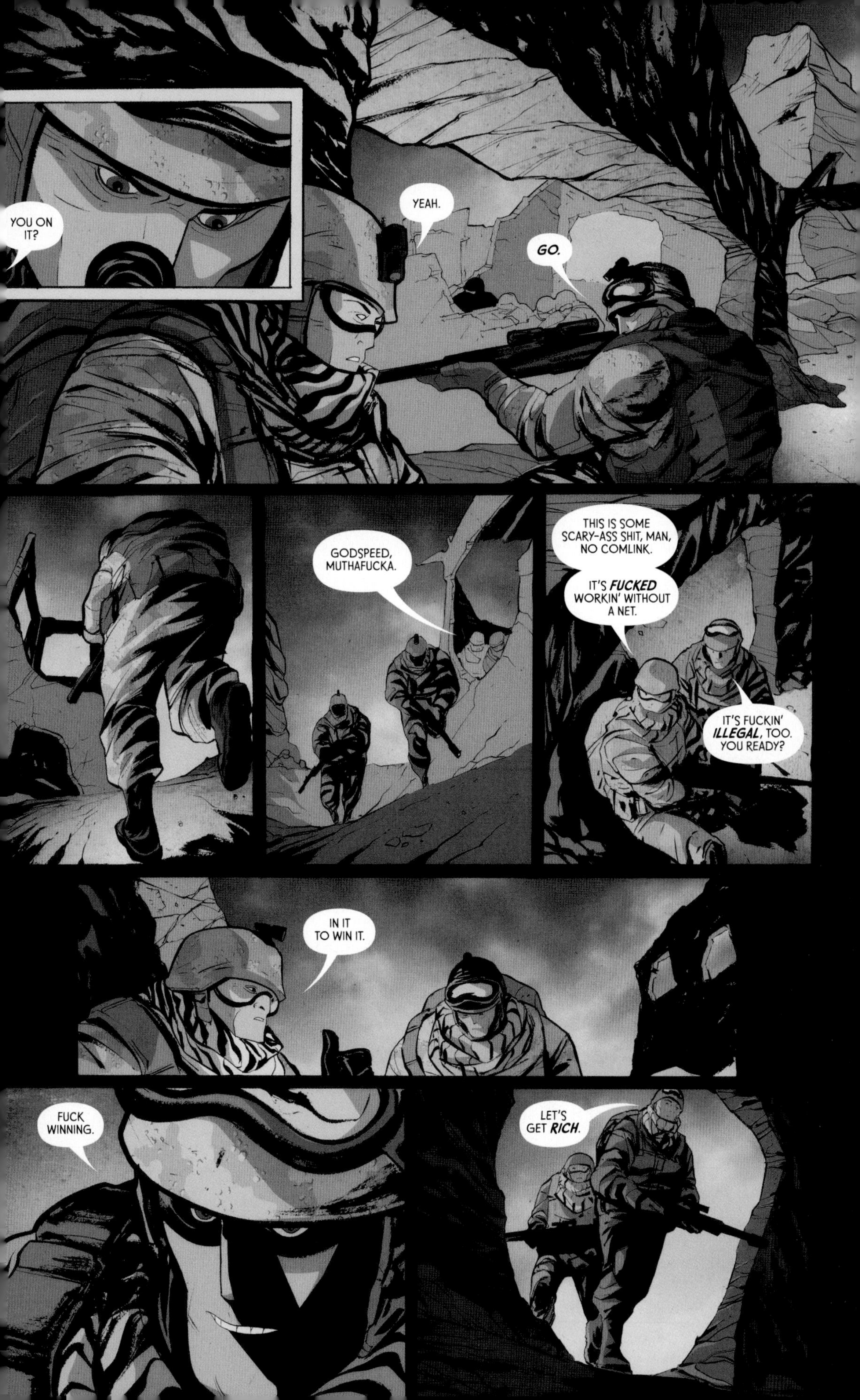
YOU ON IT?
YEAH.
GO.
GODSPEED, MUTHAFUCKA.
THIS IS SOME SCARY-ASS SHIT, MAN, NO COMLINK.
IT'S **FUCKED** WORKIN' WITHOUT A NET.
IT'S FUCKIN' ***ILLEGAL***, TOO. YOU READY?
IN IT TO WIN IT.
FUCK WINNING.
LET'S GET ***RICH***.

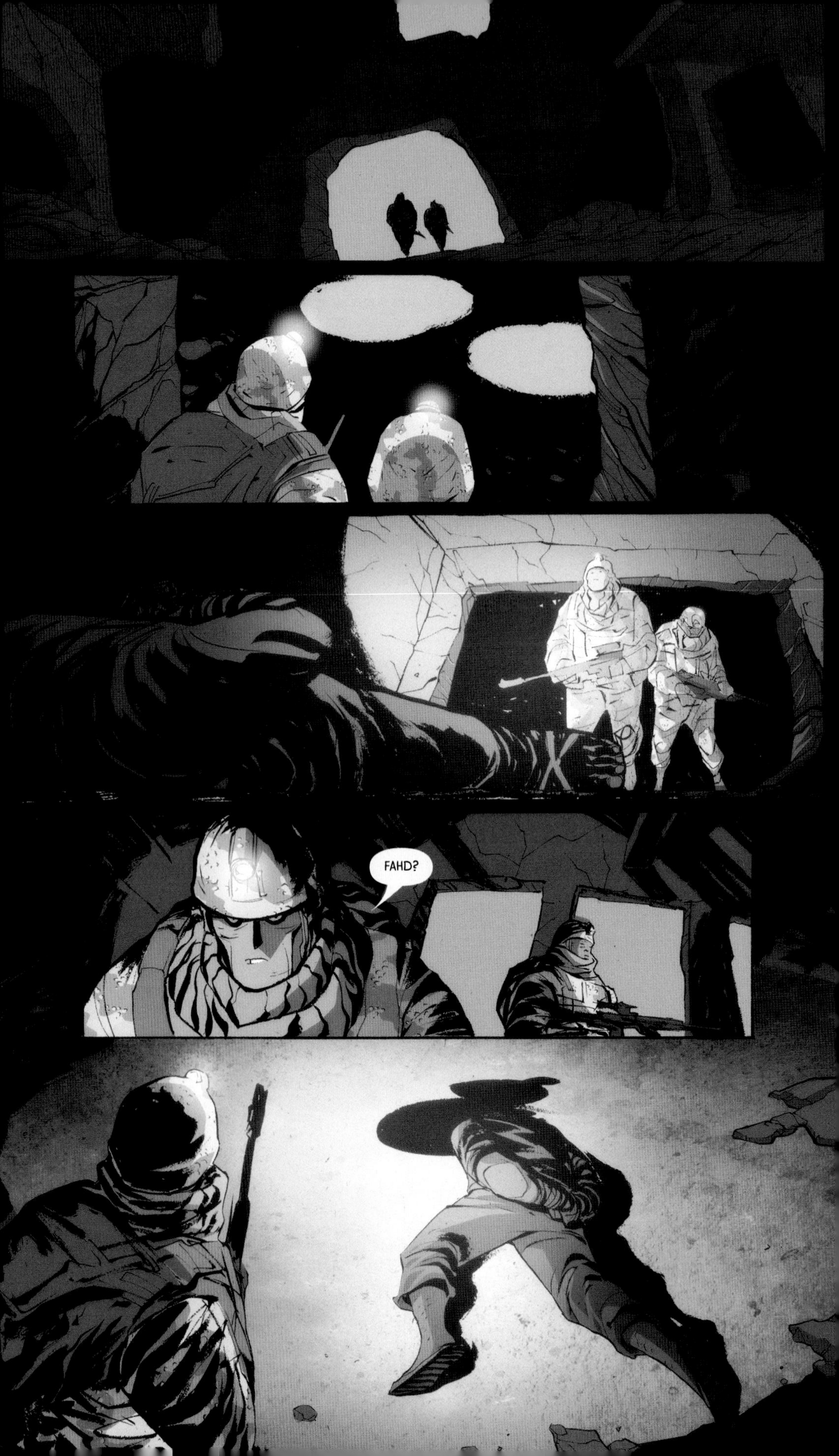
FAHD?

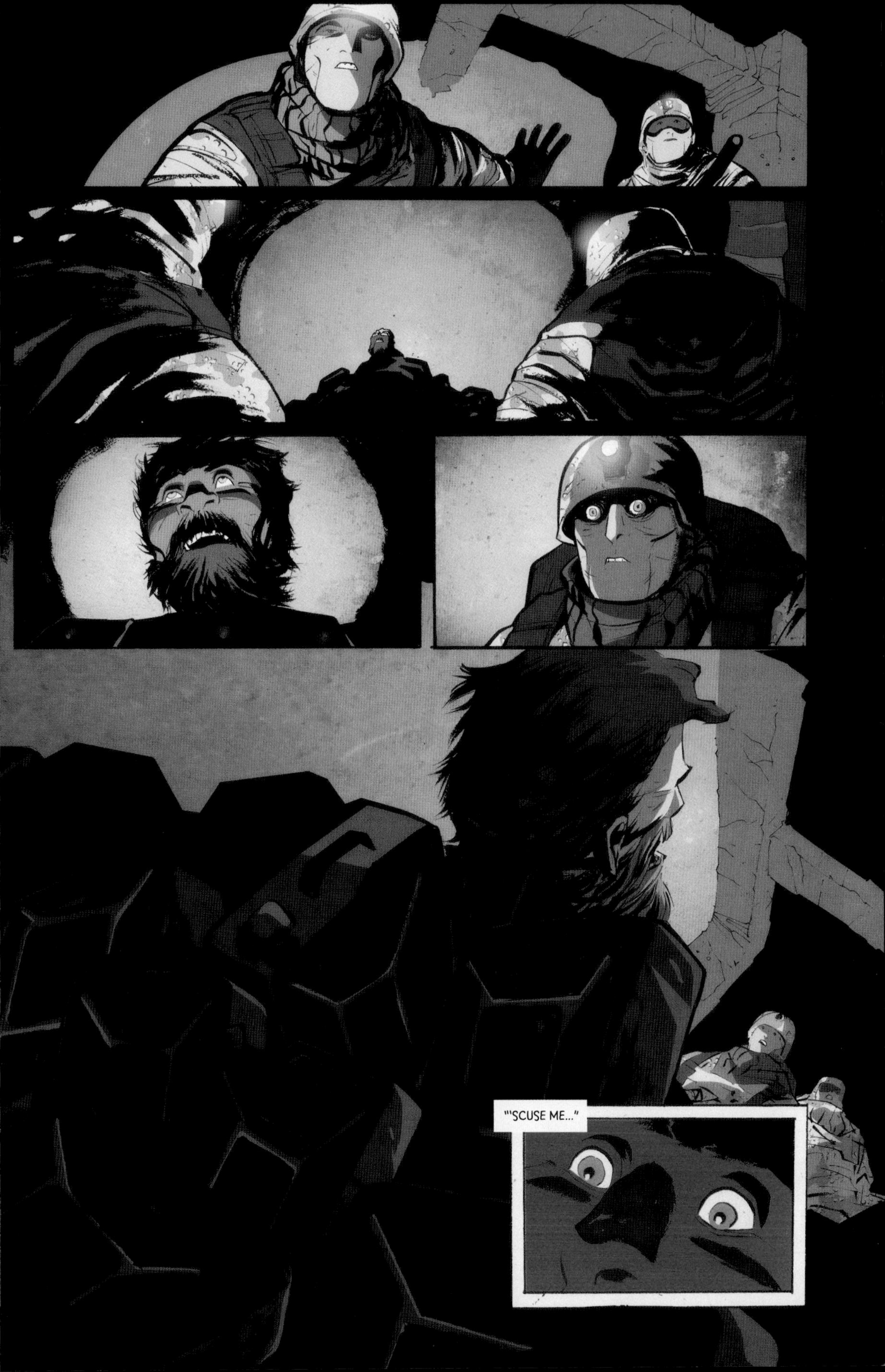
"'SCUSE ME..."

...I GOT THAT.
DON' NEED YOUR CHARITY.
IT'S NOT THAT. IT'S APPRECIATION.
YOU'RE A **VETERAN**. LET ME GET THAT DRINK.
AH.
SO I GO TO WAR, AN' I JUST GET A **BEER** OUT OF IT?
I...I JUST WANTED TO--
BLOW ME.
WHAT? I--
BLOW ME.
A BEER? FUCK. WHO GIVES A SHIT...
BLOW ME-- I'M A VETERAN. YOU OWE ME A **BEEJAY** AT THE VERY LEAST.
UNFORTUNATELY THOUGH, I CAN'T COLLECT--BUT I CAN BUY MY OWN BEER. SO...
...BLOW ME.
HEY--HE'S JUST TRYIN' TO BE **NICE**. LAY OFF, ASSHOLE.

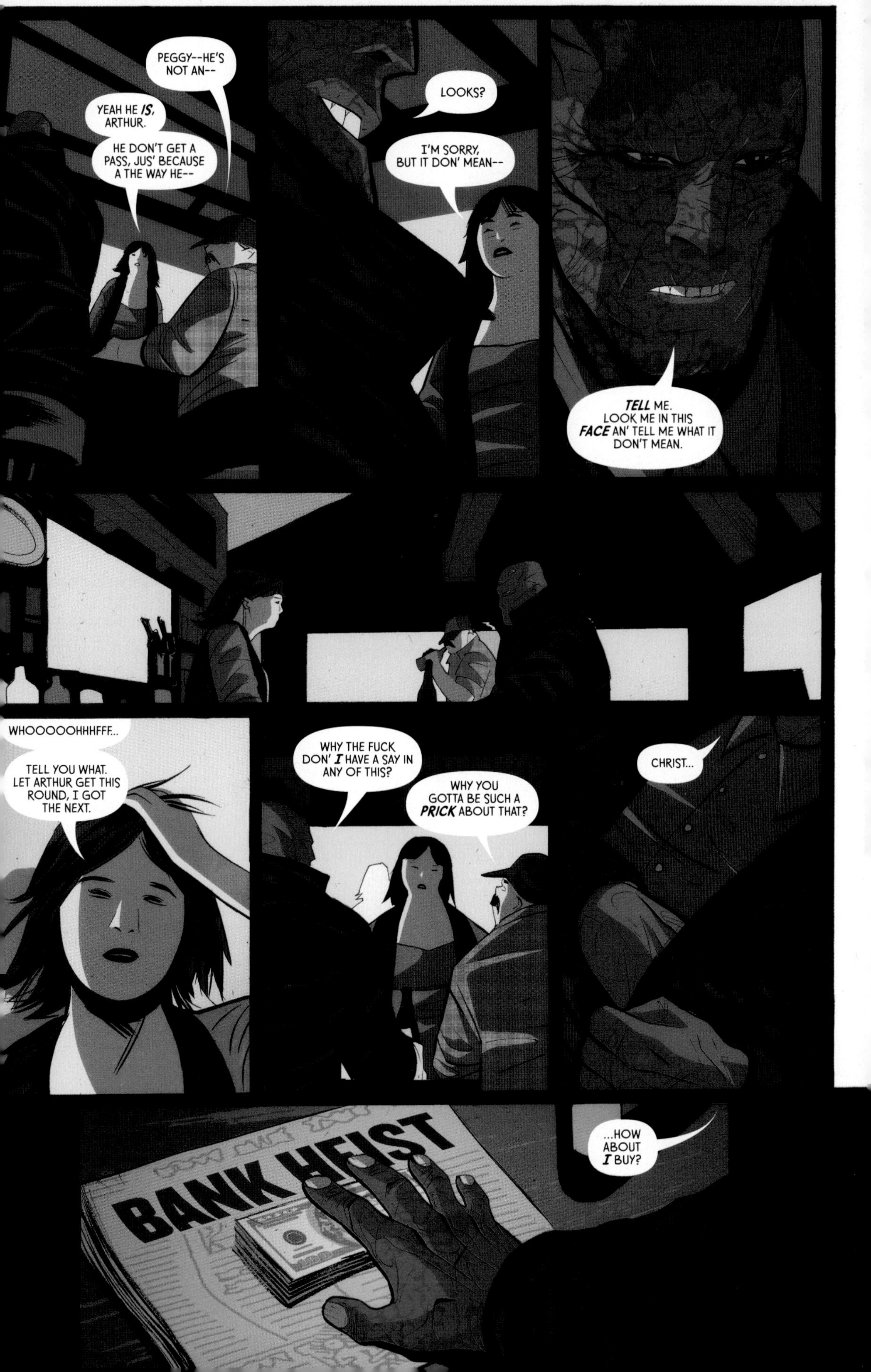
PEGGY--HE'S NOT AN--
YEAH HE *IS*, ARTHUR.
HE DON'T GET A PASS, JUS' BECAUSE A THE WAY HE--
LOOKS?
I'M SORRY, BUT IT DON' MEAN--
TELL ME. LOOK ME IN THIS *FACE* AN' TELL ME WHAT IT DON'T MEAN.
WHOOOOOOHHHFFF...
TELL YOU WHAT. LET ARTHUR GET THIS ROUND, I GOT THE NEXT.
WHY THE FUCK DON' *I* HAVE A SAY IN ANY OF THIS?
WHY YOU GOTTA BE SUCH A *PRICK* ABOUT THAT?
CHRIST...
BANK HEIST
...HOW ABOUT *I* BUY?

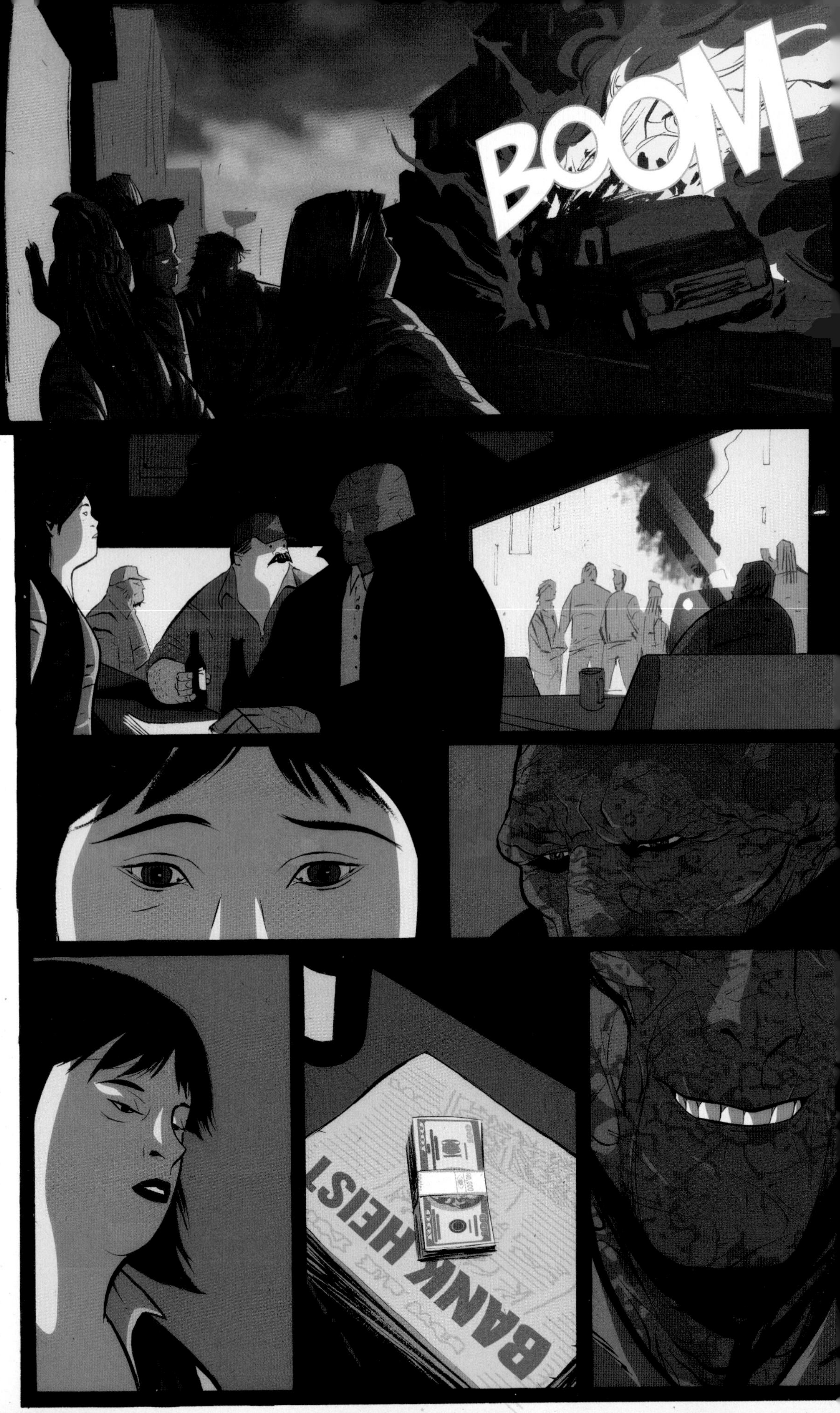
BOOM
BANK HEIST

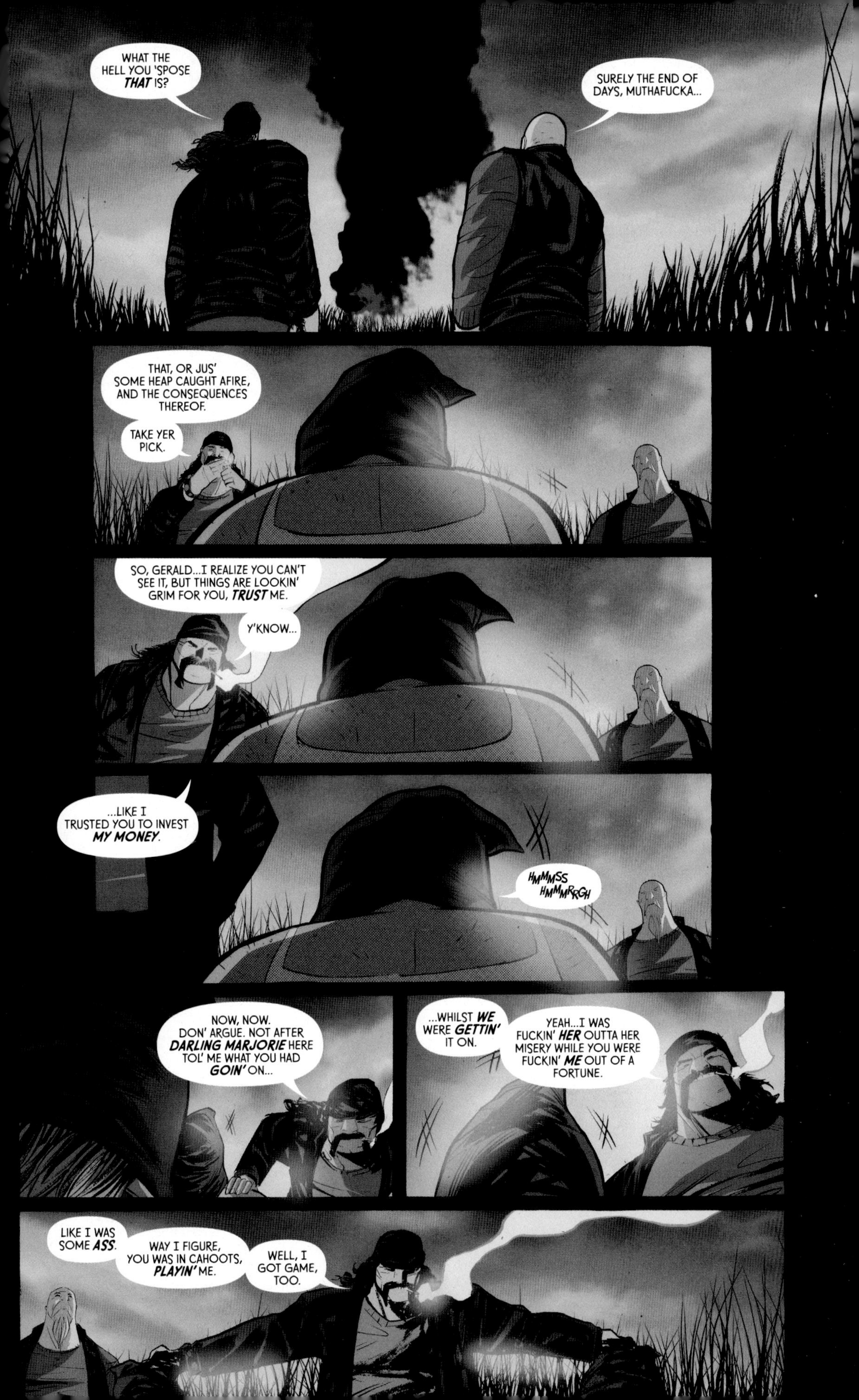

WHAT THE HELL YOU 'SPOSE THAT IS?
SURELY THE END OF DAYS, MUTHAFUCKA...
THAT, OR JUS' SOME HEAP CAUGHT AFIRE, AND THE CONSEQUENCES THEREOF.
TAKE YER PICK.
SO, GERALD...I REALIZE YOU CAN'T SEE IT, BUT THINGS ARE LOOKIN' GRIM FOR YOU, TRUST ME.
Y'KNOW...
...LIKE I TRUSTED YOU TO INVEST MY MONEY.
HMMMSS HMMMRGH
NOW, NOW. DON' ARGUE. NOT AFTER DARLING MARJORIE HERE TOL' ME WHAT YOU HAD GOIN' ON...
...WHILST WE WERE GETTIN' IT ON.
YEAH...I WAS FUCKIN' HER OUTTA HER MISERY WHILE YOU WERE FUCKIN' ME OUT OF A FORTUNE.
LIKE I WAS SOME ASS.
WAY I FIGURE, YOU WAS IN CAHOOTS, PLAYIN' ME.
WELL, I GOT GAME, TOO.

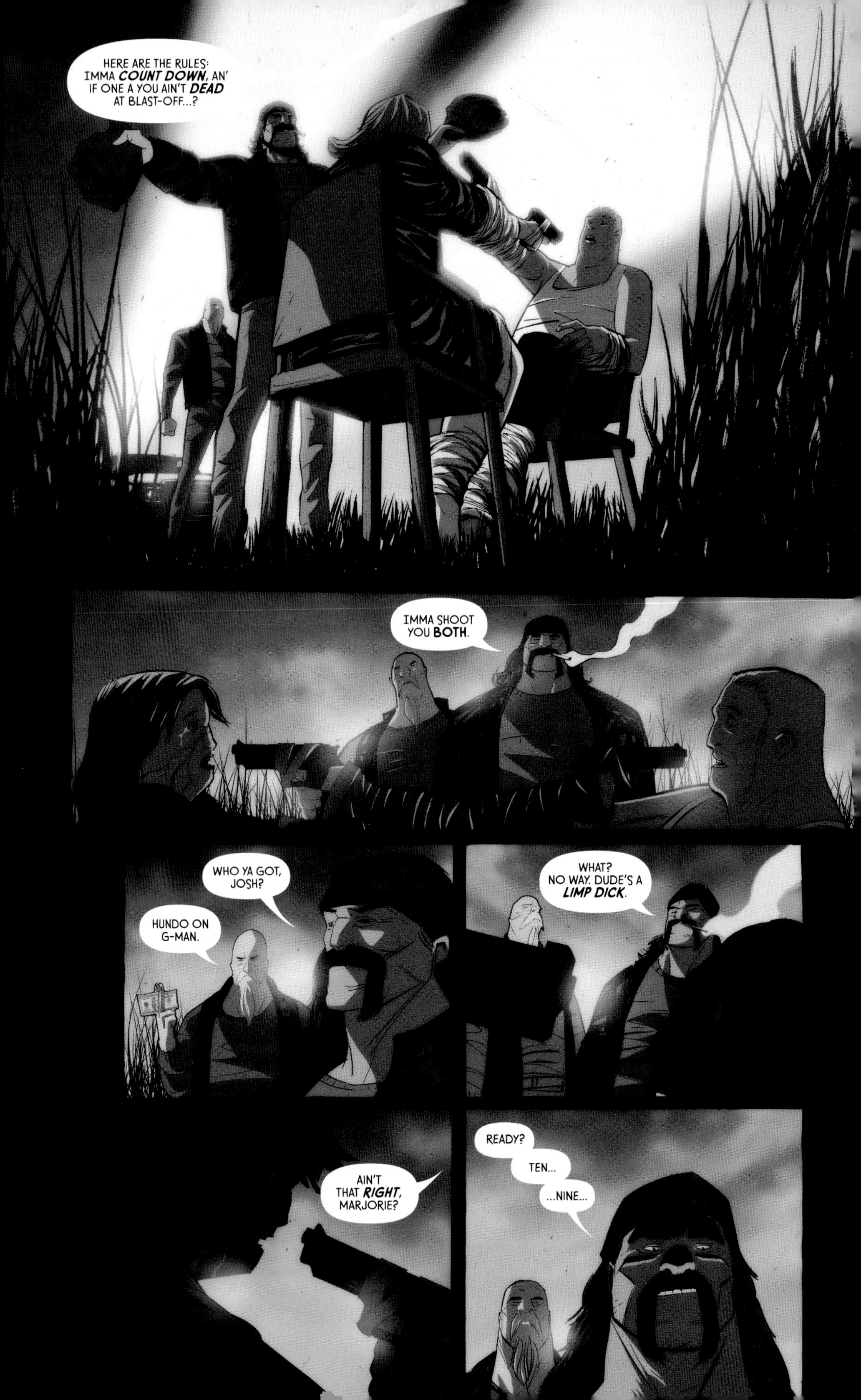
HERE ARE THE RULES: IMMA COUNT DOWN, AN' IF ONE A YOU AIN'T DEAD AT BLAST-OFF...?
IMMA SHOOT YOU BOTH.
WHO YA GOT, JOSH?
HUNDO ON G-MAN.
WHAT? NO WAY. DUDE'S A LIMP DICK.
AIN'T THAT RIGHT, MARJORIE?
READY?
TEN...
...NINE...

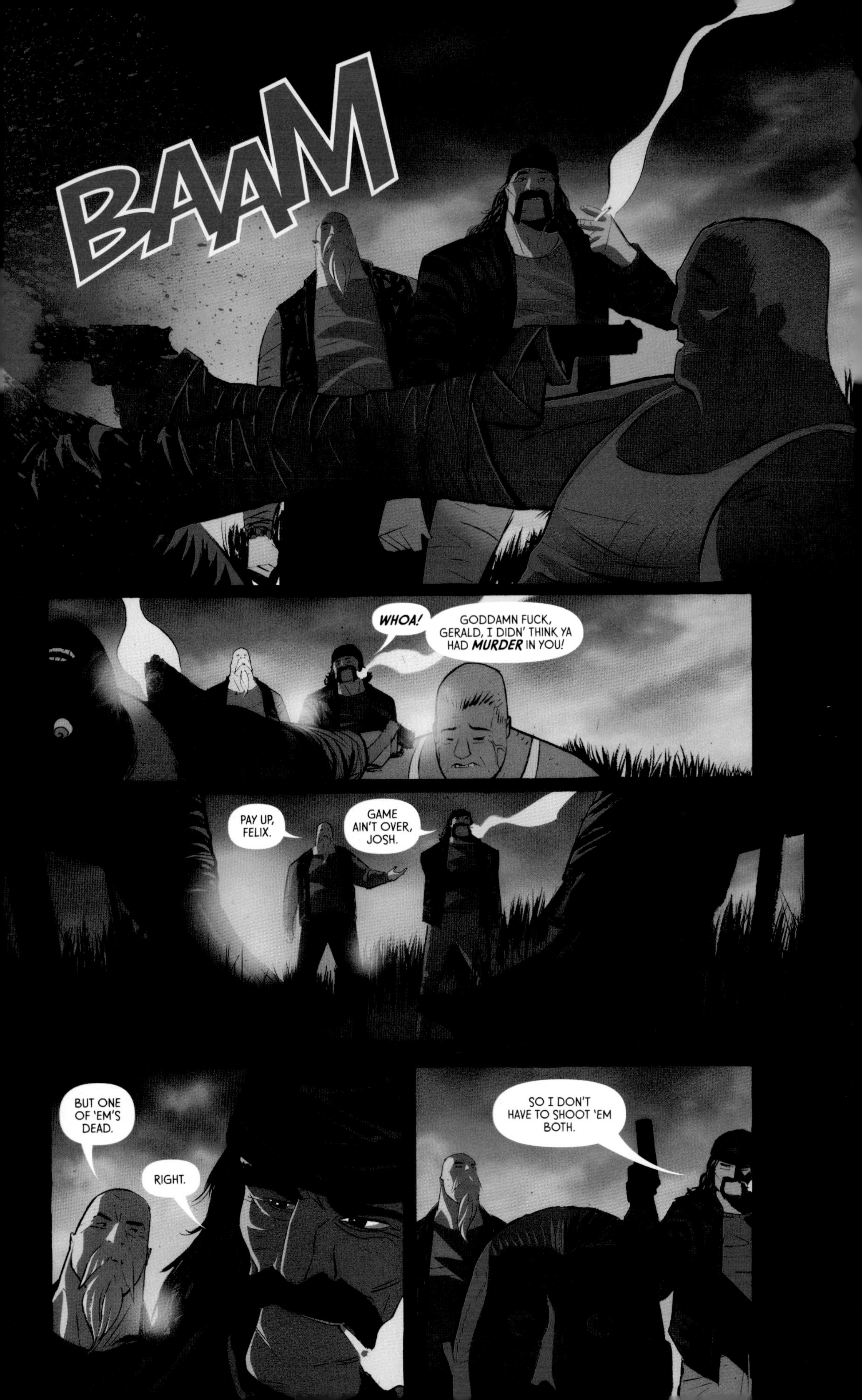
BAAM
WHOA!
GODDAMN FUCK, GERALD, I DIDN' THINK YA HAD MURDER IN YOU!
PAY UP, FELIX.
GAME AIN'T OVER, JOSH.
BUT ONE OF 'EM'S DEAD.
RIGHT.
SO I DON'T HAVE TO SHOOT 'EM BOTH.

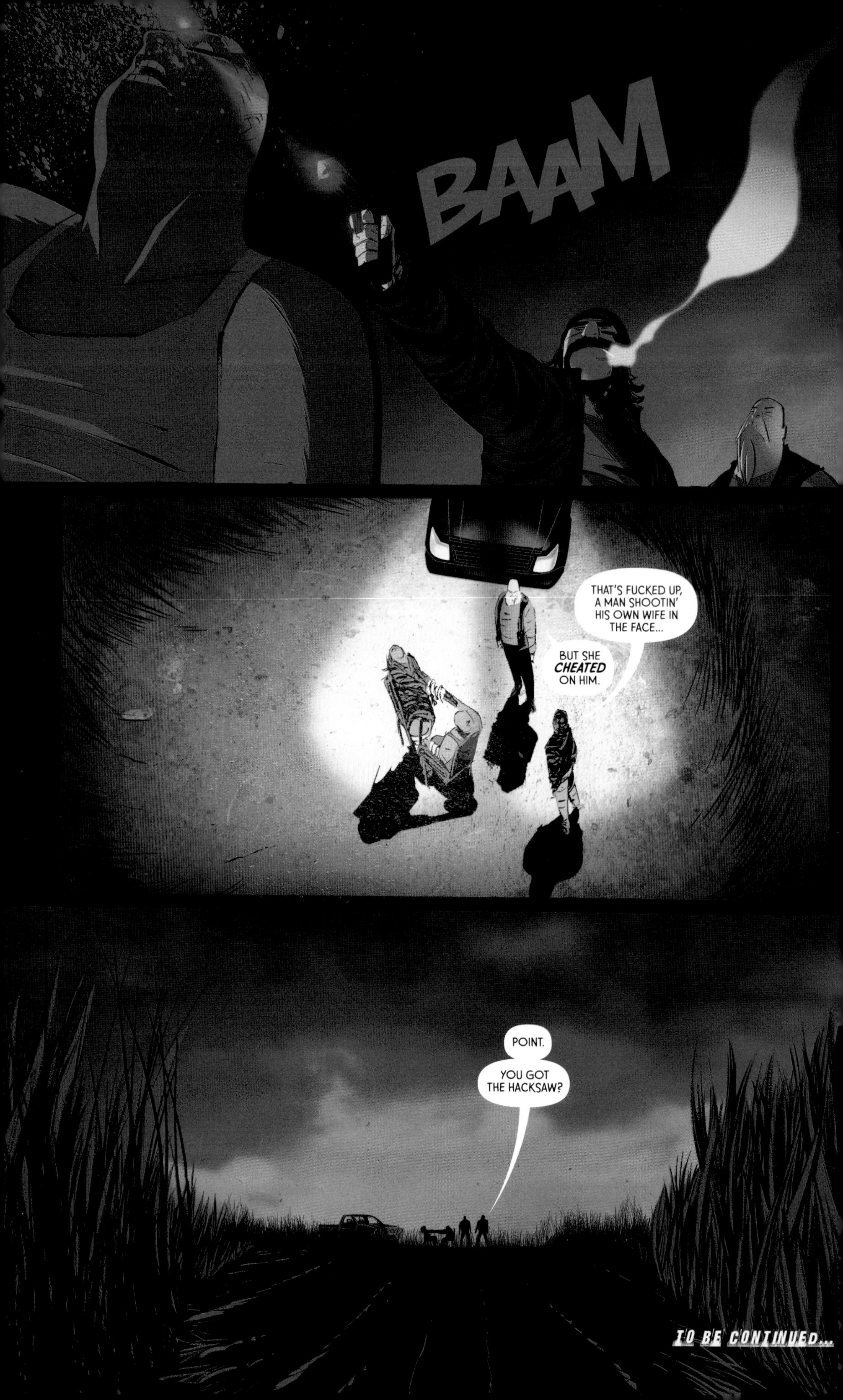
BAAM
THAT'S FUCKED UP, A MAN SHOOTIN' HIS OWN WIFE IN THE FACE...
BUT SHE CHEATED ON HIM.
POINT.
YOU GOT THE HACKSAW?
TO BE CONTINUED...

2

"ROADKILL"

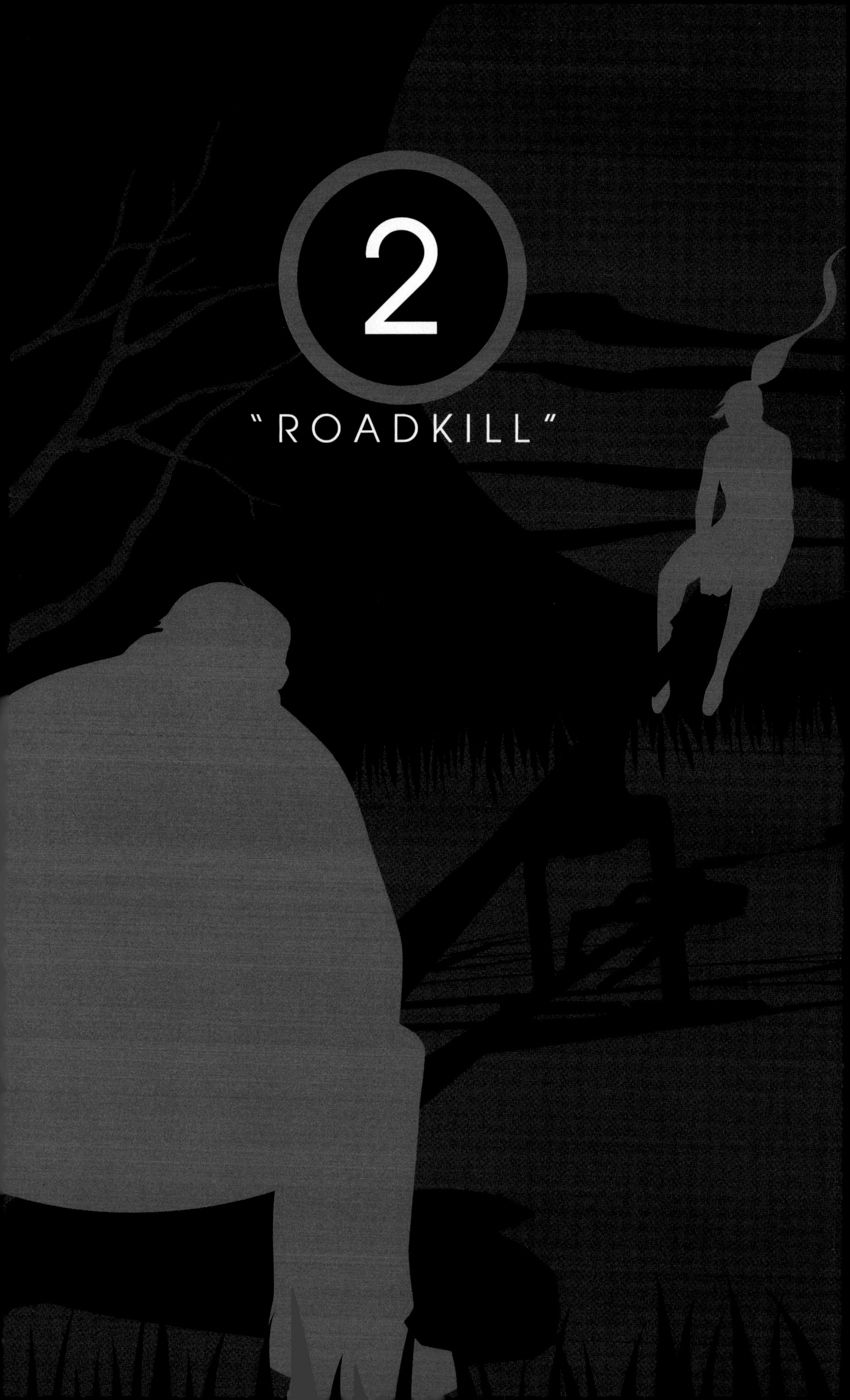

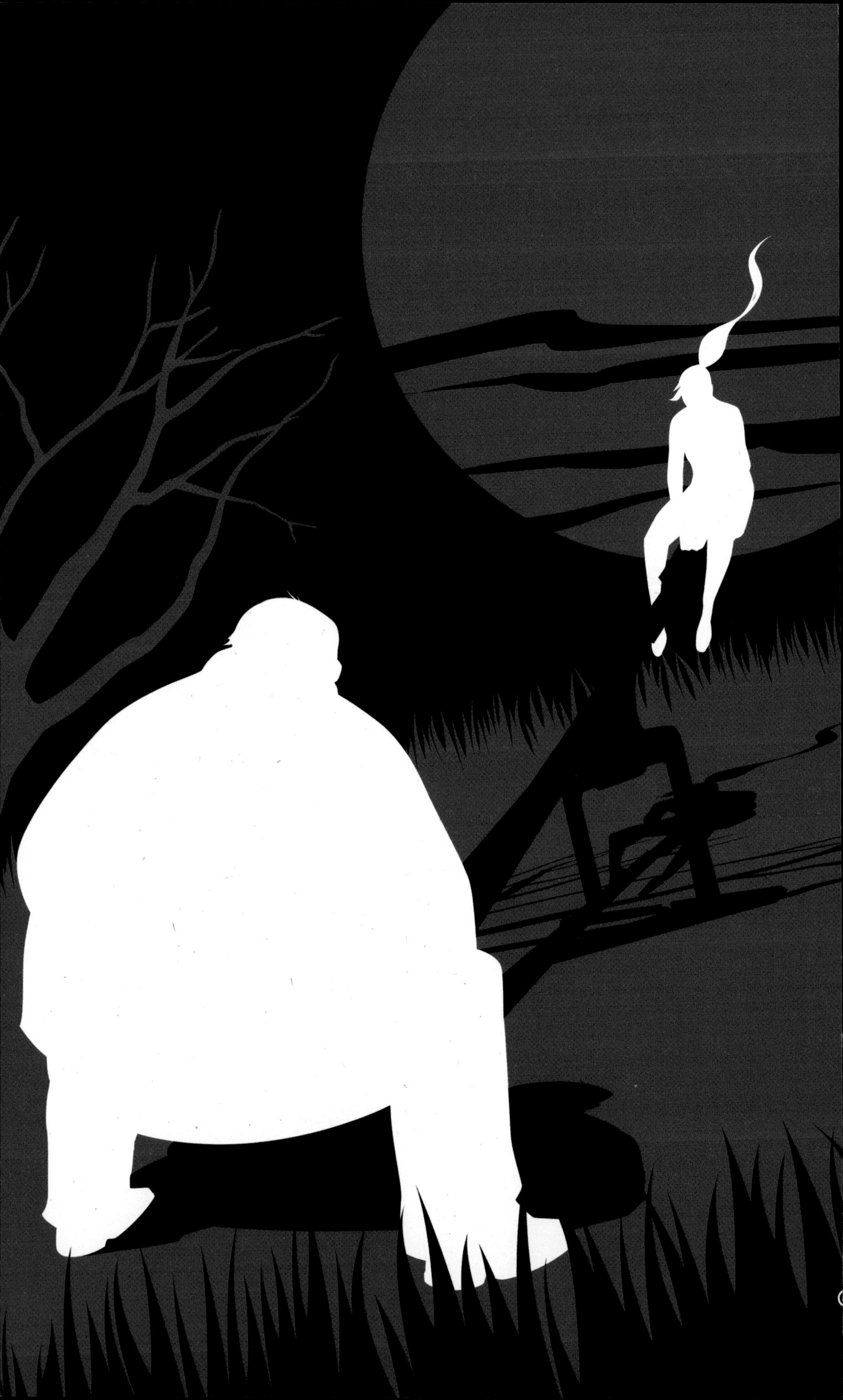

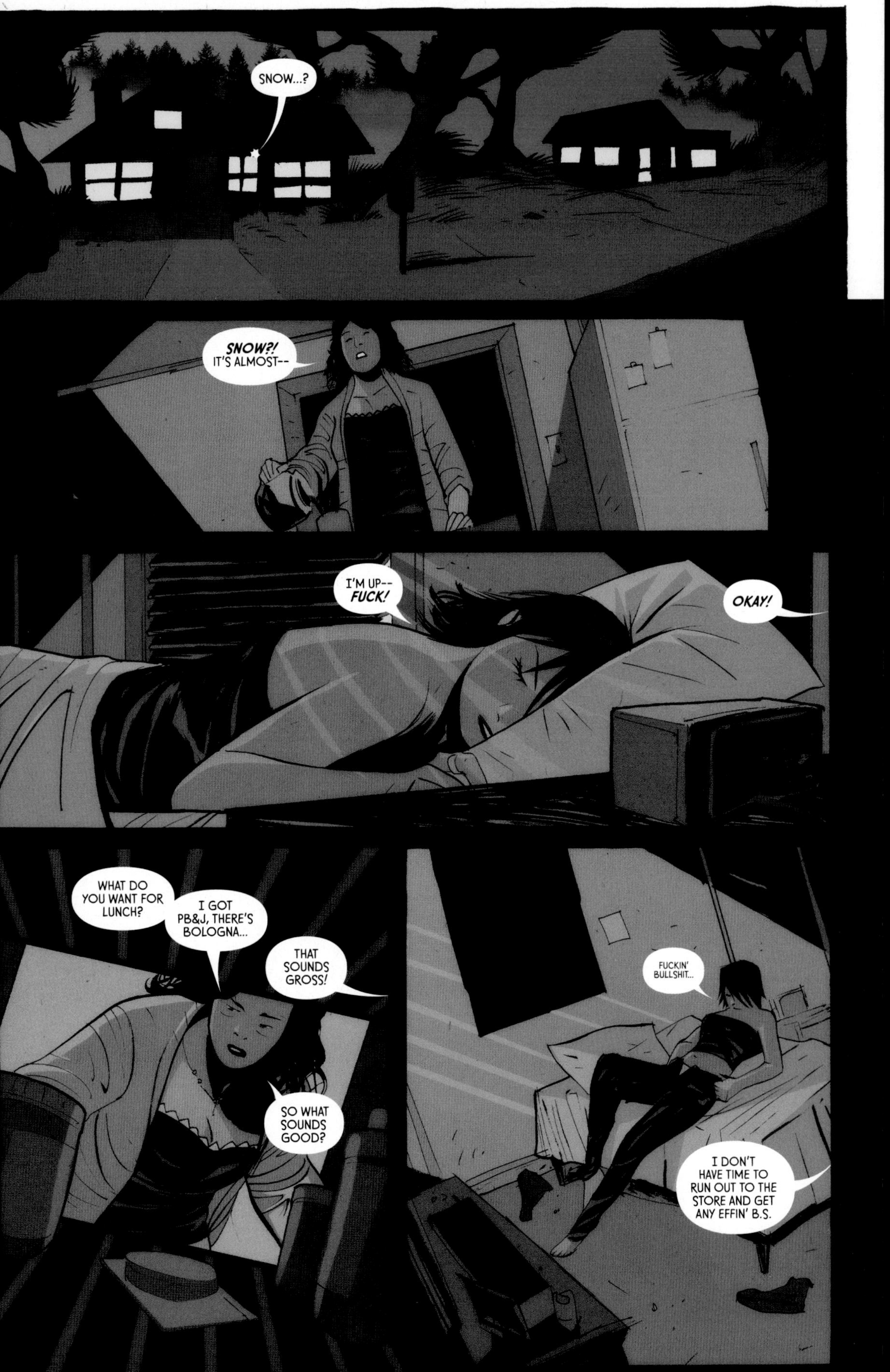
SNOW...?
SNOW?! IT'S ALMOST--
I'M UP-- FUCK!
OKAY!
WHAT DO YOU WANT FOR LUNCH?
I GOT PB&J, THERE'S BOLOGNA...
THAT SOUNDS GROSS!
SO WHAT SOUNDS GOOD?
FUCKIN' BULLSHIT...
I DON'T HAVE TIME TO RUN OUT TO THE STORE AND GET ANY EFFIN' B.S.

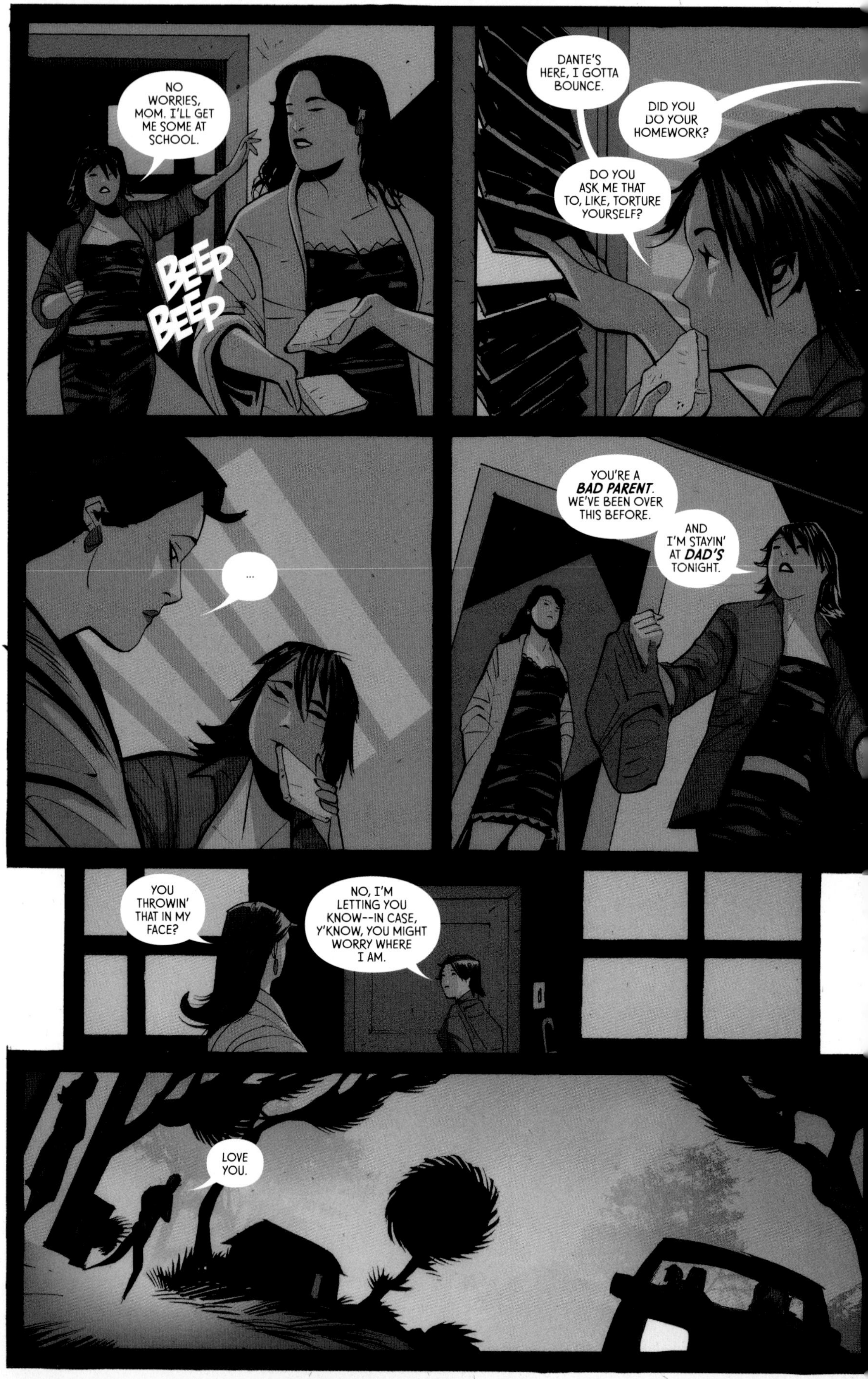
NO WORRIES, MOM. I'LL GET ME SOME AT SCHOOL.
BEEP BEEP
DANTE'S HERE, I GOTTA BOUNCE.
DID YOU DO YOUR HOMEWORK?
DO YOU ASK ME THAT TO, LIKE, TORTURE YOURSELF?
...
YOU'RE A **BAD PARENT**. WE'VE BEEN OVER THIS BEFORE.
AND I'M STAYIN' AT **DAD'S** TONIGHT.
YOU THROWIN' THAT IN MY FACE?
NO, I'M LETTING YOU KNOW--IN CASE, Y'KNOW, YOU MIGHT WORRY WHERE I AM.
LOVE YOU.

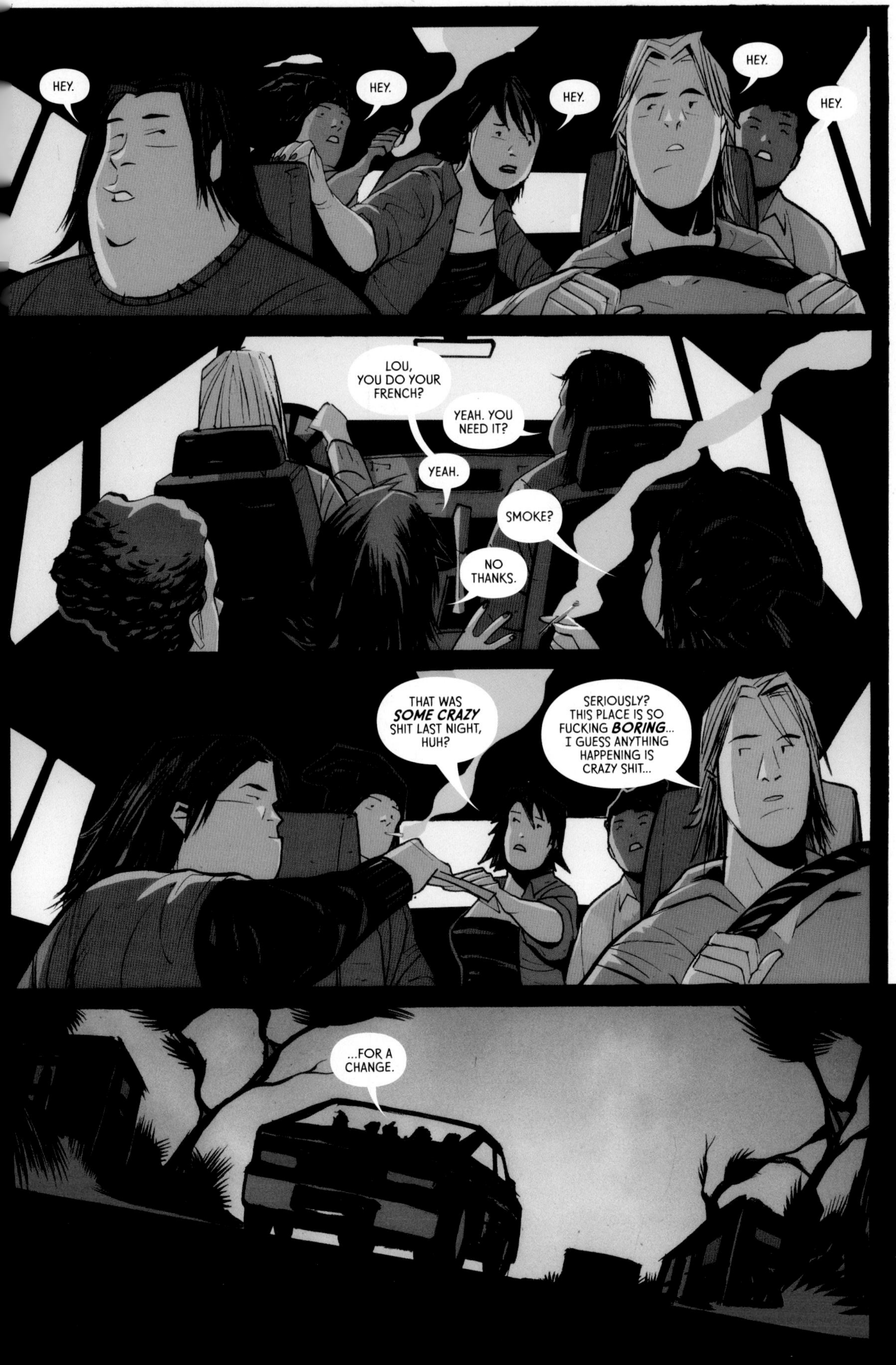
HEY.
HEY.
HEY.
HEY.
HEY.
LOU, YOU DO YOUR FRENCH?
YEAH. YOU NEED IT?
YEAH.
SMOKE?
NO THANKS.
THAT WAS **SOME CRAZY** SHIT LAST NIGHT, HUH?
SERIOUSLY? THIS PLACE IS SO FUCKING **BORING**... I GUESS ANYTHING HAPPENING IS CRAZY SHIT...
...FOR A CHANGE.

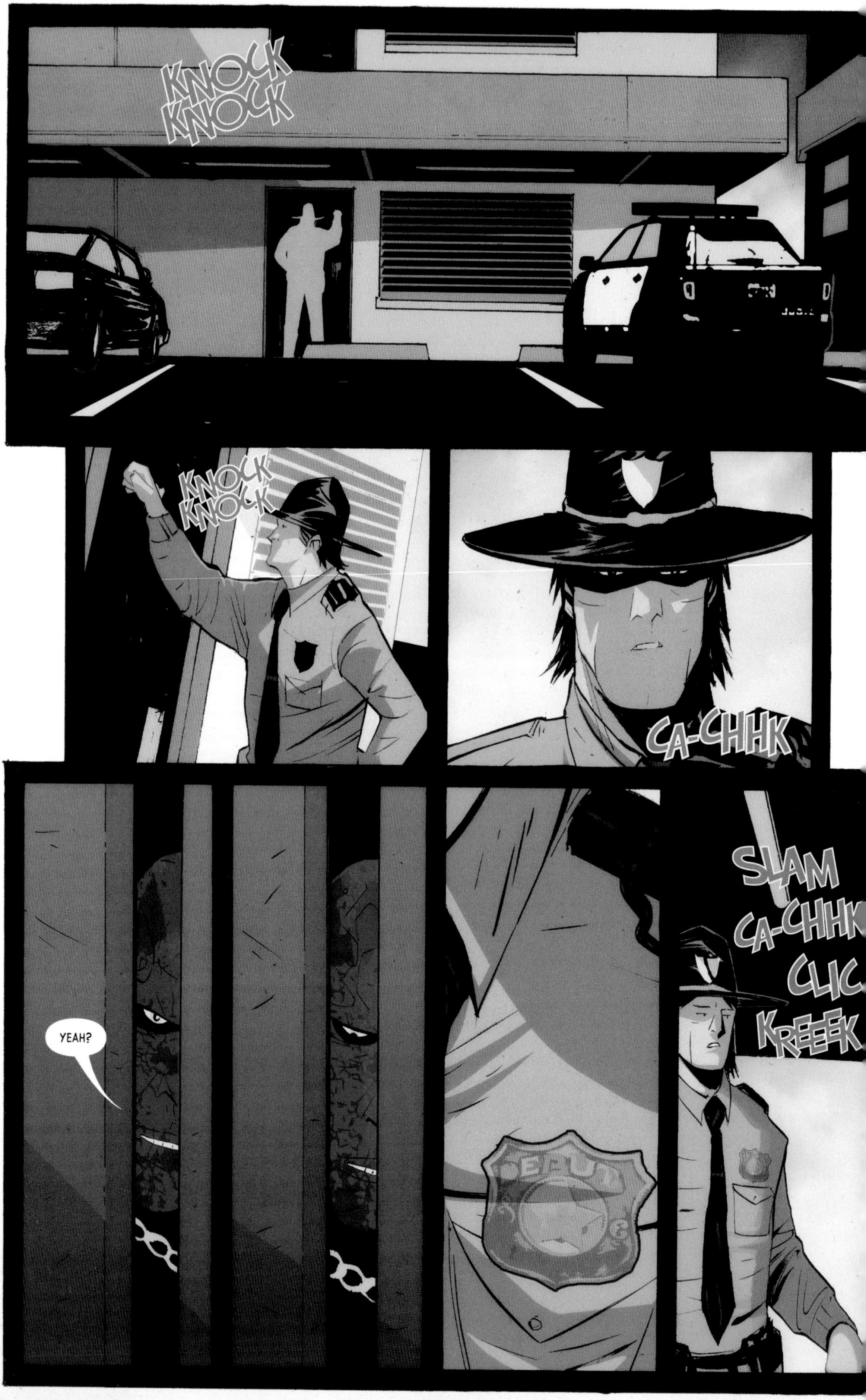
KNOCK KNOCK
KNOCK KNOCK
CA-CHHK
YEAH?
SLAM
CA-CHHK
CLIC
KREEEK

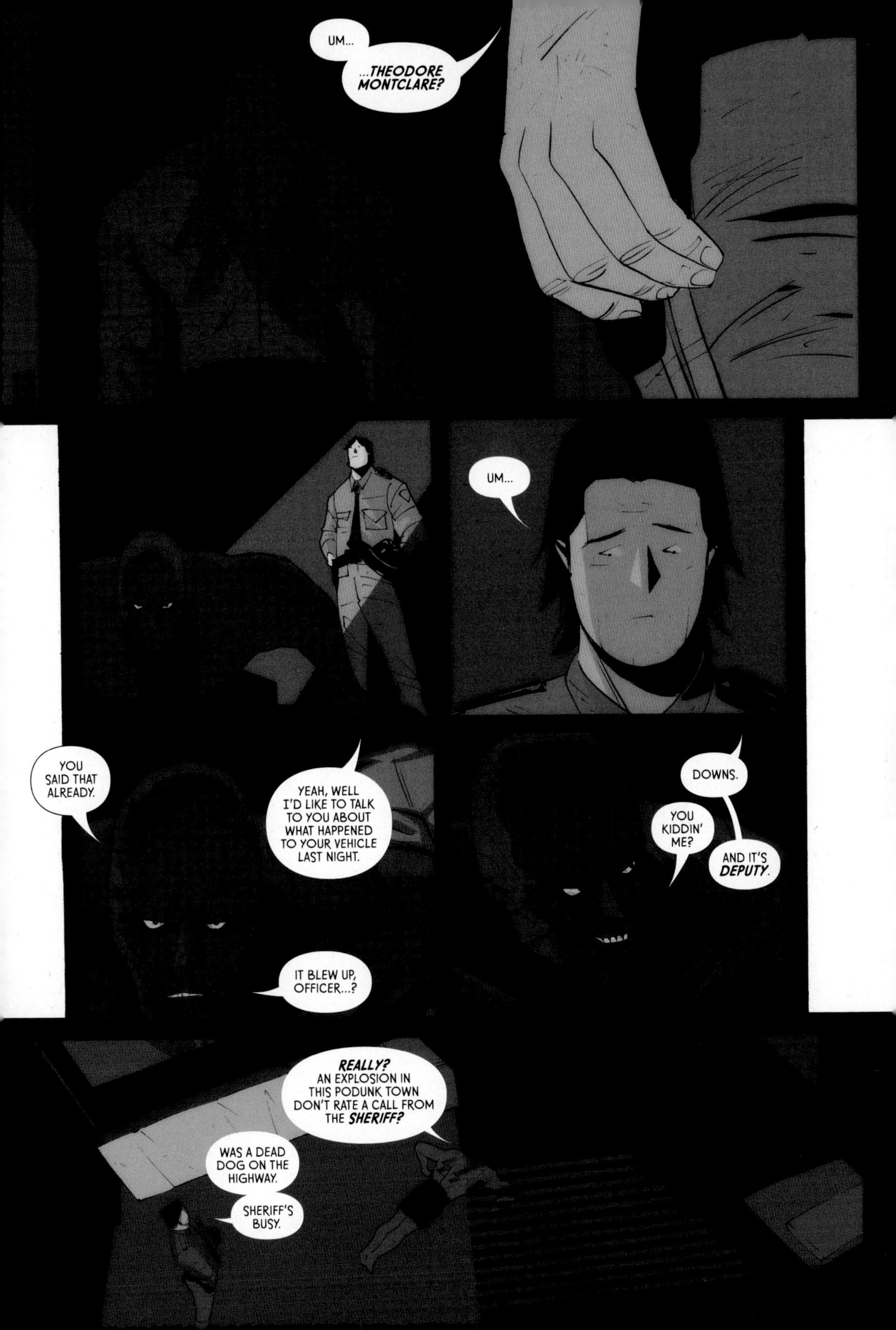

UM...
...THEODORE MONTCLARE?
UM...
YOU SAID THAT ALREADY.
YEAH, WELL I'D LIKE TO TALK TO YOU ABOUT WHAT HAPPENED TO YOUR VEHICLE LAST NIGHT.
IT BLEW UP, OFFICER...?
DOWNS.
YOU KIDDIN' ME?
AND IT'S DEPUTY.
REALLY? AN EXPLOSION IN THIS PODUNK TOWN DON'T RATE A CALL FROM THE SHERIFF?
WAS A DEAD DOG ON THE HIGHWAY.
SHERIFF'S BUSY.

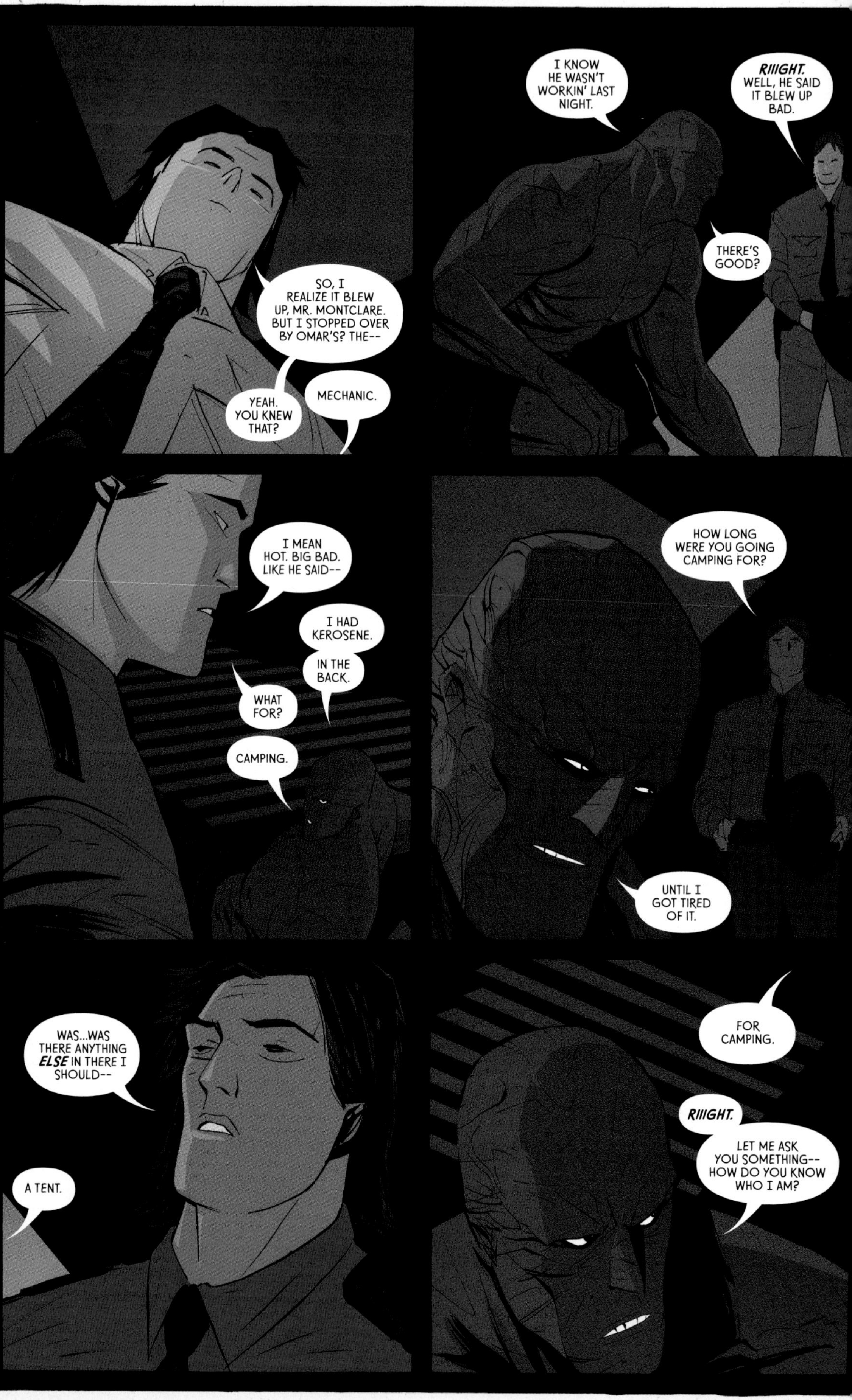
SO, I REALIZE IT BLEW UP, MR. MONTCLARE. BUT I STOPPED OVER BY OMAR'S? THE--
MECHANIC.
YEAH. YOU KNEW THAT?
I KNOW HE WASN'T WORKIN' LAST NIGHT.
RIIIGHT. WELL, HE SAID IT BLEW UP BAD.
THERE'S GOOD?
I MEAN HOT. BIG BAD. LIKE HE SAID--
I HAD KEROSENE.
IN THE BACK.
WHAT FOR?
CAMPING.
HOW LONG WERE YOU GOING CAMPING FOR?
UNTIL I GOT TIRED OF IT.
WAS...WAS THERE ANYTHING *ELSE* IN THERE I SHOULD--
A TENT.
FOR CAMPING.
RIIIGHT.
LET ME ASK YOU SOMETHING-- HOW DO YOU KNOW WHO I AM?

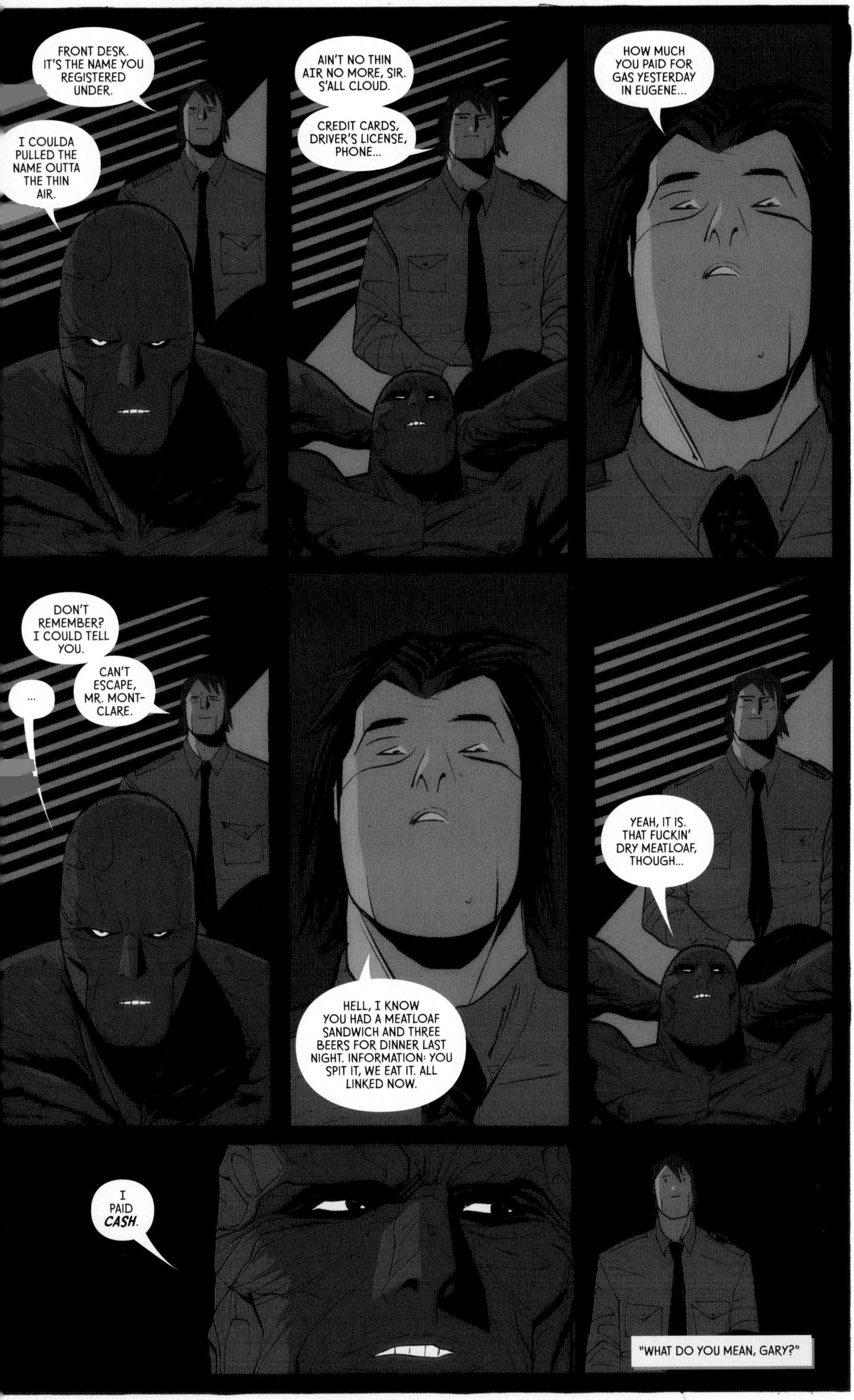

FRONT DESK. IT'S THE NAME YOU REGISTERED UNDER.
I COULDA PULLED THE NAME OUTTA THE THIN AIR.
AIN'T NO THIN AIR NO MORE, SIR. S'ALL CLOUD.
CREDIT CARDS, DRIVER'S LICENSE, PHONE...
HOW MUCH YOU PAID FOR GAS YESTERDAY IN EUGENE...
DON'T REMEMBER? I COULD TELL YOU.
...
CAN'T ESCAPE, MR. MONT-CLARE.
HELL, I KNOW YOU HAD A MEATLOAF SANDWICH AND THREE BEERS FOR DINNER LAST NIGHT. INFORMATION: YOU SPIT IT, WE EAT IT. ALL LINKED NOW.
YEAH, IT IS. THAT FUCKIN' DRY MEATLOAF, THOUGH...
I PAID *CASH*.
"WHAT DO YOU MEAN, GARY?"

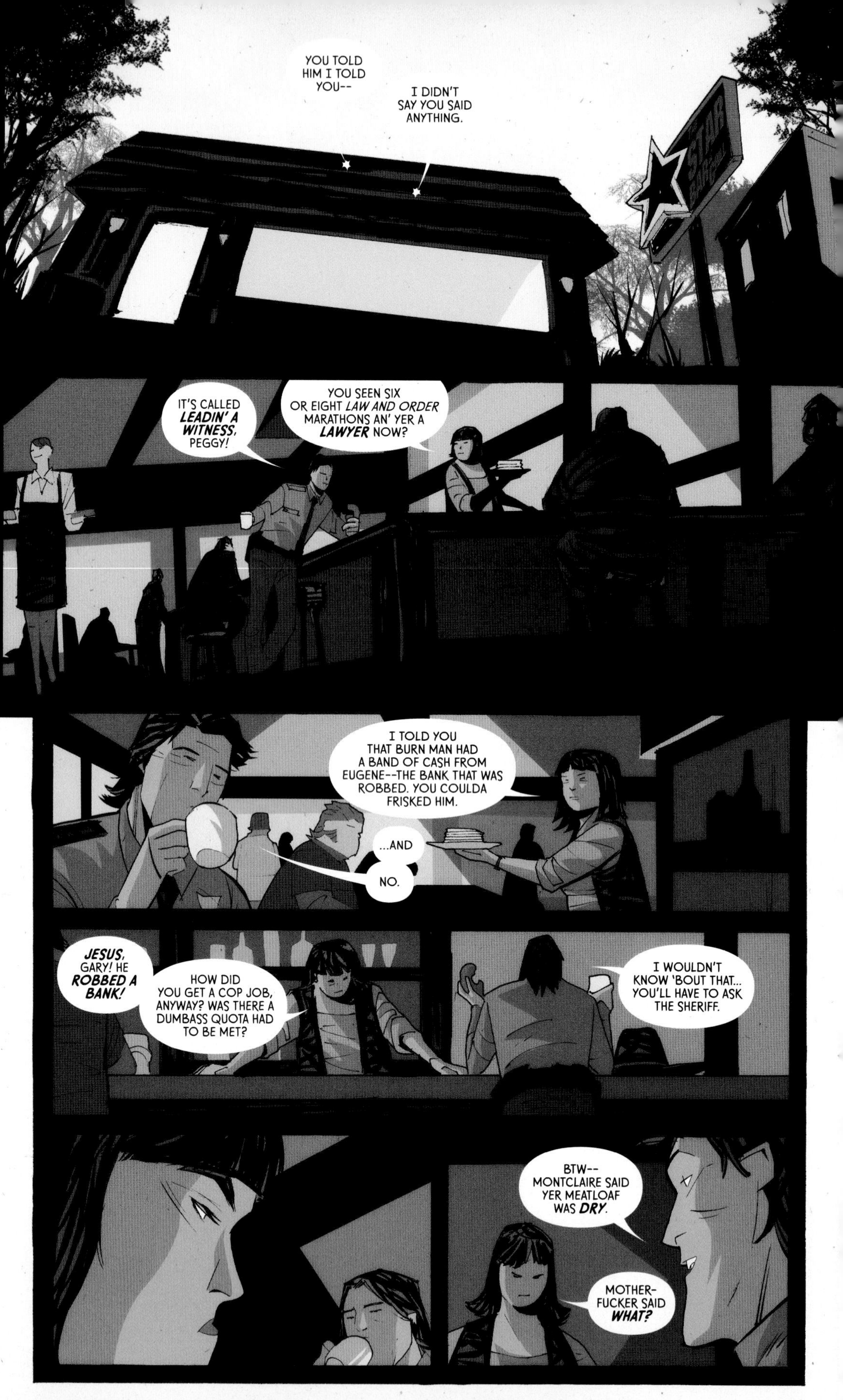
YOU TOLD HIM I TOLD YOU--
I DIDN'T SAY YOU SAID ANYTHING.
THE STAR BAR & GRILL
IT'S CALLED *LEADIN' A WITNESS*, PEGGY!
YOU SEEN SIX OR EIGHT *LAW AND ORDER* MARATHONS AN' YER A *LAWYER* NOW?
I TOLD YOU THAT BURN MAN HAD A BAND OF CASH FROM EUGENE--THE BANK THAT WAS ROBBED. YOU COULDA FRISKED HIM.
...AND
NO.
JESUS, GARY! HE *ROBBED A BANK!*
HOW DID YOU GET A COP JOB, ANYWAY? WAS THERE A DUMBASS QUOTA HAD TO BE MET?
I WOULDN'T KNOW 'BOUT THAT... YOU'LL HAVE TO ASK THE SHERIFF.
BTW-- MONTCLAIRE SAID YER MEATLOAF WAS *DRY*.
MOTHER-FUCKER SAID *WHAT?*

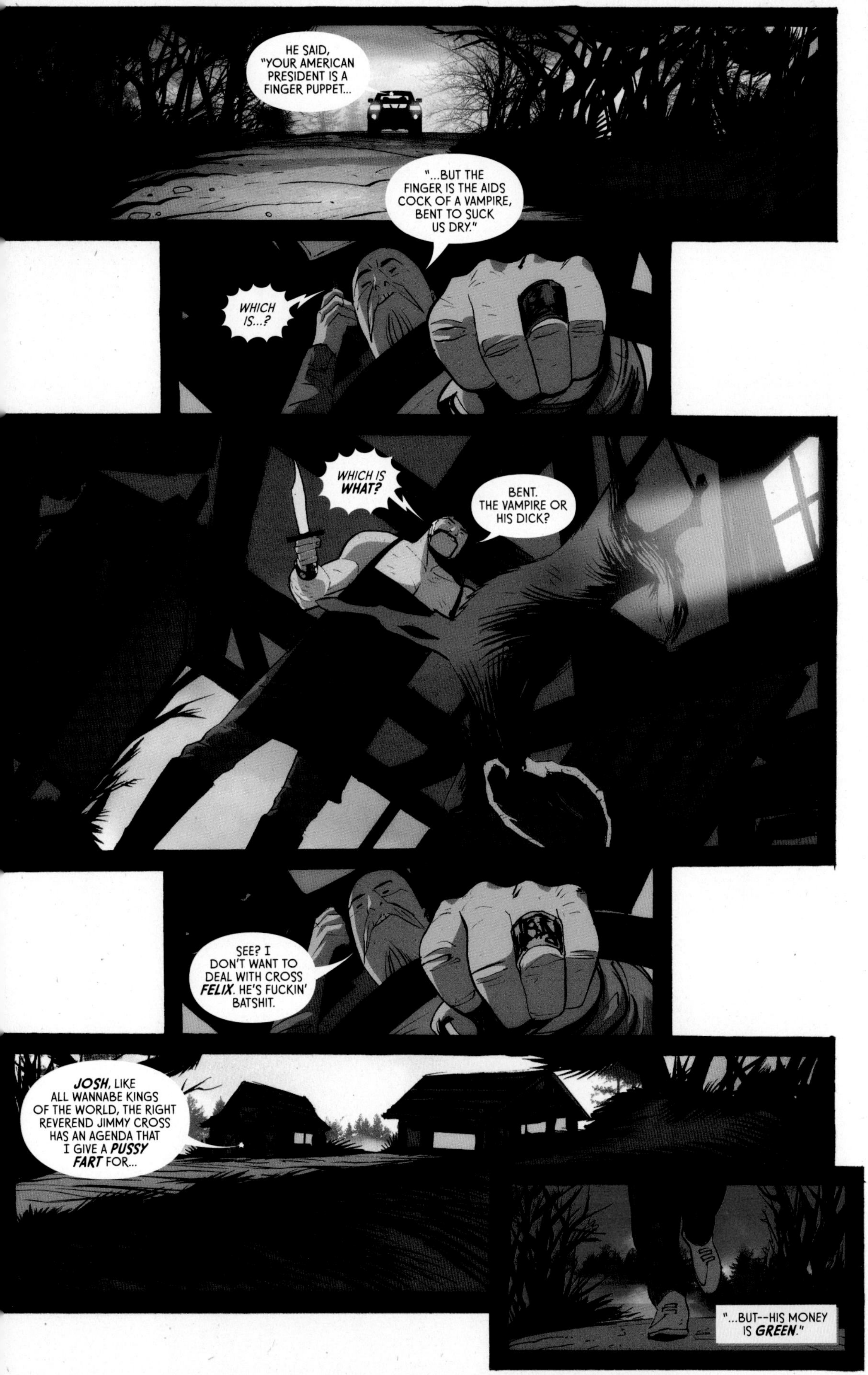
HE SAID, "YOUR AMERICAN PRESIDENT IS A FINGER PUPPET...
"...BUT THE FINGER IS THE AIDS COCK OF A VAMPIRE, BENT TO SUCK US DRY."
WHICH IS...?
WHICH IS WHAT?
BENT. THE VAMPIRE OR HIS DICK?
SEE? I DON'T WANT TO DEAL WITH CROSS FELIX. HE'S FUCKIN' BATSHIT.
JOSH, LIKE ALL WANNABE KINGS OF THE WORLD, THE RIGHT REVEREND JIMMY CROSS HAS AN AGENDA THAT I GIVE A PUSSY FART FOR...
"...BUT--HIS MONEY IS GREEN."

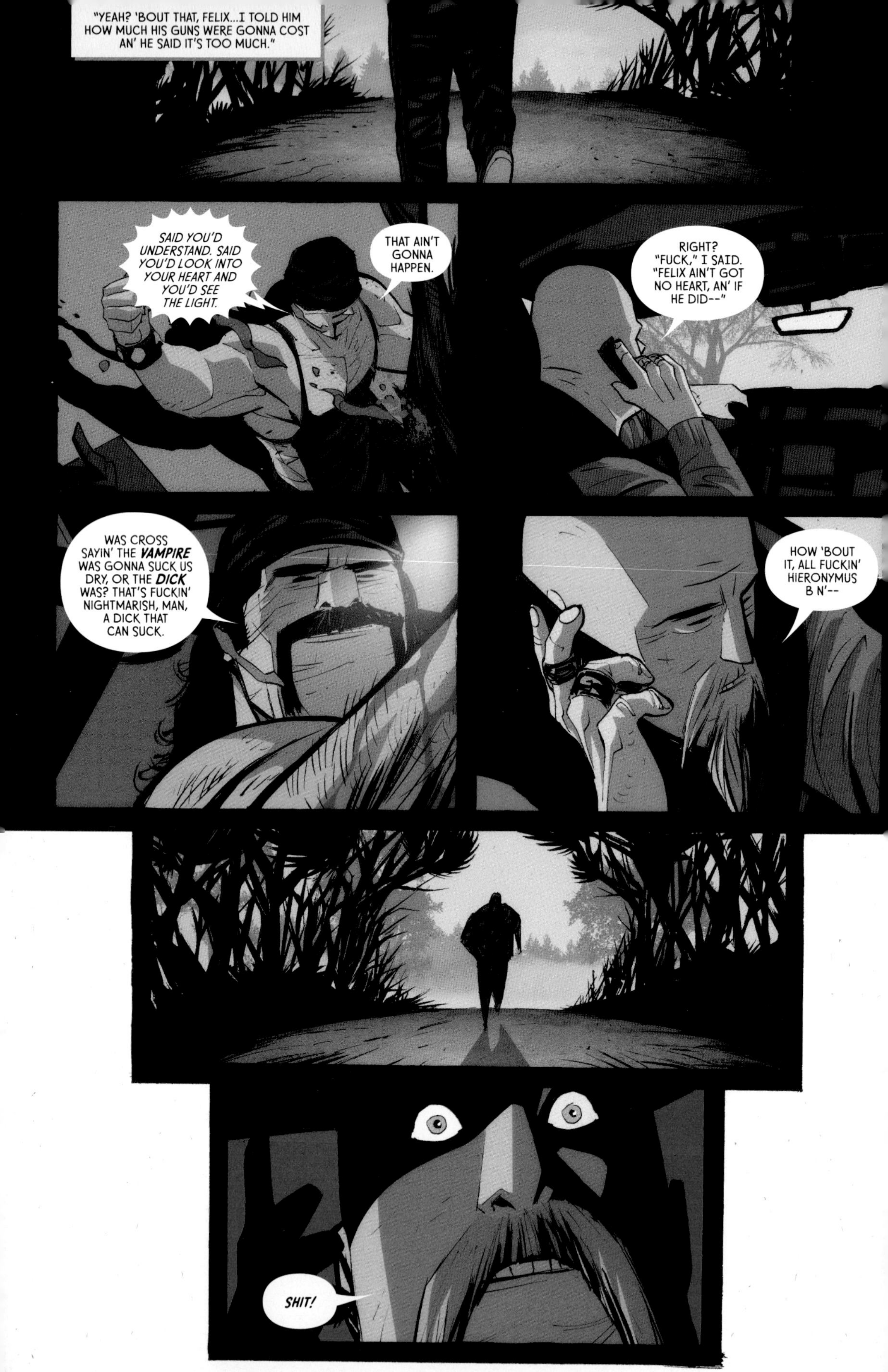
"YEAH? 'BOUT THAT, FELIX...I TOLD HIM HOW MUCH HIS GUNS WERE GONNA COST AN' HE SAID IT'S TOO MUCH."
SAID YOU'D UNDERSTAND. SAID YOU'D LOOK INTO YOUR HEART AND YOU'D SEE THE LIGHT.
THAT AIN'T GONNA HAPPEN.
RIGHT? "FUCK," I SAID. "FELIX AIN'T GOT NO HEART, AN' IF HE DID--"
WAS CROSS SAYIN' THE VAMPIRE WAS GONNA SUCK US DRY, OR THE DICK WAS? THAT'S FUCKIN' NIGHTMARISH, MAN, A DICK THAT CAN SUCK.
HOW 'BOUT IT, ALL FUCKIN' HIERONYMUS B N'--
SHIT!

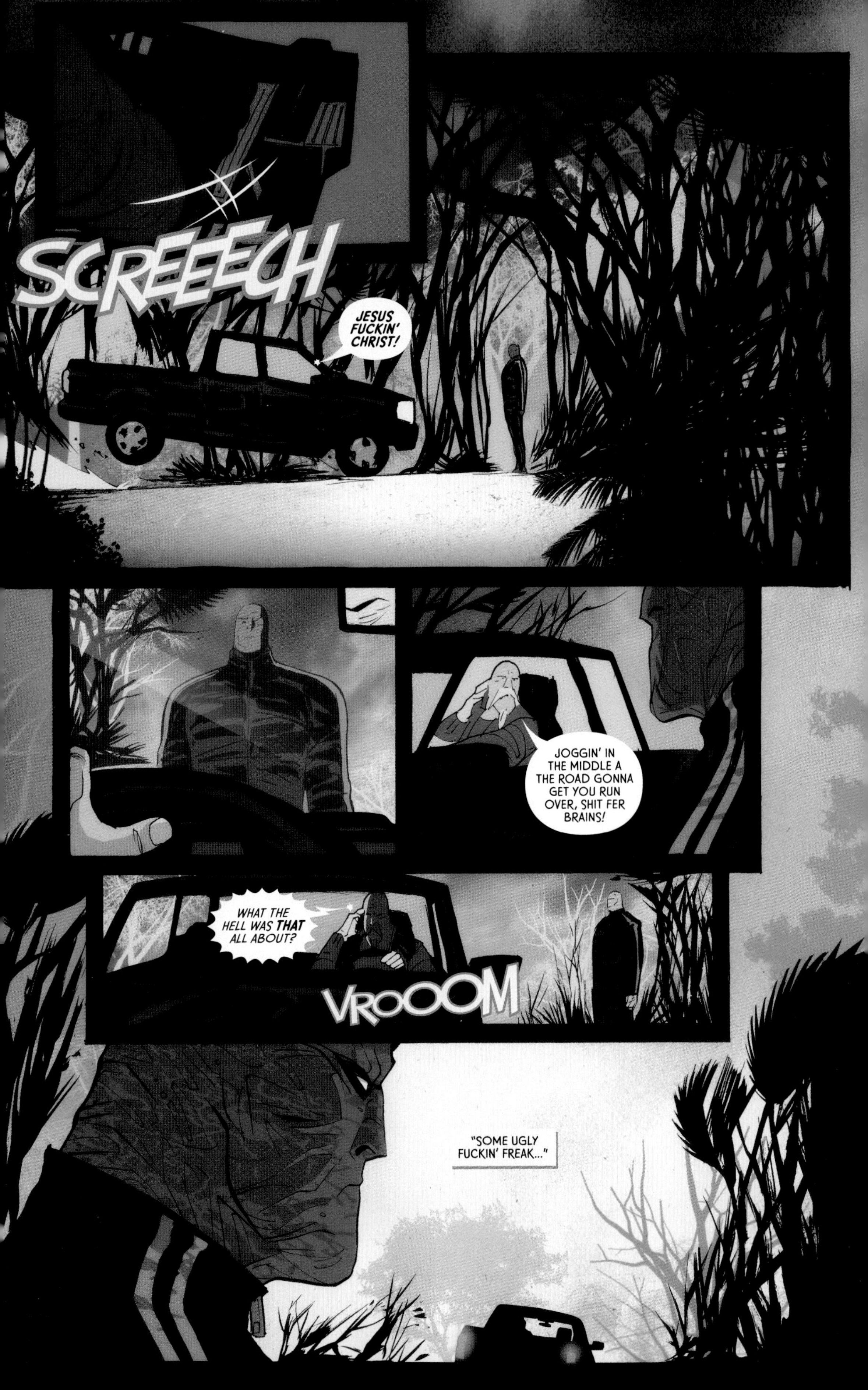
SCREEECH
JESUS FUCKIN' CHRIST!
JOGGIN' IN THE MIDDLE A THE ROAD GONNA GET YOU RUN OVER, SHIT FER BRAINS!
WHAT THE HELL WAS THAT ALL ABOUT?
VROOOM
"SOME UGLY FUCKIN' FREAK..."

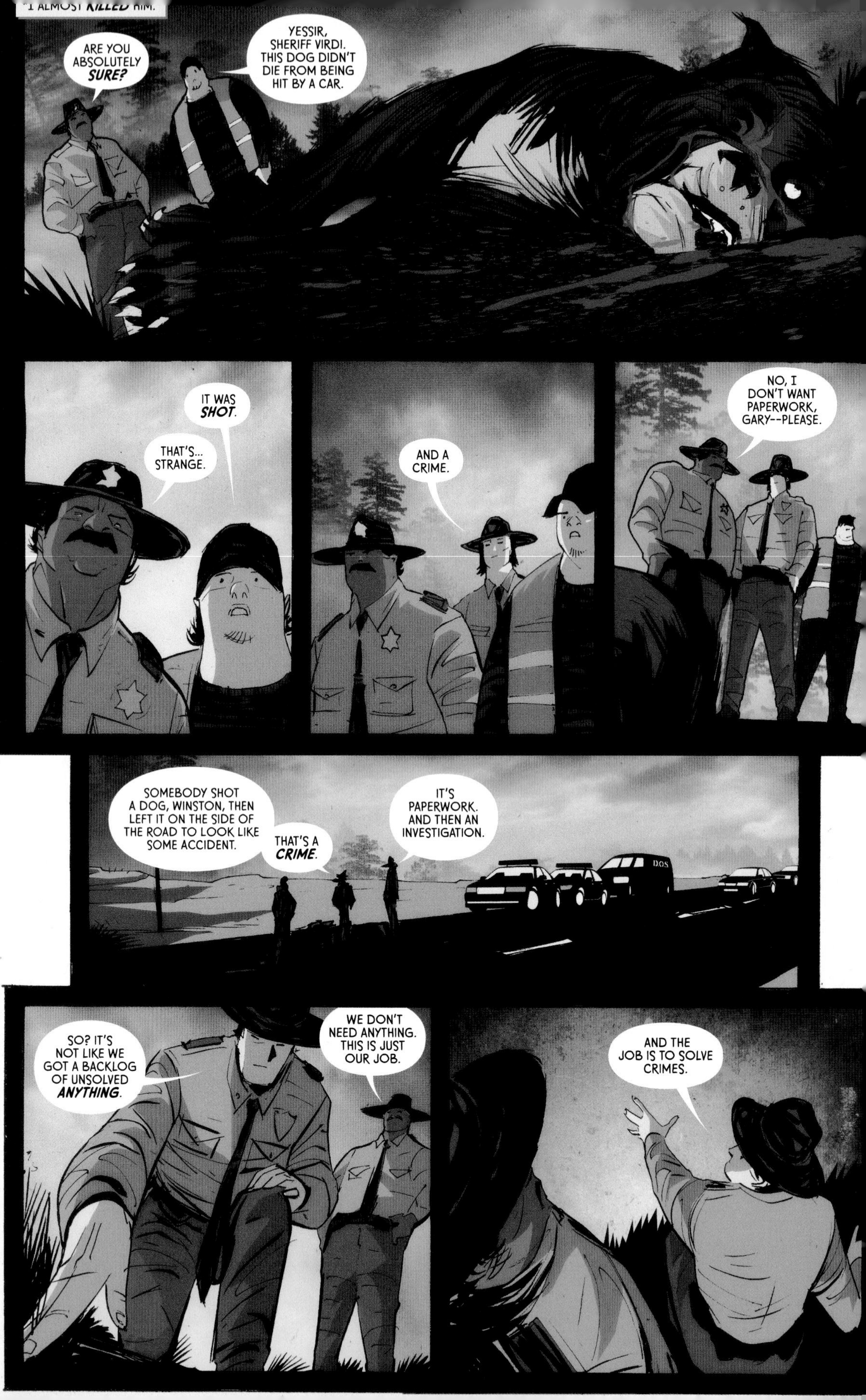
"I ALMOST KILLED HIM.
ARE YOU ABSOLUTELY ***SURE?***
YESSIR, SHERIFF VIRDI. THIS DOG DIDN'T DIE FROM BEING HIT BY A CAR.
IT WAS ***SHOT***.
THAT'S... STRANGE.
AND A CRIME.
NO, I DON'T WANT PAPERWORK, GARY--PLEASE.
SOMEBODY SHOT A DOG, WINSTON, THEN LEFT IT ON THE SIDE OF THE ROAD TO LOOK LIKE SOME ACCIDENT.
THAT'S A ***CRIME***.
IT'S PAPERWORK. AND THEN AN INVESTIGATION.
D.O.S.
SO? IT'S NOT LIKE WE GOT A BACKLOG OF UNSOLVED ***ANYTHING***.
WE DON'T NEED ANYTHING. THIS IS JUST OUR JOB.
AND THE JOB IS TO SOLVE CRIMES.

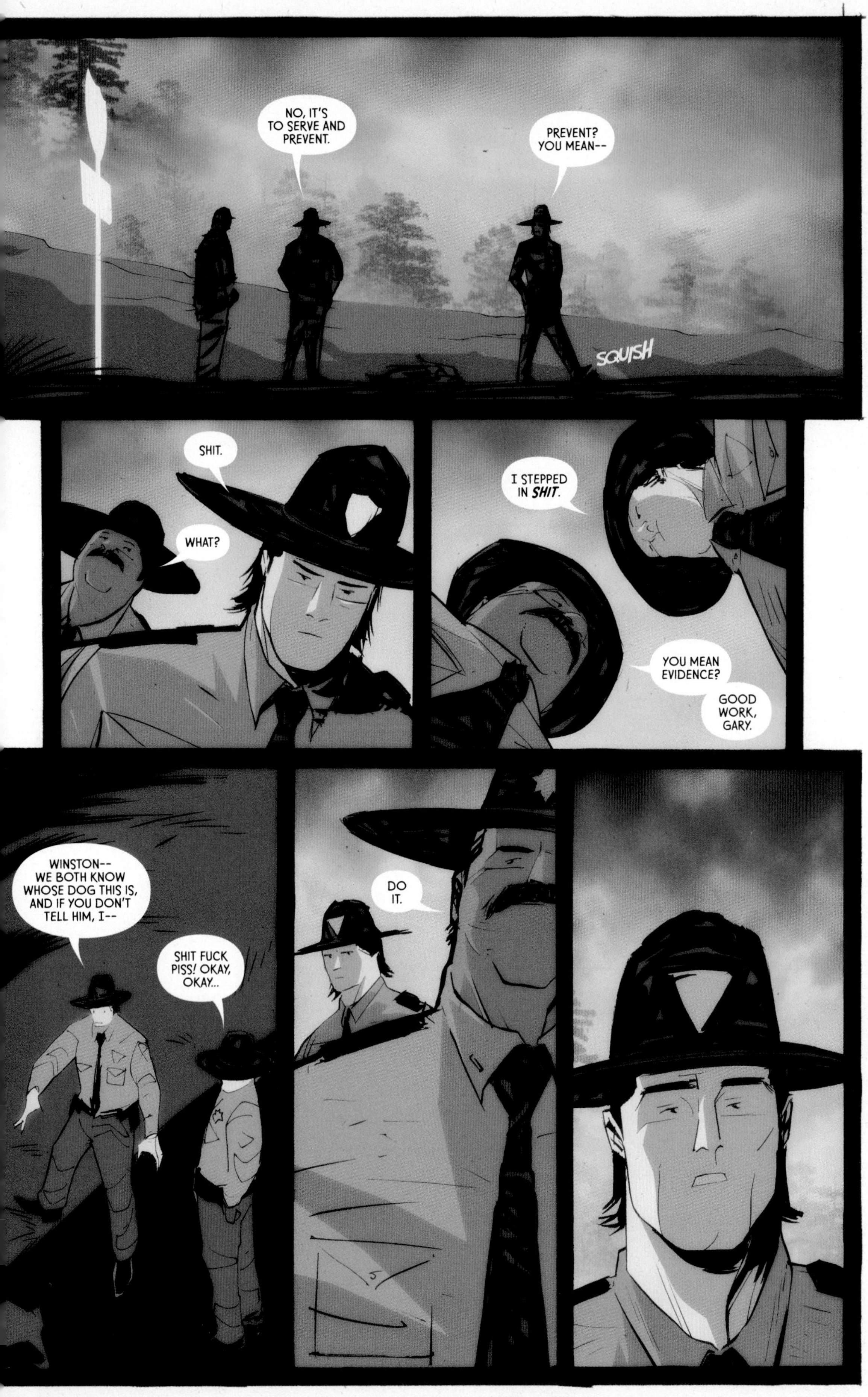
NO, IT'S TO SERVE AND PREVENT.
PREVENT? YOU MEAN--
SQUISH
SHIT.
WHAT?
I STEPPED IN *SHIT*.
YOU MEAN EVIDENCE?
GOOD WORK, GARY.
WINSTON-- WE BOTH KNOW WHOSE DOG THIS IS, AND IF YOU DON'T TELL HIM, I--
SHIT FUCK PISS! OKAY, OKAY...
DO IT.

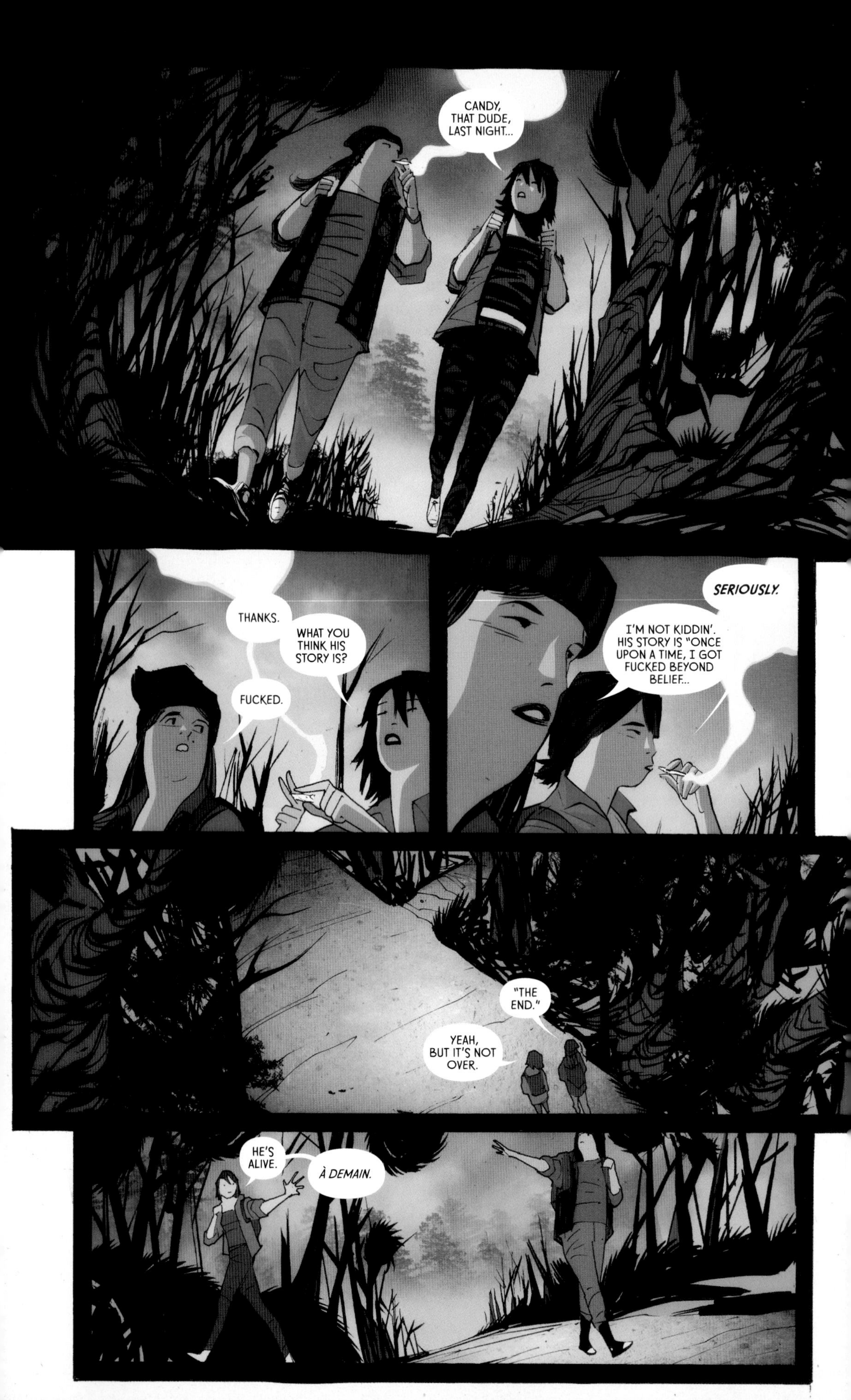
CANDY, THAT DUDE, LAST NIGHT...
THANKS.
WHAT YOU THINK HIS STORY IS?
FUCKED.
SERIOUSLY.
I'M NOT KIDDIN'. HIS STORY IS "ONCE UPON A TIME, I GOT FUCKED BEYOND BELIEF...
"THE END."
YEAH, BUT IT'S NOT OVER.
HE'S ALIVE.
À DEMAIN.

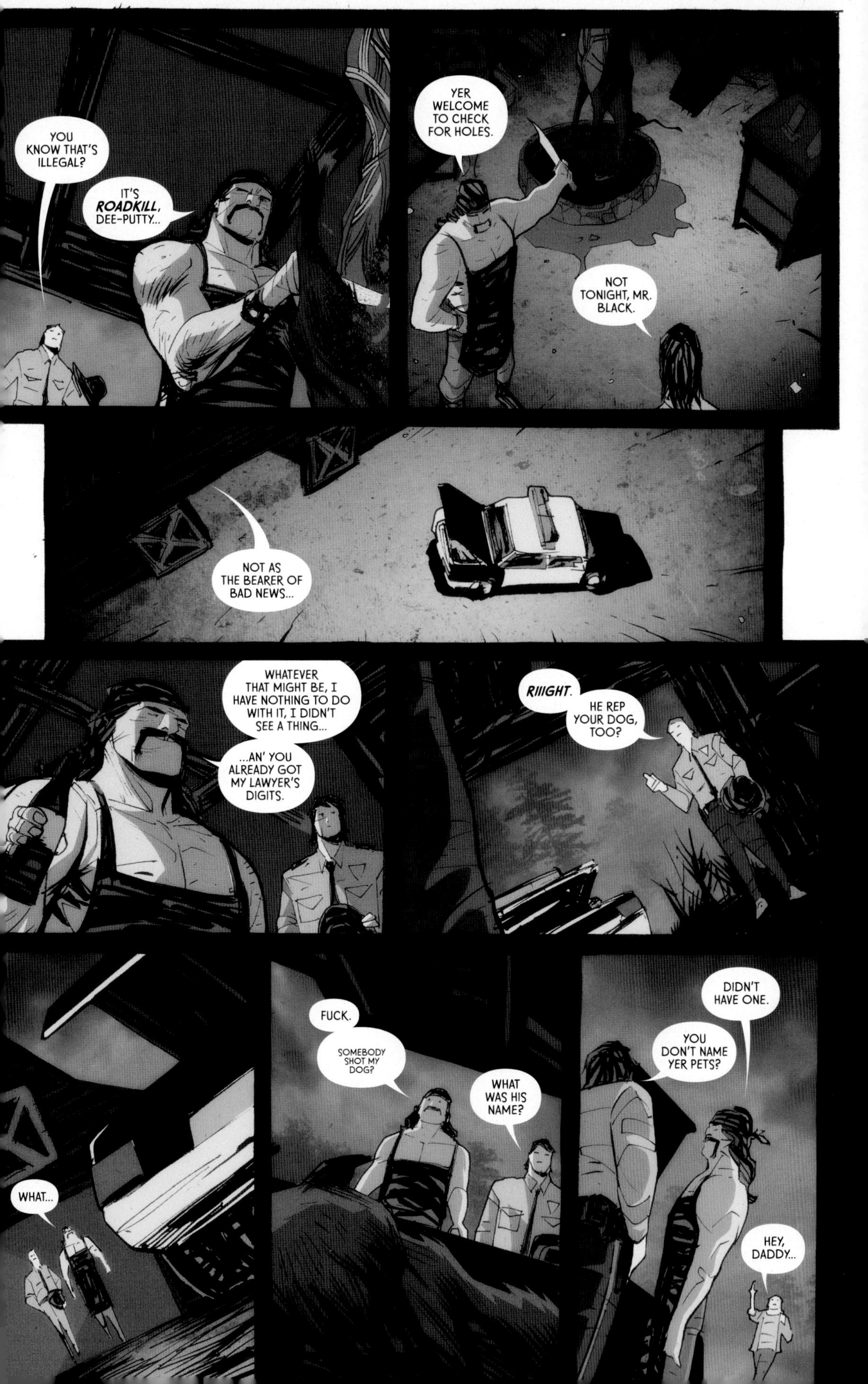

YOU KNOW THAT'S ILLEGAL?
IT'S **ROADKILL**, DEE-PUTTY...
YER WELCOME TO CHECK FOR HOLES.
NOT TONIGHT, MR. BLACK.
NOT AS THE BEARER OF BAD NEWS...
WHATEVER THAT MIGHT BE, I HAVE NOTHING TO DO WITH IT, I DIDN'T SEE A THING...
...AN' YOU ALREADY GOT MY LAWYER'S DIGITS.
RIIIGHT.
HE REP YOUR DOG, TOO?
WHAT...
FUCK.
SOMEBODY SHOT MY DOG?
WHAT WAS HIS NAME?
DIDN'T HAVE ONE.
YOU DON'T NAME YER PETS?
HEY, DADDY...

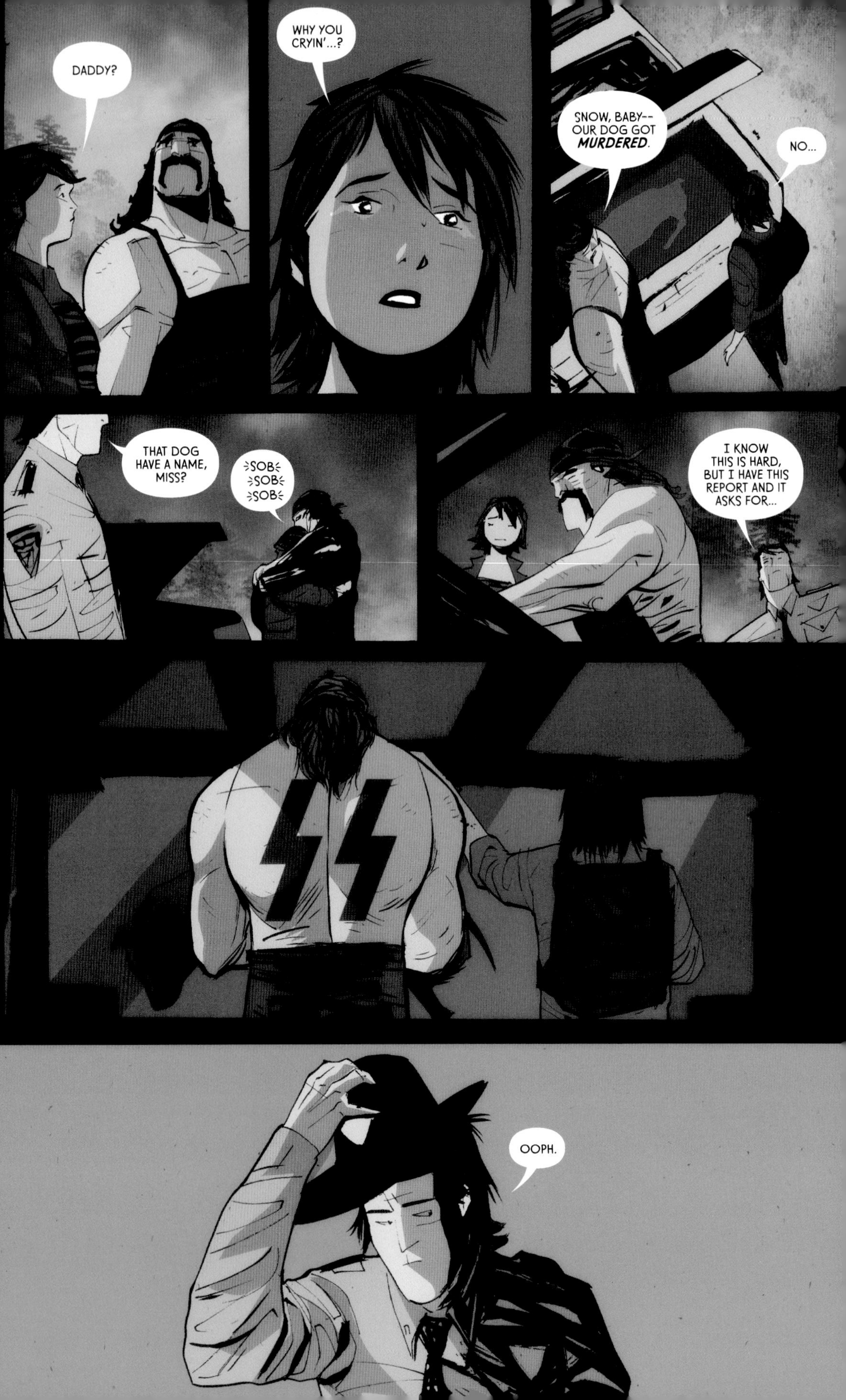
DADDY?
WHY YOU CRYIN'...?
SNOW, BABY-- OUR DOG GOT *MURDERED*.
NO...
THAT DOG HAVE A NAME, MISS?
SOB SOB SOB
I KNOW THIS IS HARD, BUT I HAVE THIS REPORT AND IT ASKS FOR...
OOPH.

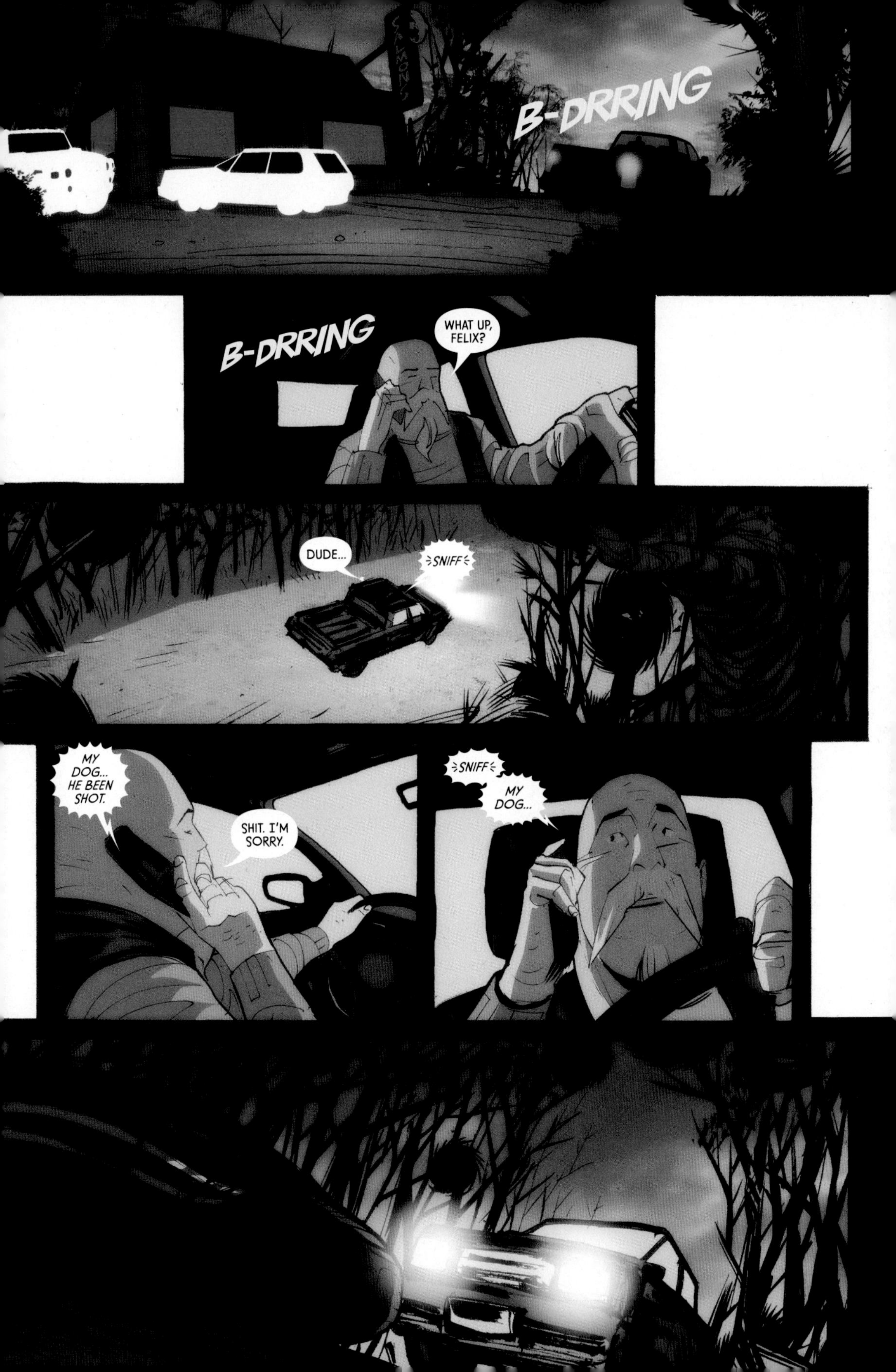
B-DRRING
B-DRRING
WHAT UP, FELIX?
DUDE...
SNIFF
MY DOG... HE BEEN SHOT.
SHIT. I'M SORRY.
SNIFF
MY DOG...

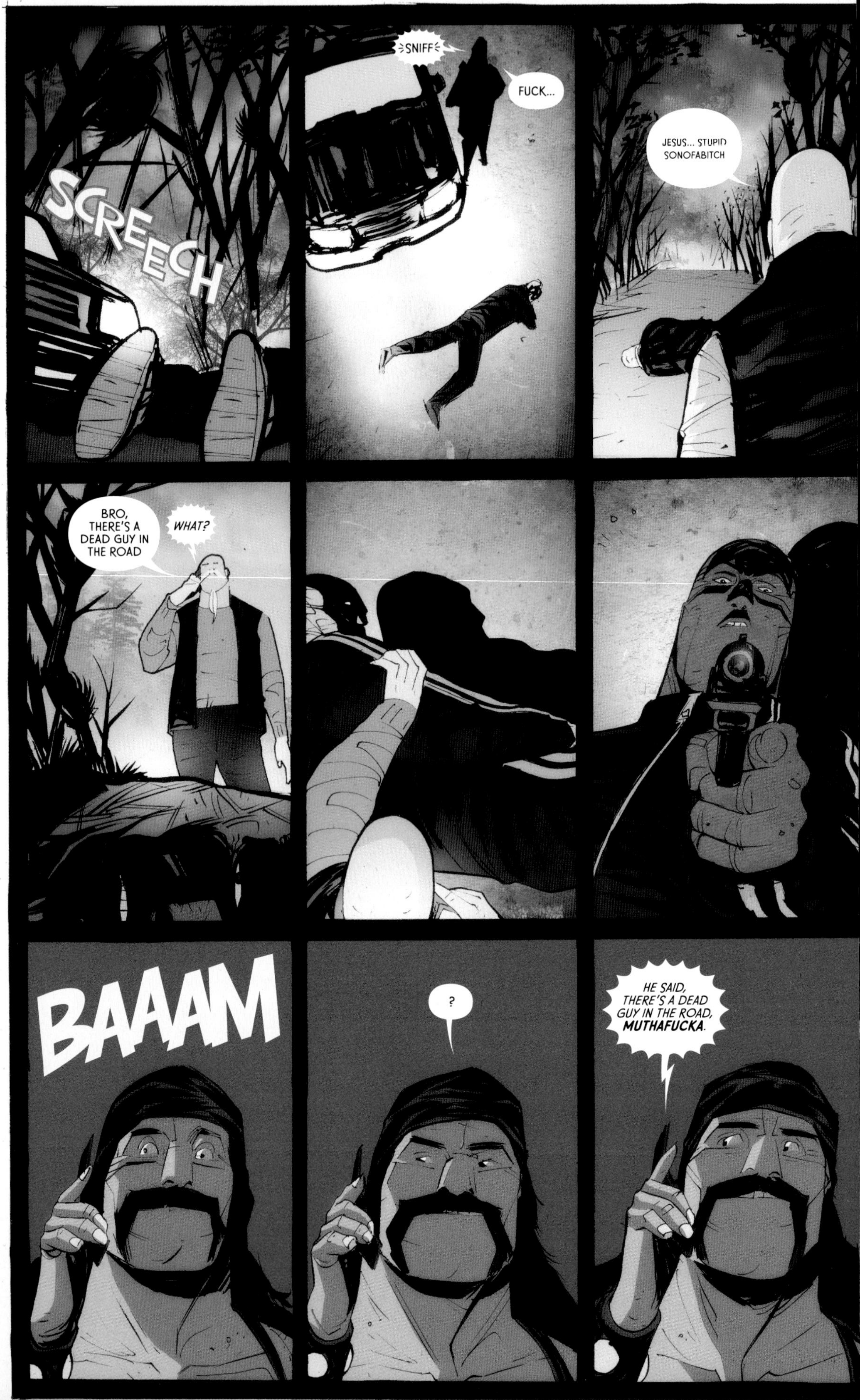
SCREEECH
SNIFF
FUCK...
JESUS... STUPID SONOFABITCH
BRO, THERE'S A DEAD GUY IN THE ROAD
WHAT?
BAAAM
?
HE SAID, THERE'S A DEAD GUY IN THE ROAD, MUTHAFUCKA.

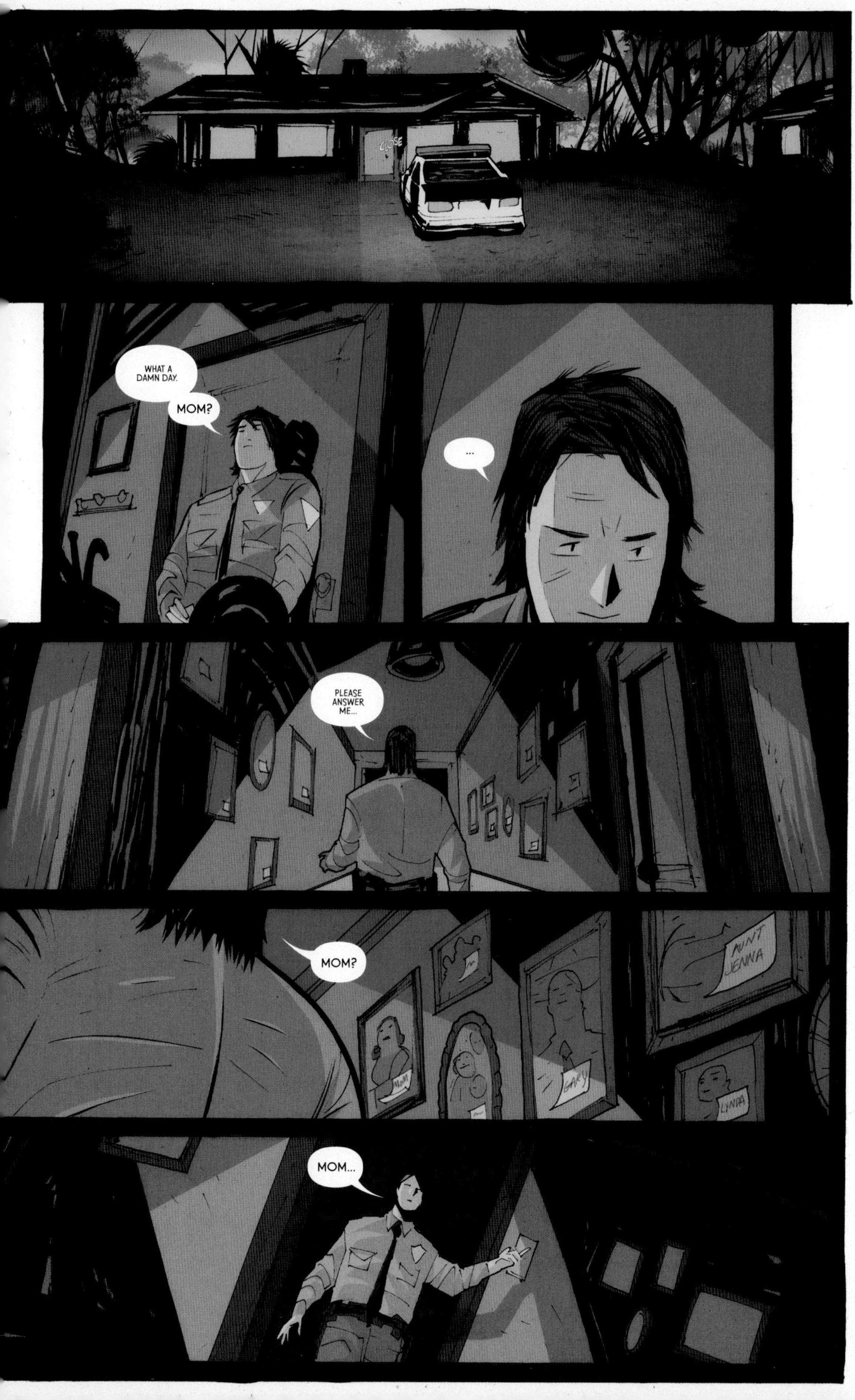
CLOSE
WHAT A DAMN DAY.
MOM?
...
PLEASE ANSWER ME...
MOM?
AUNT JENNA
MOM
GARY
LYNDA
MOM...

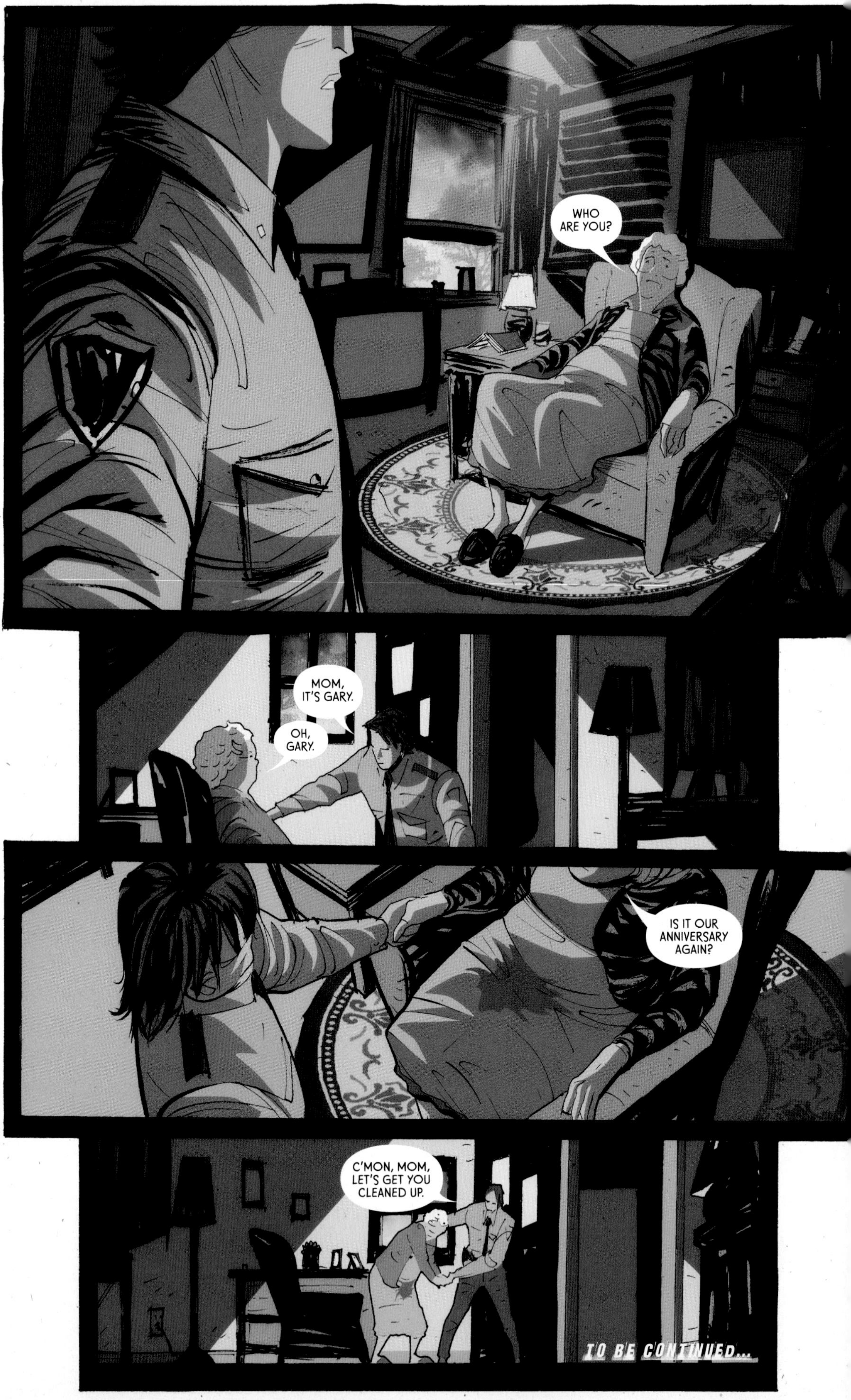
WHO ARE YOU?
MOM, IT'S GARY.
OH, GARY.
IS IT OUR ANNIVERSARY AGAIN?
C'MON, MOM, LET'S GET YOU CLEANED UP.
TO BE CONTINUED...

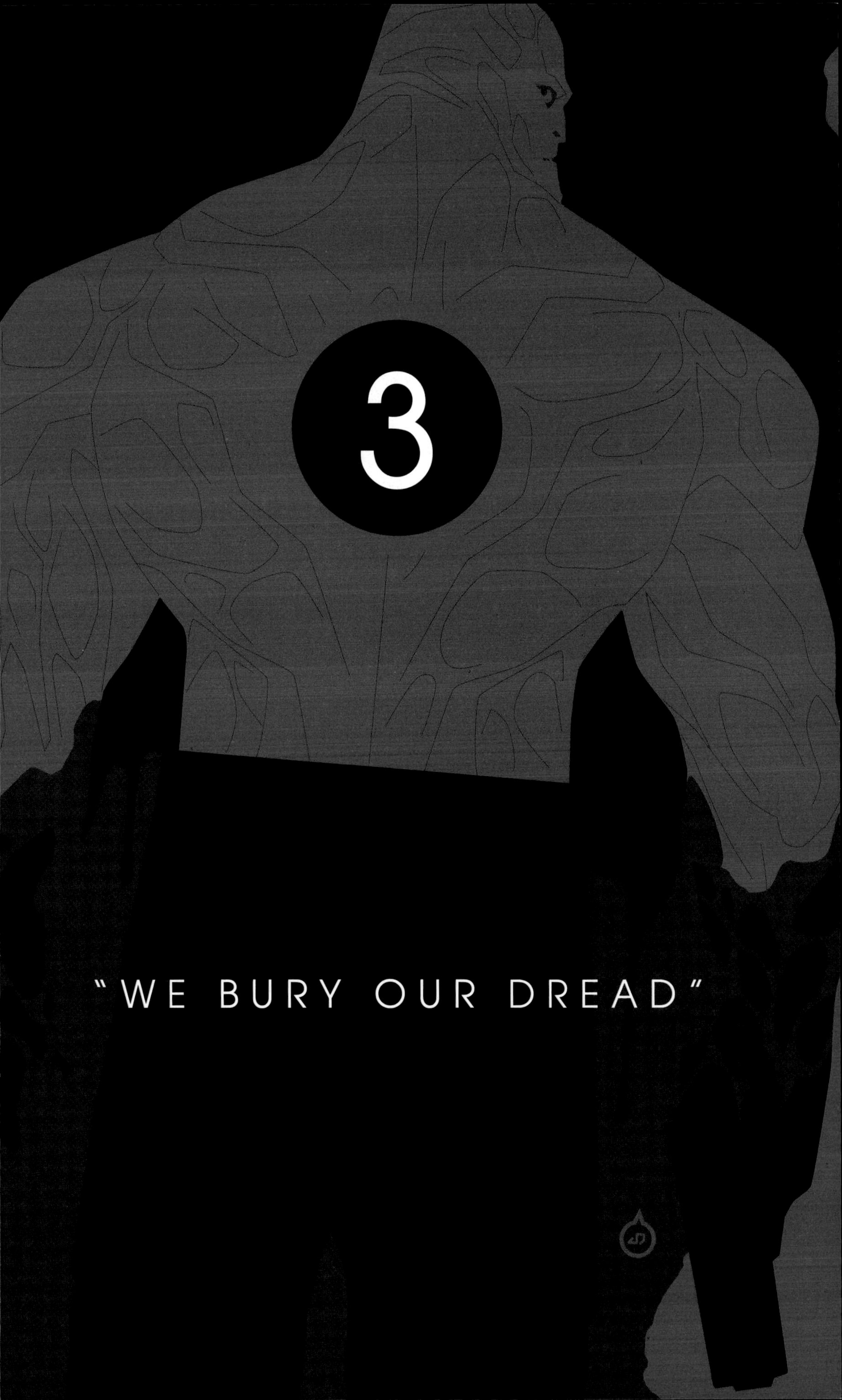
3
"WE BURY OUR DREAD"

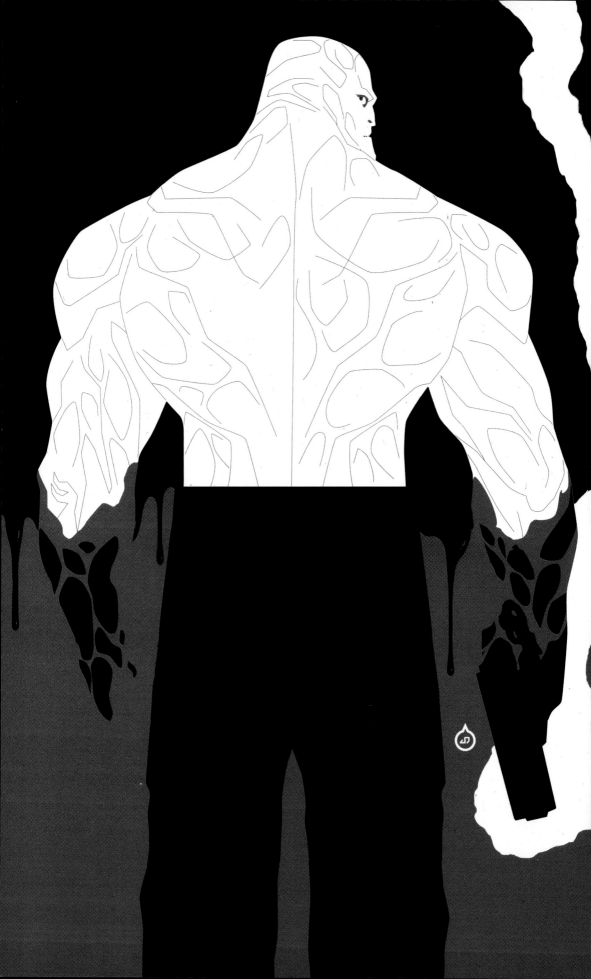

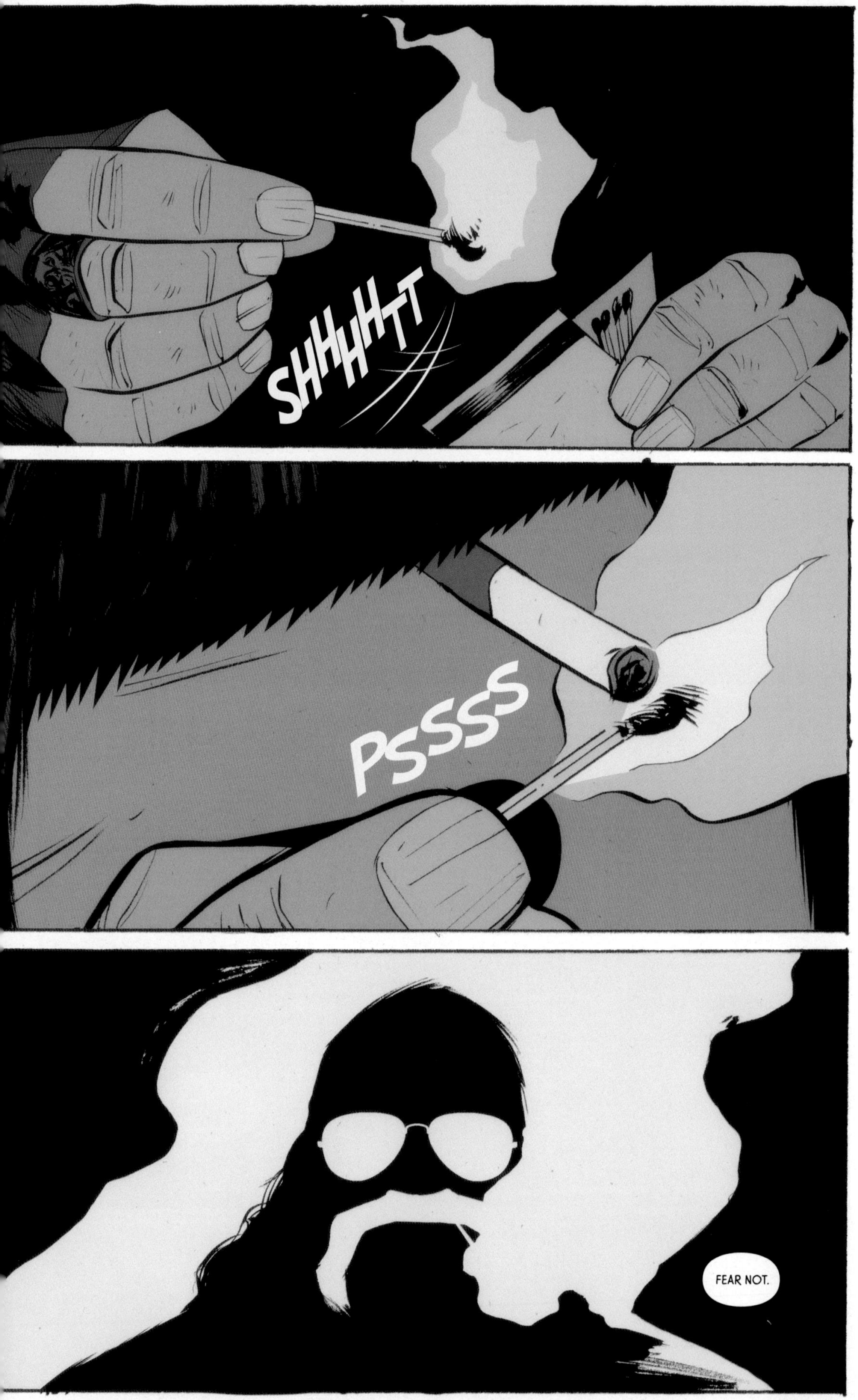
SHHHHTT
PSSSSS
FEAR NOT.

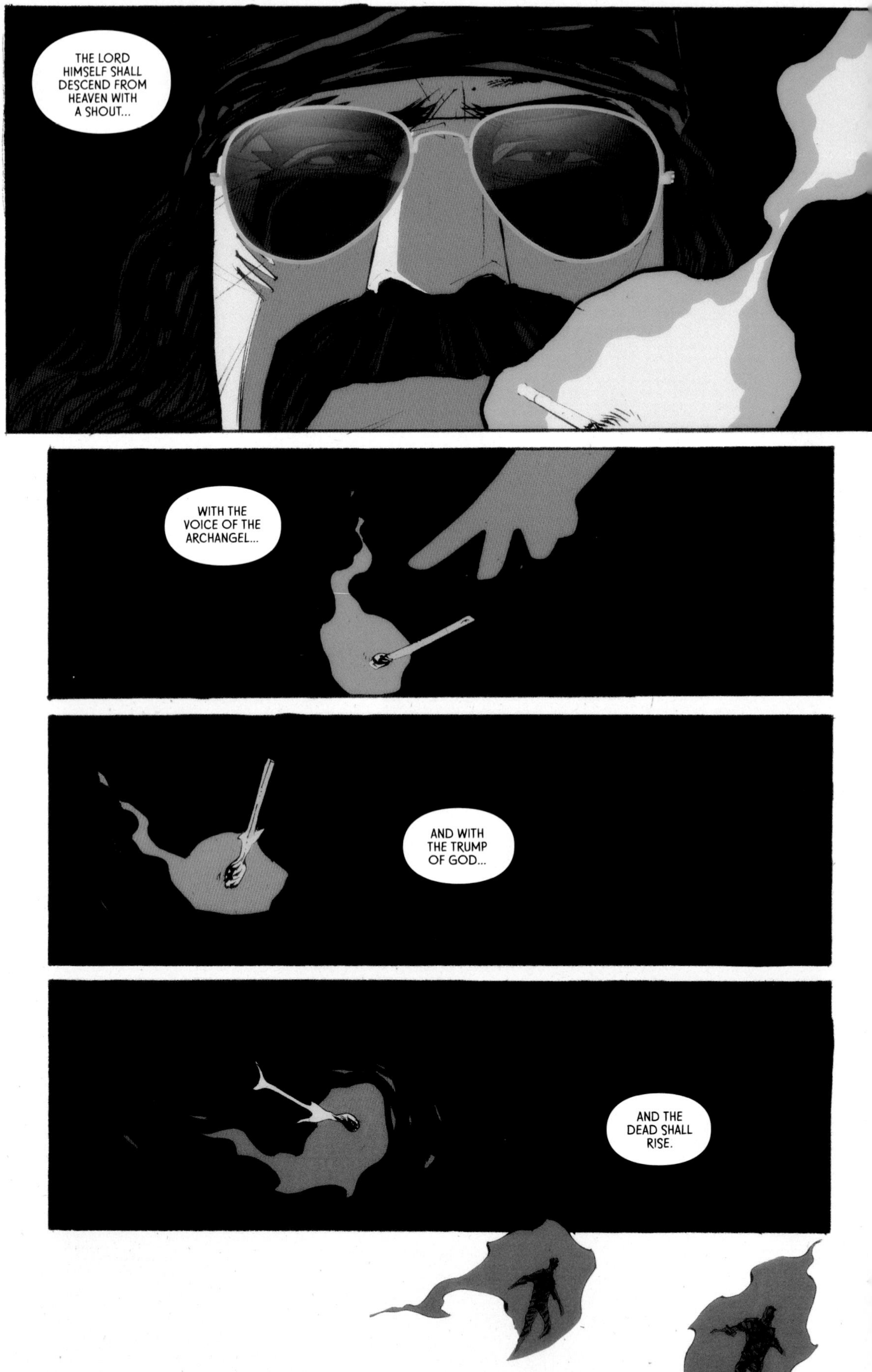
THE LORD HIMSELF SHALL DESCEND FROM HEAVEN WITH A SHOUT...
WITH THE VOICE OF THE ARCHANGEL...
AND WITH THE TRUMP OF GOD...
AND THE DEAD SHALL RISE.

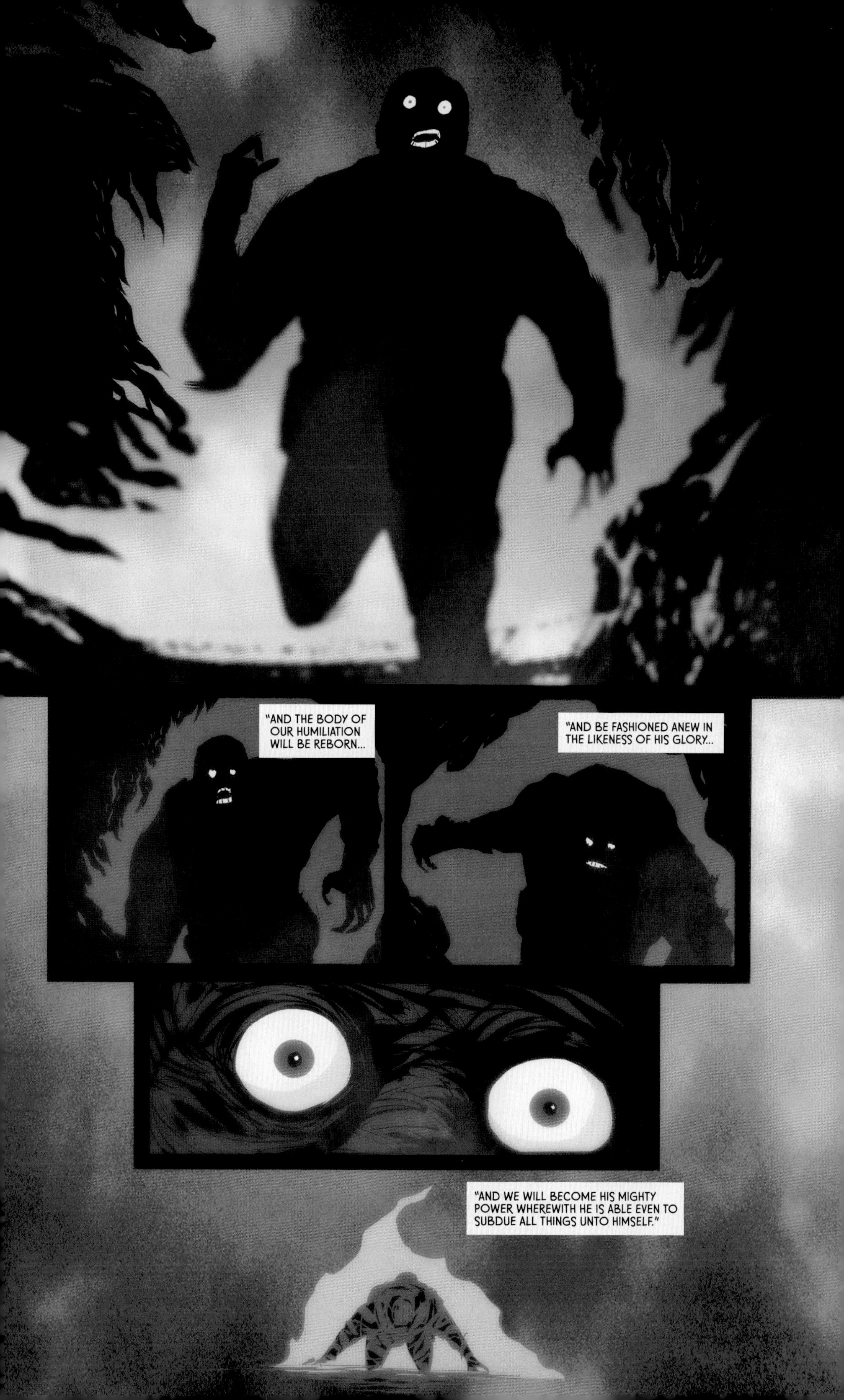
"AND THE BODY OF OUR HUMILIATION WILL BE REBORN...
"AND BE FASHIONED ANEW IN THE LIKENESS OF HIS GLORY...
"AND WE WILL BECOME HIS MIGHTY POWER WHEREWITH HE IS ABLE EVEN TO SUBDUE ALL THINGS UNTO HIMSELF."

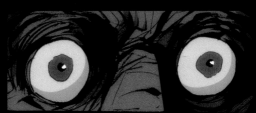

"TERRIBLE THOUGH IT MAY SEEM, DEATH IS NOT AN ENDING...

"BUT A RETURN TO GRACE."

ASHES TO ASHES, DUST TO--

DUDE...

CONNER, RED-- GET IN THAT FUCKIN' MUD HUT! WE SENT TWO MEN IN...

...HOW THE FUCK DID ONE *GET OUT?*

NO WORRIES, BROTHER...

...I GOT'CHER BACK.

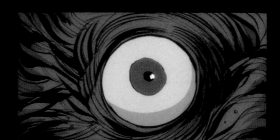

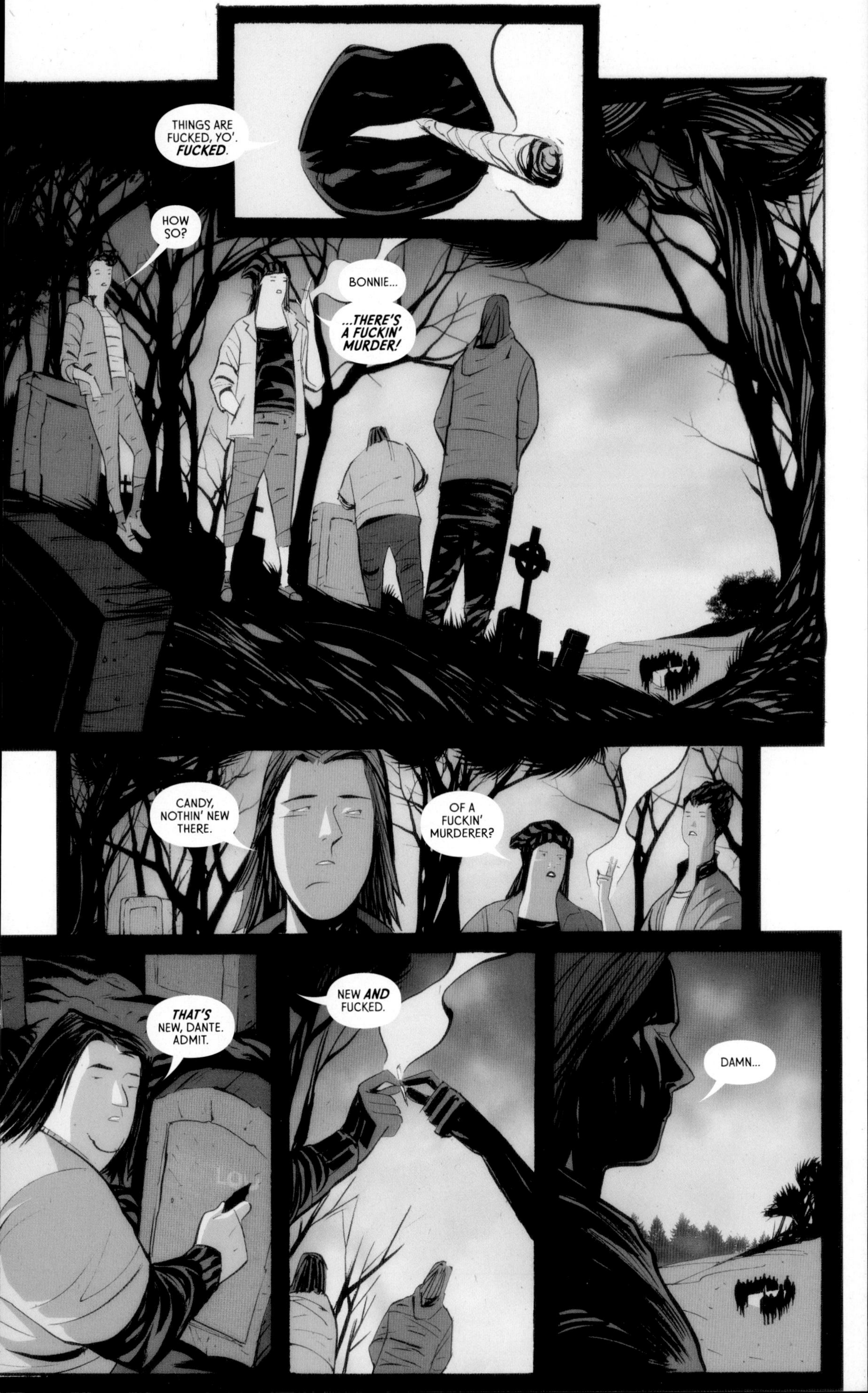
THINGS ARE FUCKED, YO'. ***FUCKED***.
HOW SO?
BONNIE...
...THERE'S A FUCKIN' MURDER!
CANDY, NOTHIN' NEW THERE.
OF A FUCKIN' MURDERER?
THAT'S NEW, DANTE. ADMIT.
NEW ***AND*** FUCKED.
DAMN...

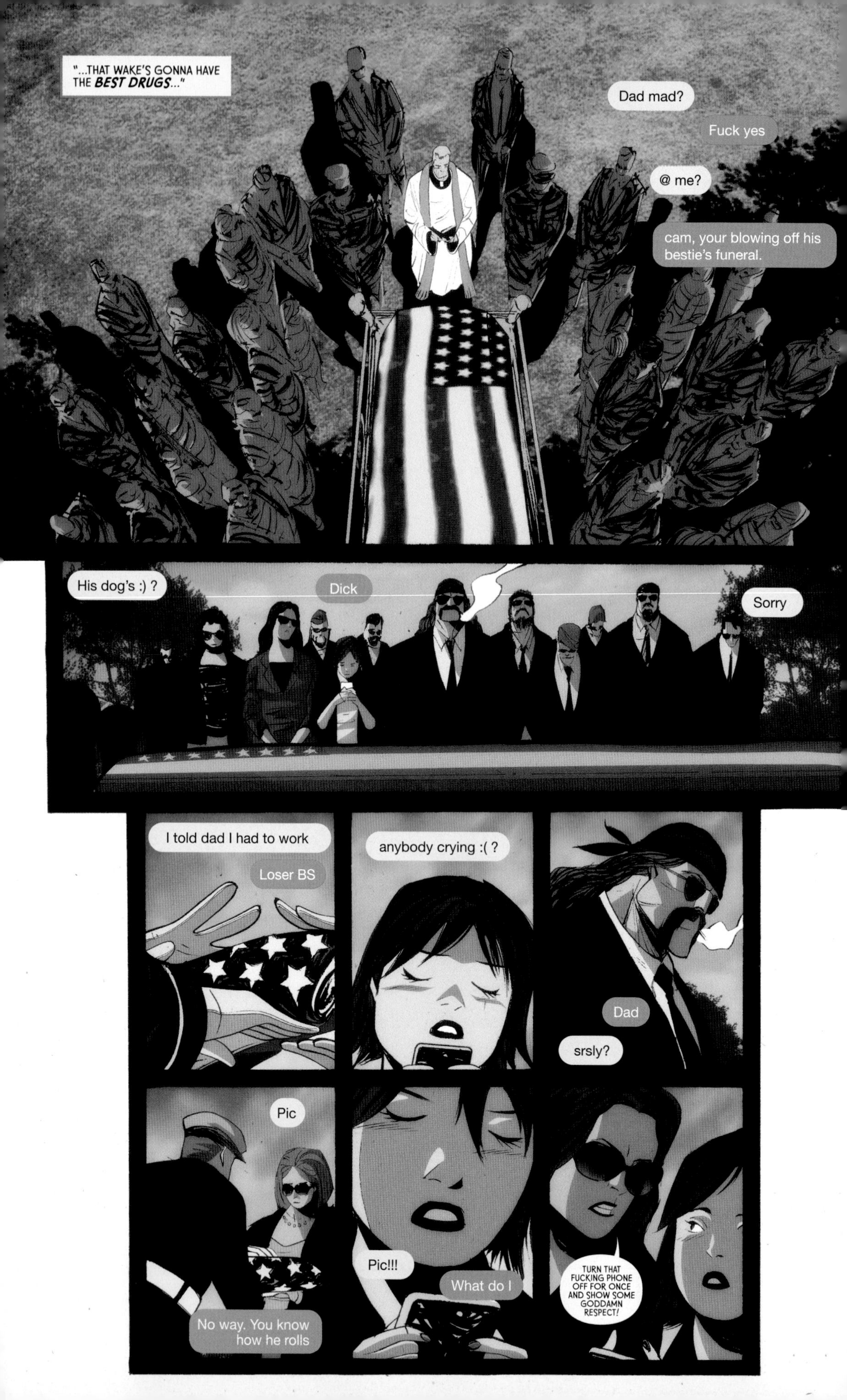
"...THAT WAKE'S GONNA HAVE THE **BEST DRUGS**..."
Dad mad?
Fuck yes
@ me?
cam, your blowing off his bestie's funeral.
His dog's :) ?
Dick
Sorry
I told dad I had to work
Loser BS
anybody crying :(?
Dad
srsly?
Pic
No way. You know how he rolls
Pic!!!
What do I
TURN THAT FUCKING PHONE OFF FOR ONCE AND SHOW SOME GODDAMN RESPECT!

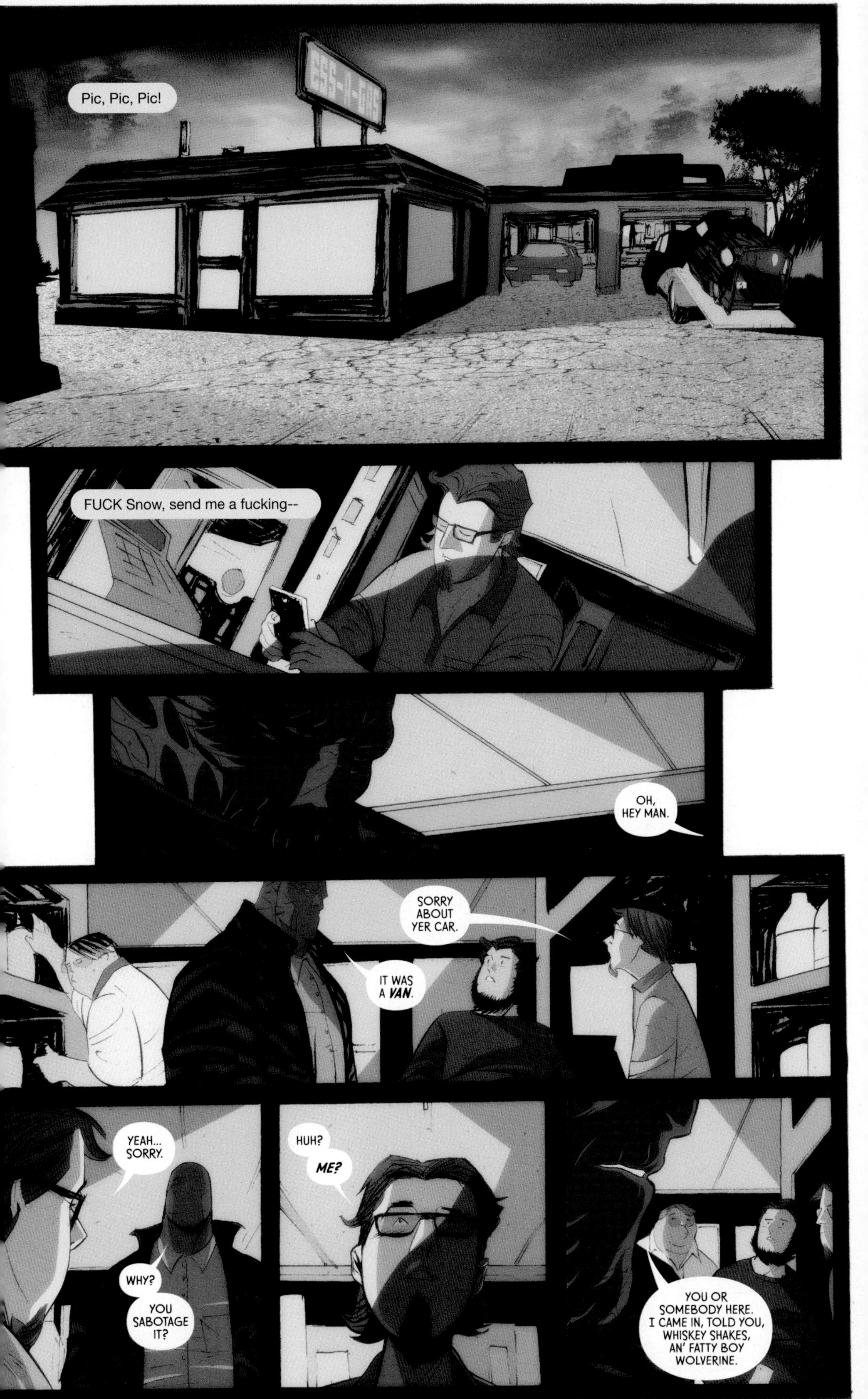
Pic, Pic, Pic!
FUCK Snow, send me a fucking--
OH, HEY MAN.
SORRY ABOUT YER CAR.
IT WAS A **VAN**.
YEAH... SORRY.
WHY?
YOU SABOTAGE IT?
HUH?
ME?
YOU OR SOMEBODY HERE. I CAME IN, TOLD YOU, WHISKEY SHAKES, AN' FATTY BOY WOLVERINE.

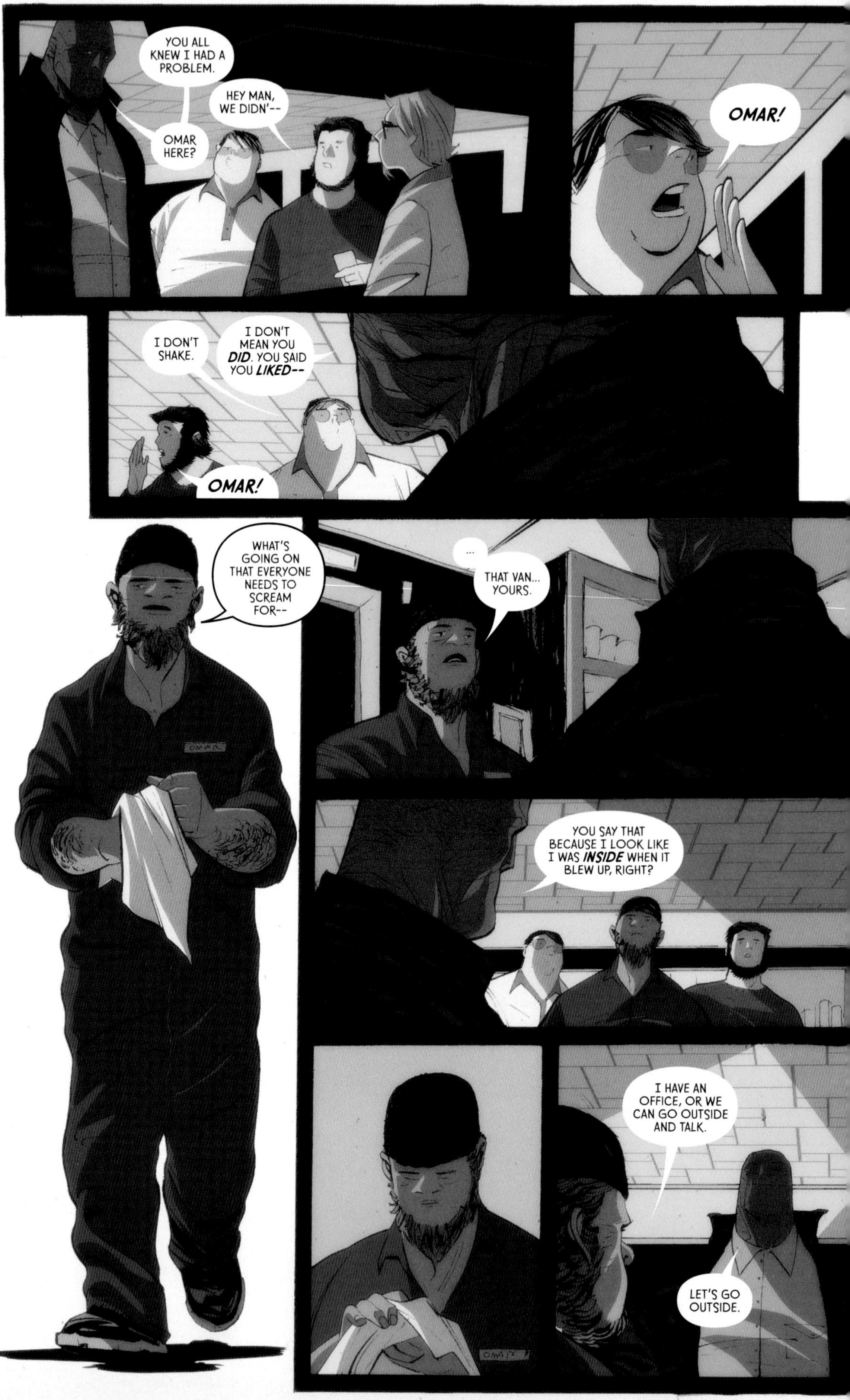
YOU ALL KNEW I HAD A PROBLEM.
OMAR HERE?
HEY MAN, WE DIDN'--
OMAR!
I DON'T SHAKE.
I DON'T MEAN YOU DID. YOU SAID YOU LIKED--
OMAR!
WHAT'S GOING ON THAT EVERYONE NEEDS TO SCREAM FOR--
...
THAT VAN... YOURS.
YOU SAY THAT BECAUSE I LOOK LIKE I WAS INSIDE WHEN IT BLEW UP, RIGHT?
I HAVE AN OFFICE, OR WE CAN GO OUTSIDE AND TALK.
LET'S GO OUTSIDE.

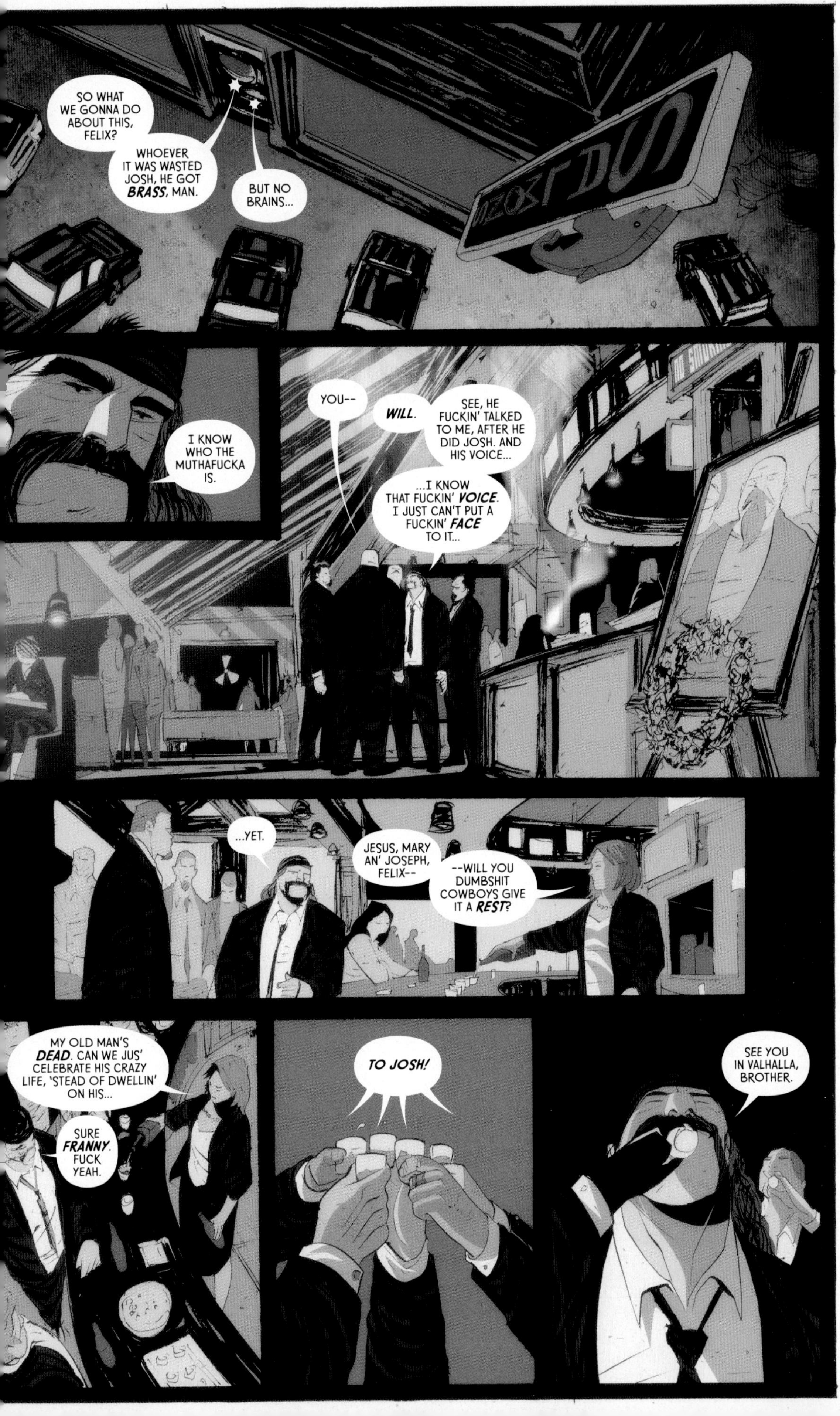

SO WHAT WE GONNA DO ABOUT THIS, FELIX?
WHOEVER IT WAS WASTED JOSH, HE GOT BRASS, MAN.
BUT NO BRAINS...
I KNOW WHO THE MUTHAFUCKA IS.
YOU--
WILL.
SEE, HE FUCKIN' TALKED TO ME, AFTER HE DID JOSH. AND HIS VOICE...
...I KNOW THAT FUCKIN' VOICE. I JUST CAN'T PUT A FUCKIN' FACE TO IT...
...YET.
JESUS, MARY AN' JOSEPH, FELIX--
--WILL YOU DUMBSHIT COWBOYS GIVE IT A REST?
MY OLD MAN'S DEAD. CAN WE JUS' CELEBRATE HIS CRAZY LIFE, 'STEAD OF DWELLIN' ON HIS...
SURE FRANNY. FUCK YEAH.
TO JOSH!
SEE YOU IN VALHALLA, BROTHER.

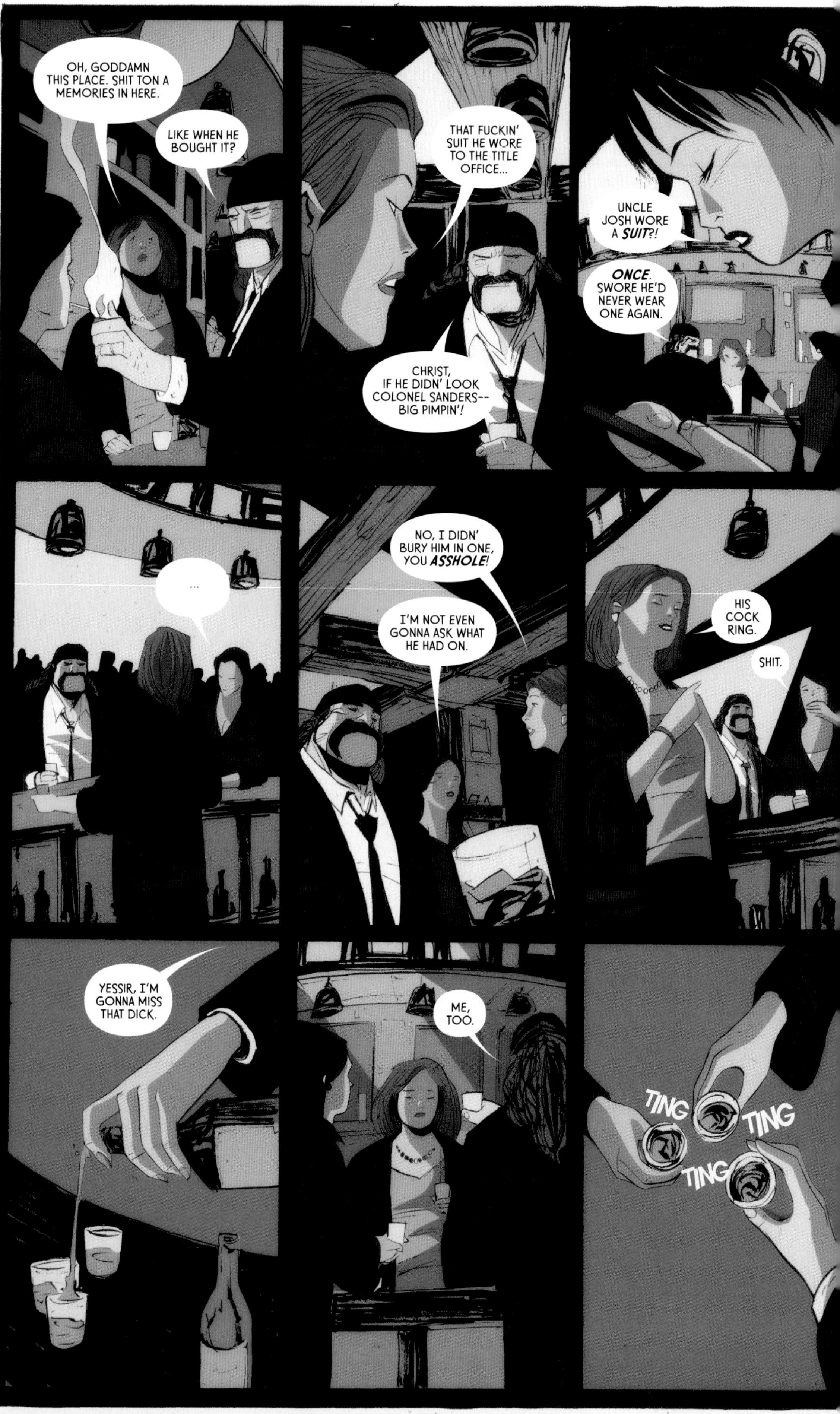
OH, GODDAMN THIS PLACE. SHIT TON A MEMORIES IN HERE.
LIKE WHEN HE BOUGHT IT?
THAT FUCKIN' SUIT HE WORE TO THE TITLE OFFICE...
CHRIST, IF HE DIDN' LOOK COLONEL SANDERS-- BIG PIMPIN'!
UNCLE JOSH WORE A *SUIT*?!
ONCE. SWORE HE'D NEVER WEAR ONE AGAIN.
...
NO, I DIDN' BURY HIM IN ONE, YOU *ASSHOLE*!
I'M NOT EVEN GONNA ASK WHAT HE HAD ON.
HIS COCK RING.
SHIT.
YESSIR, I'M GONNA MISS THAT DICK.
ME, TOO.
TING
TING
TING

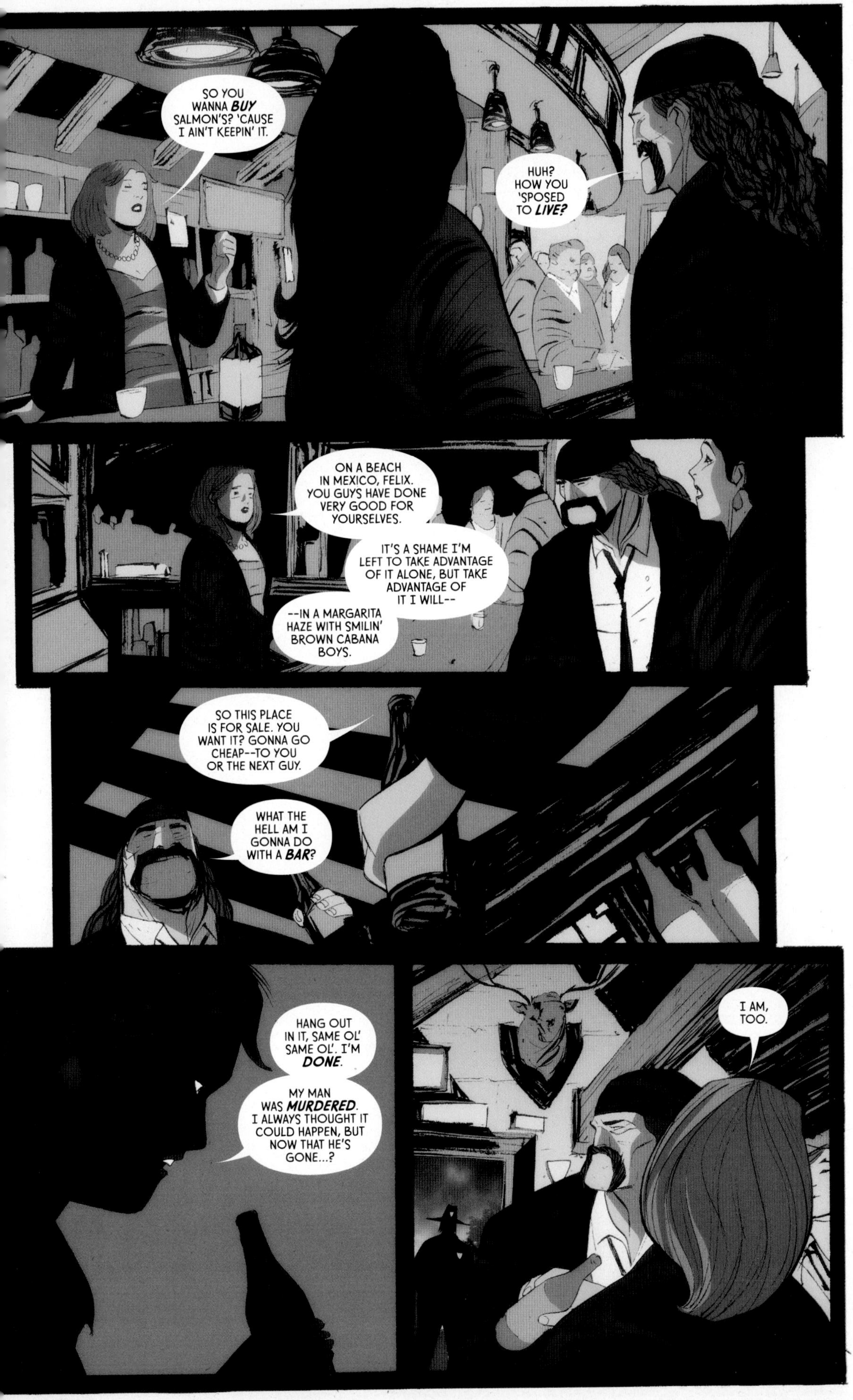
SO YOU WANNA **BUY** SALMON'S? 'CAUSE I AIN'T KEEPIN' IT.
HUH? HOW YOU 'SPOSED TO **LIVE?**
ON A BEACH IN MEXICO, FELIX. YOU GUYS HAVE DONE VERY GOOD FOR YOURSELVES.
IT'S A SHAME I'M LEFT TO TAKE ADVANTAGE OF IT ALONE, BUT TAKE ADVANTAGE OF IT I WILL--
--IN A MARGARITA HAZE WITH SMILIN' BROWN CABANA BOYS.
SO THIS PLACE IS FOR SALE. YOU WANT IT? GONNA GO CHEAP--TO YOU OR THE NEXT GUY.
WHAT THE HELL AM I GONNA DO WITH A **BAR**?
HANG OUT IN IT, SAME OL' SAME OL'. I'M **DONE**.
MY MAN WAS **MURDERED**. I ALWAYS THOUGHT IT COULD HAPPEN, BUT NOW THAT HE'S GONE...?
I AM, TOO.

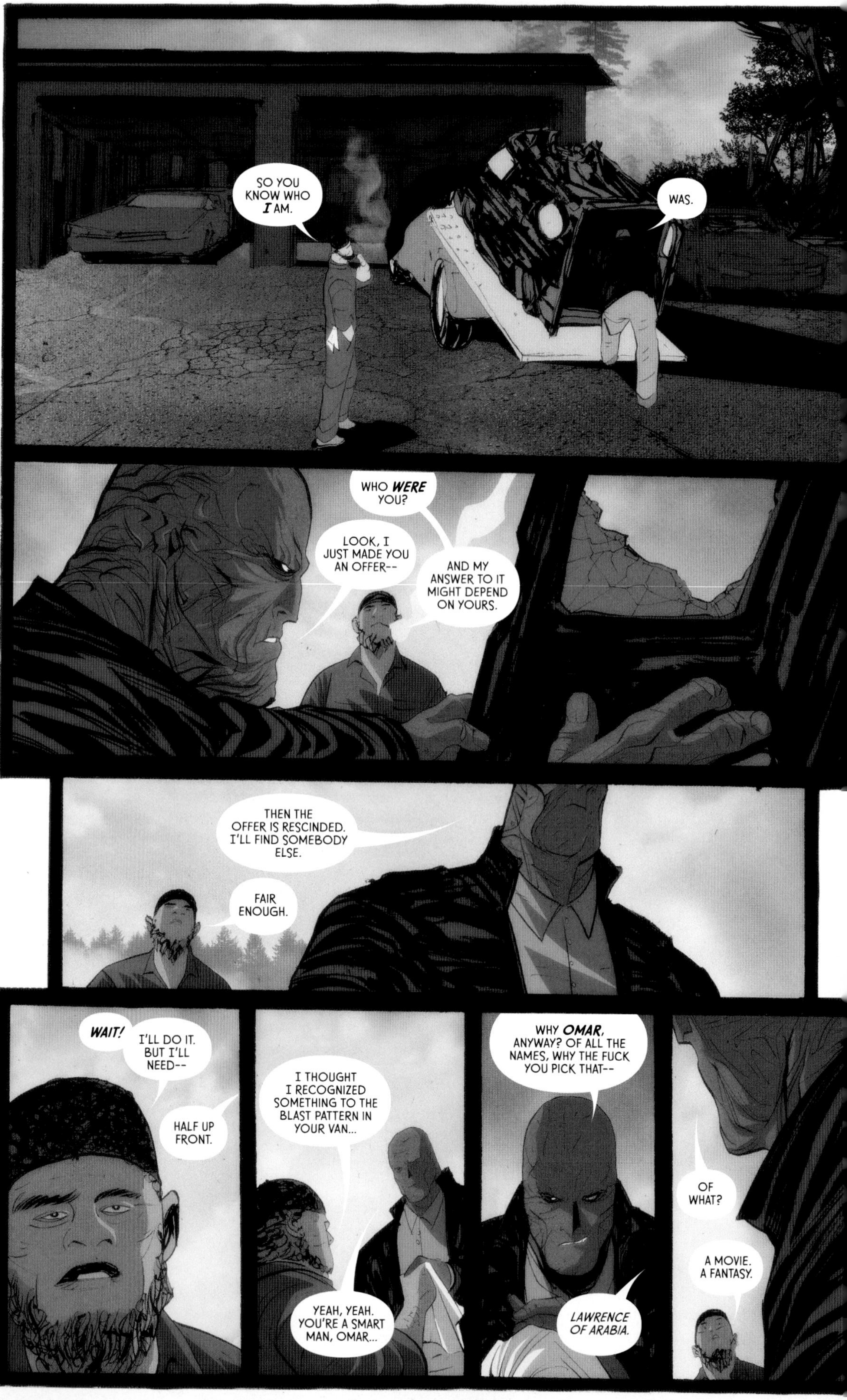
SO YOU KNOW WHO *I* AM.
WAS.
WHO ***WERE*** YOU?
LOOK, I JUST MADE YOU AN OFFER--
AND MY ANSWER TO IT MIGHT DEPEND ON YOURS.
THEN THE OFFER IS RESCINDED. I'LL FIND SOMEBODY ELSE.
FAIR ENOUGH.
WAIT!
I'LL DO IT. BUT I'LL NEED--
HALF UP FRONT.
I THOUGHT I RECOGNIZED SOMETHING TO THE BLAST PATTERN IN YOUR VAN...
YEAH, YEAH. YOU'RE A SMART MAN, OMAR...
WHY ***OMAR***, ANYWAY? OF ALL THE NAMES, WHY THE FUCK YOU PICK THAT--
LAWRENCE OF ARABIA.
OF WHAT?
A MOVIE. A FANTASY.

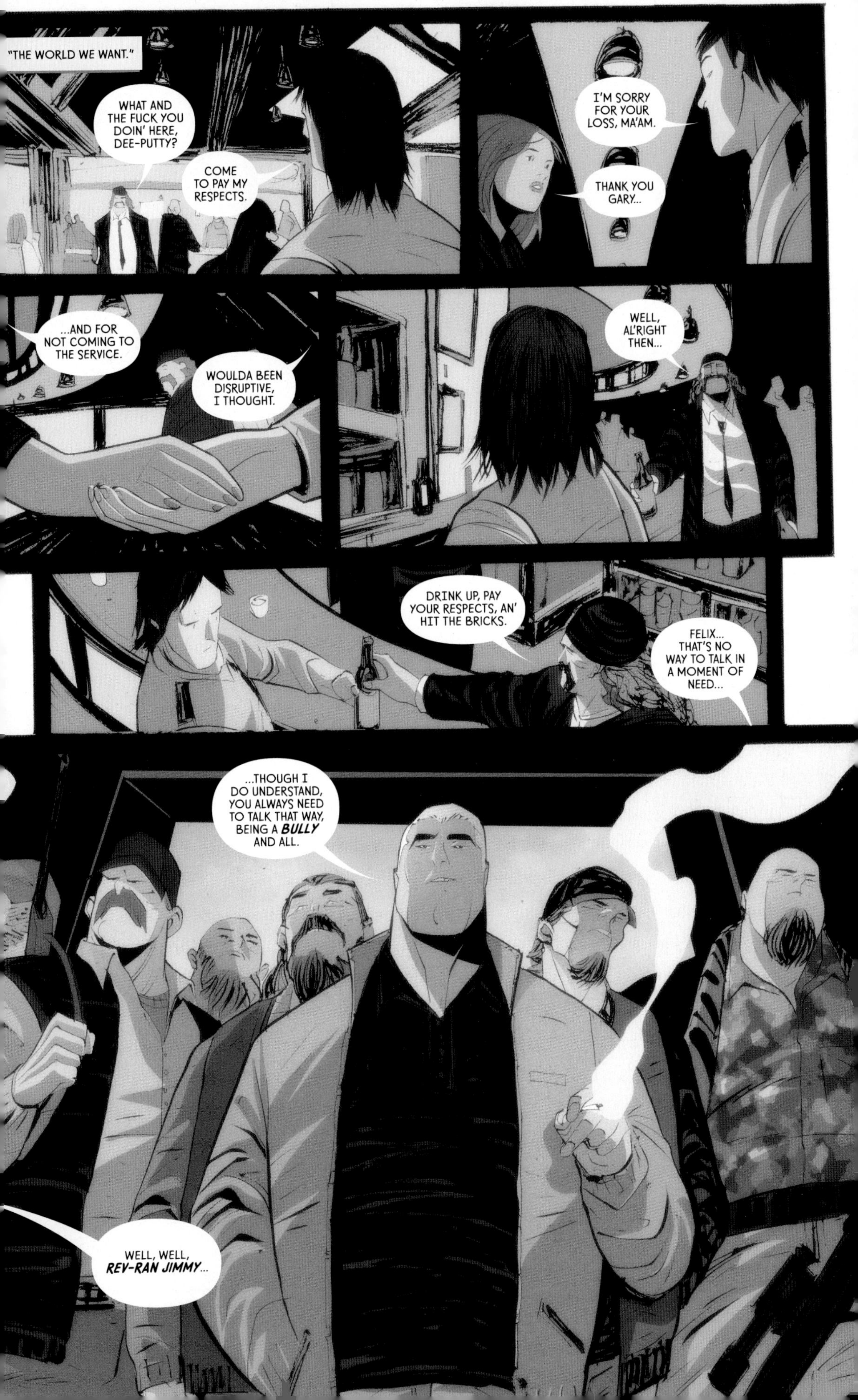
"THE WORLD WE WANT."
WHAT AND THE FUCK YOU DOIN' HERE, DEE-PUTTY?
COME TO PAY MY RESPECTS.
I'M SORRY FOR YOUR LOSS, MA'AM.
THANK YOU GARY...
...AND FOR NOT COMING TO THE SERVICE.
WOULDA BEEN DISRUPTIVE, I THOUGHT.
WELL, AL'RIGHT THEN...
DRINK UP, PAY YOUR RESPECTS, AN' HIT THE BRICKS.
FELIX... THAT'S NO WAY TO TALK IN A MOMENT OF NEED...
...THOUGH I DO UNDERSTAND, YOU ALWAYS NEED TO TALK THAT WAY, BEING A BULLY AND ALL.
WELL, WELL, REV-RAN JIMMY...

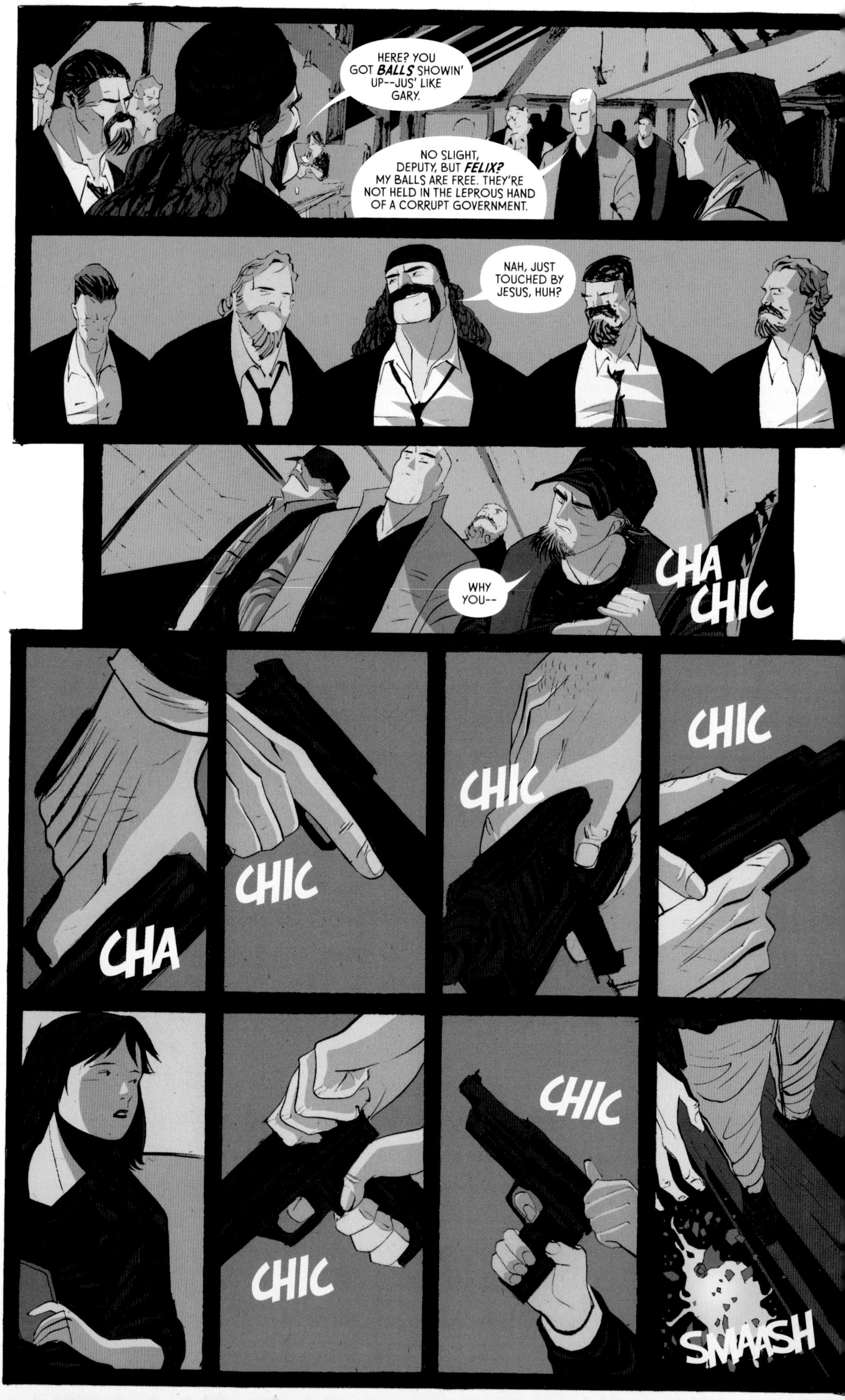
HERE? YOU GOT **BALLS** SHOWIN' UP--JUS' LIKE GARY.
NO SLIGHT, DEPUTY, BUT ***FELIX?*** MY BALLS ARE FREE. THEY'RE NOT HELD IN THE LEPROUS HAND OF A CORRUPT GOVERNMENT.
NAH, JUST TOUCHED BY JESUS, HUH?
WHY YOU--
CHA CHIC
CHA
CHIC
CHIC
CHIC
CHIC
CHIC
SMAASH

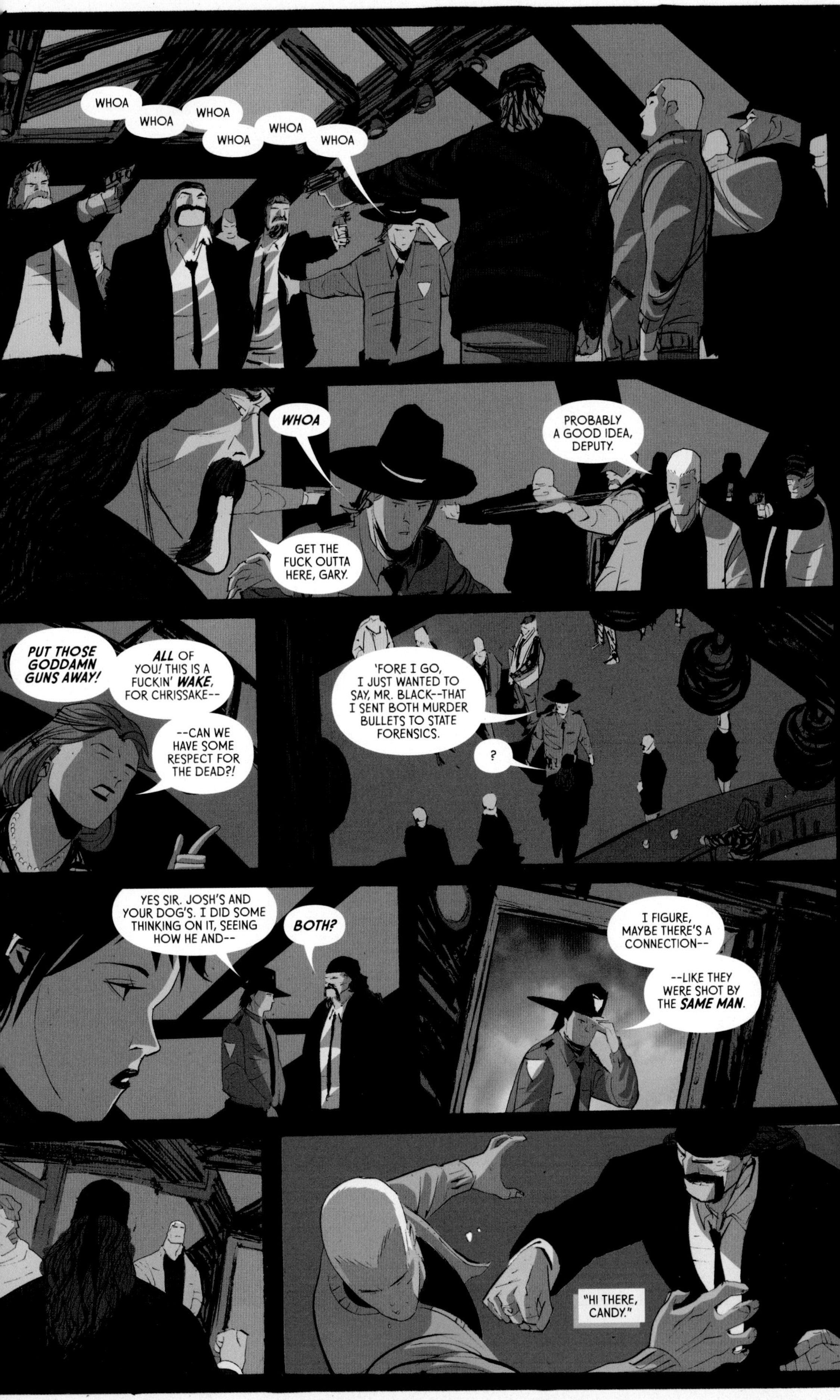

WHOA
WHOA
WHOA
WHOA
WHOA
WHOA
WHOA
PROBABLY A GOOD IDEA, DEPUTY.
GET THE FUCK OUTTA HERE, GARY.
PUT THOSE GODDAMN GUNS AWAY!
ALL OF YOU! THIS IS A FUCKIN' WAKE, FOR CHRISSAKE--
--CAN WE HAVE SOME RESPECT FOR THE DEAD?!
'FORE I GO, I JUST WANTED TO SAY, MR. BLACK--THAT I SENT BOTH MURDER BULLETS TO STATE FORENSICS.
?
YES SIR. JOSH'S AND YOUR DOG'S. I DID SOME THINKING ON IT, SEEING HOW HE AND--
BOTH?
I FIGURE, MAYBE THERE'S A CONNECTION--
--LIKE THEY WERE SHOT BY THE SAME MAN.
"HI THERE, CANDY."

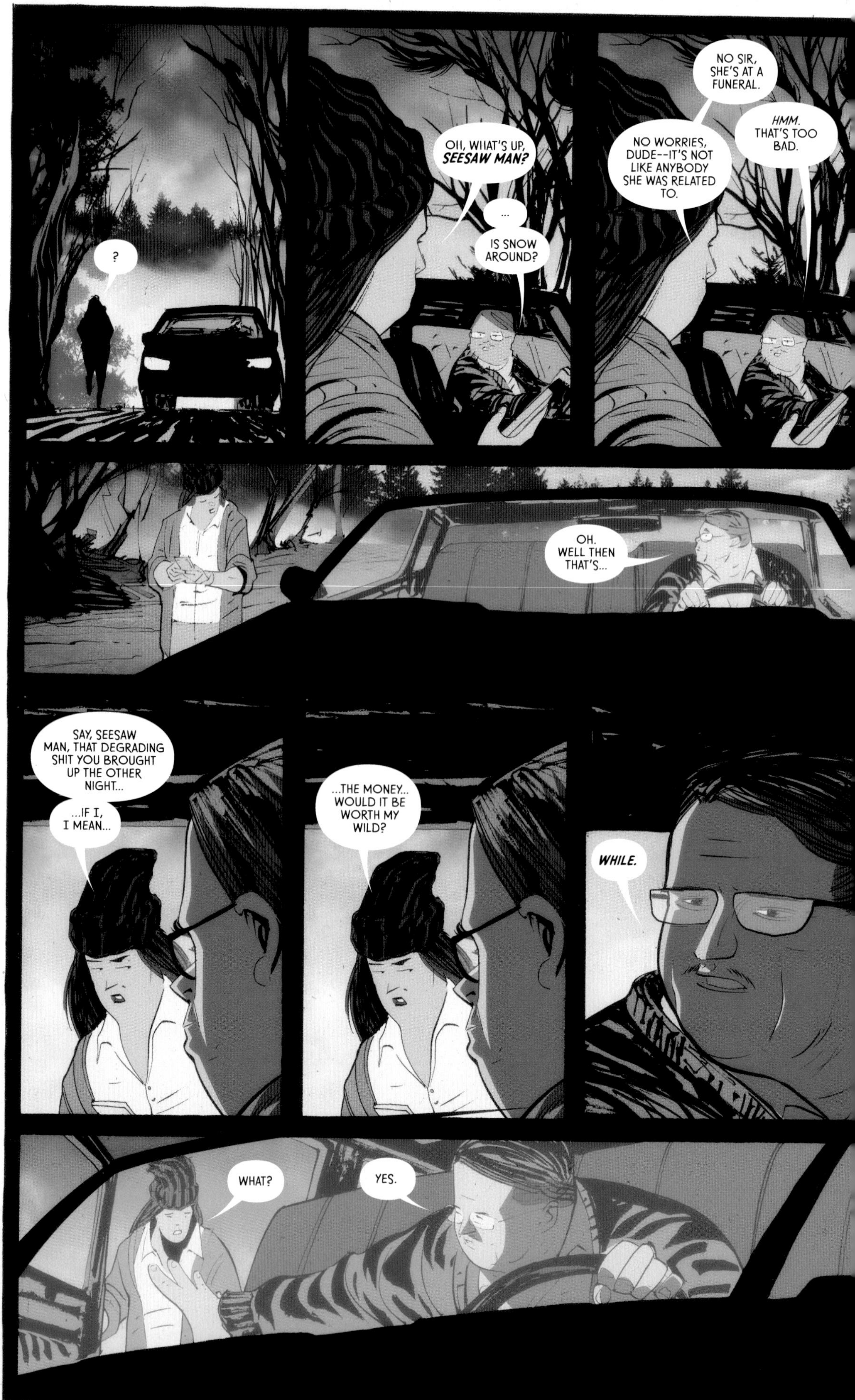
?
OH, WHAT'S UP, **SEESAW MAN?**
...
IS SNOW AROUND?
NO SIR, SHE'S AT A FUNERAL.
NO WORRIES, DUDE--IT'S NOT LIKE ANYBODY SHE WAS RELATED TO.
HMM. THAT'S TOO BAD.
OH. WELL THEN THAT'S...
SAY, SEESAW MAN, THAT DEGRADING SHIT YOU BROUGHT UP THE OTHER NIGHT...
...IF I, I MEAN...
...THE MONEY... WOULD IT BE WORTH MY WILD?
WHILE.
WHAT?
YES.

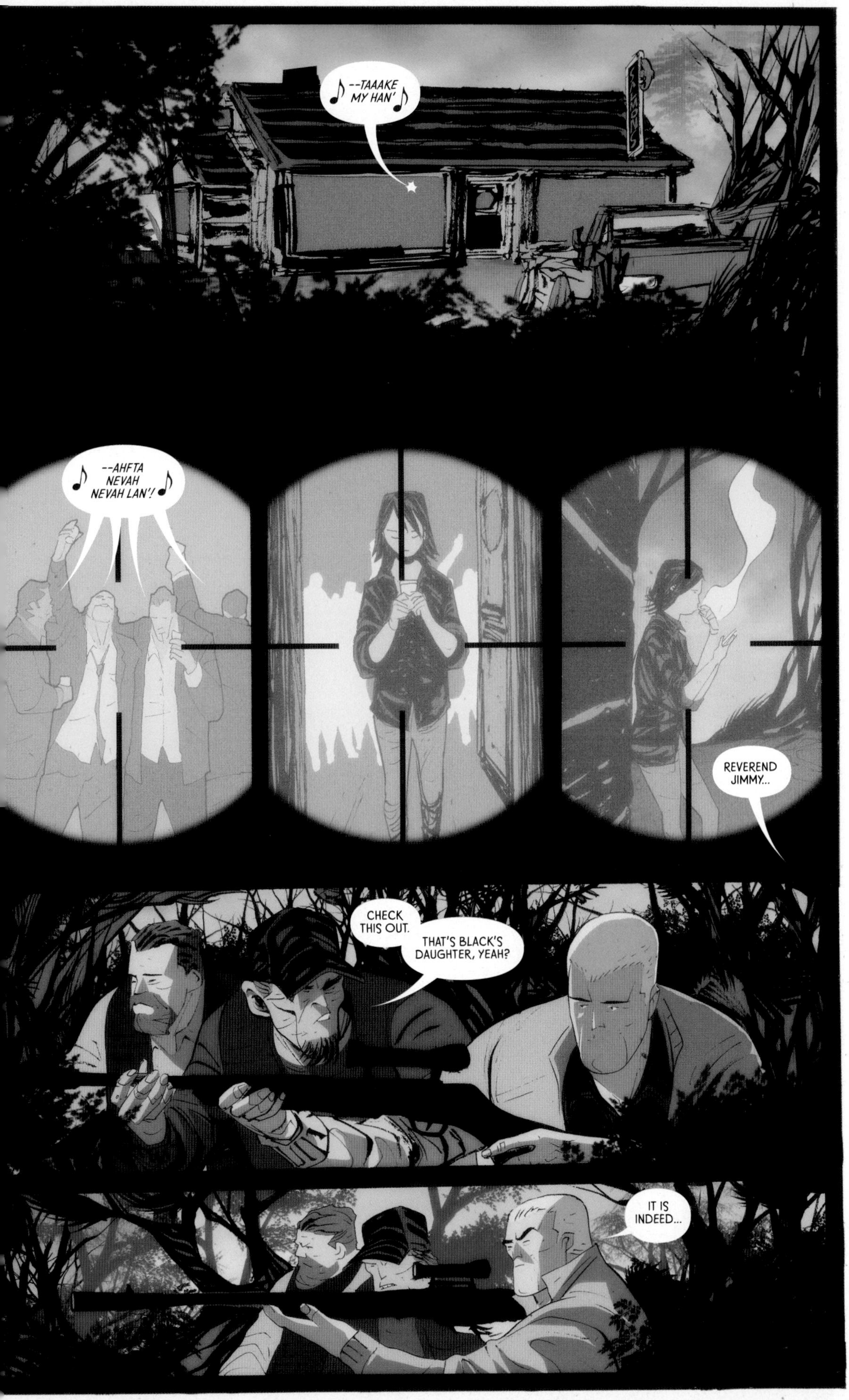
♪ --TAAAKE MY HAN' ♪
♪ --AHFTA NEVAH NEVAH LAN'! ♪
REVEREND JIMMY...
CHECK THIS OUT.
THAT'S BLACK'S DAUGHTER, YEAH?
IT IS INDEED...

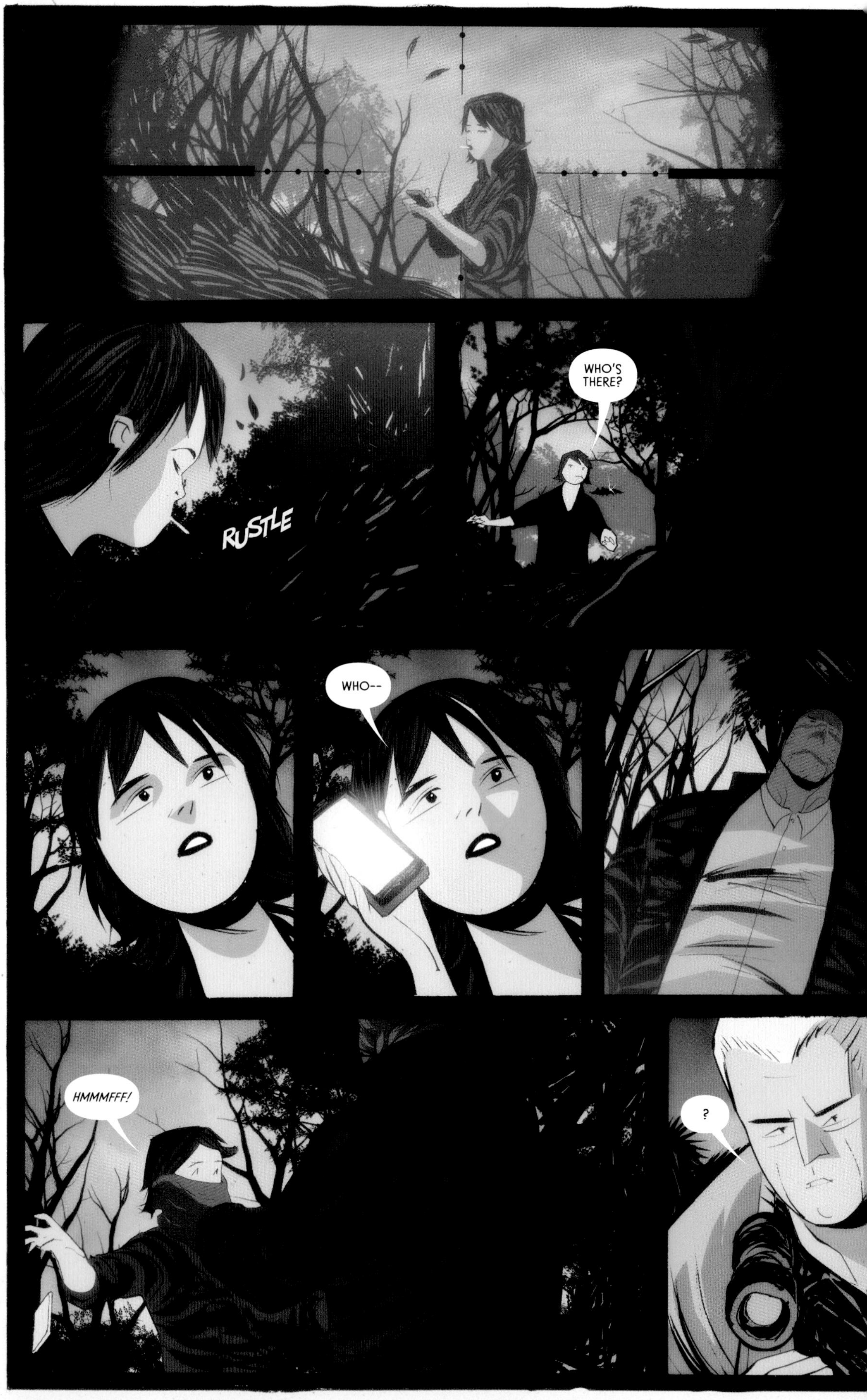
RUSTLE
WHO'S THERE?
WHO--
HMMMFFF!
?

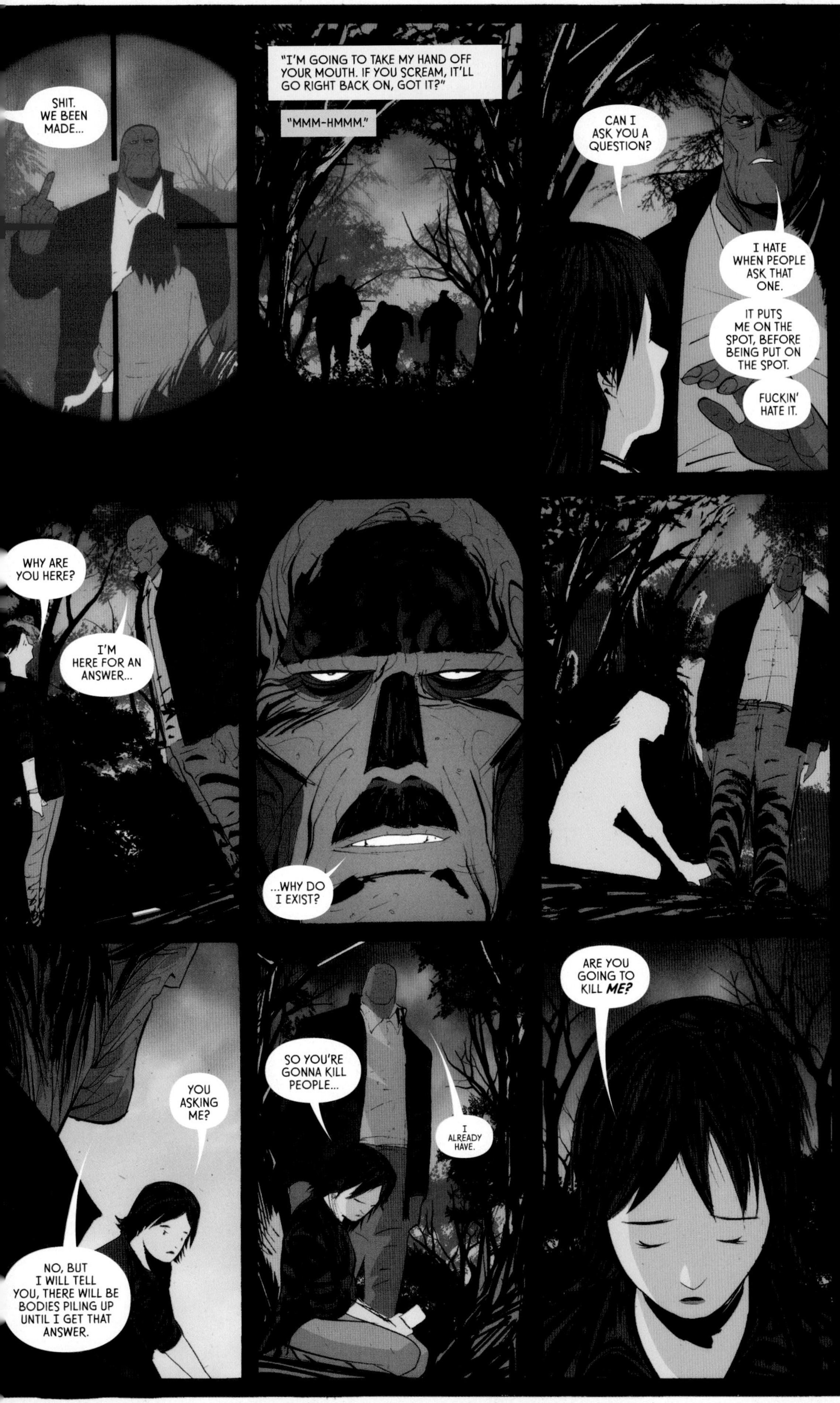
SHIT. WE BEEN MADE...
"I'M GOING TO TAKE MY HAND OFF YOUR MOUTH. IF YOU SCREAM, IT'LL GO RIGHT BACK ON, GOT IT?"
"MMM-HMMM."
CAN I ASK YOU A QUESTION?
I HATE WHEN PEOPLE ASK THAT ONE.
IT PUTS ME ON THE SPOT, BEFORE BEING PUT ON THE SPOT.
FUCKIN' HATE IT.
WHY ARE YOU HERE?
I'M HERE FOR AN ANSWER...
...WHY DO I EXIST?
YOU ASKING ME?
NO, BUT I WILL TELL YOU, THERE WILL BE BODIES PILING UP UNTIL I GET THAT ANSWER.
SO YOU'RE GONNA KILL PEOPLE...
I ALREADY HAVE.
ARE YOU GOING TO KILL *ME?*

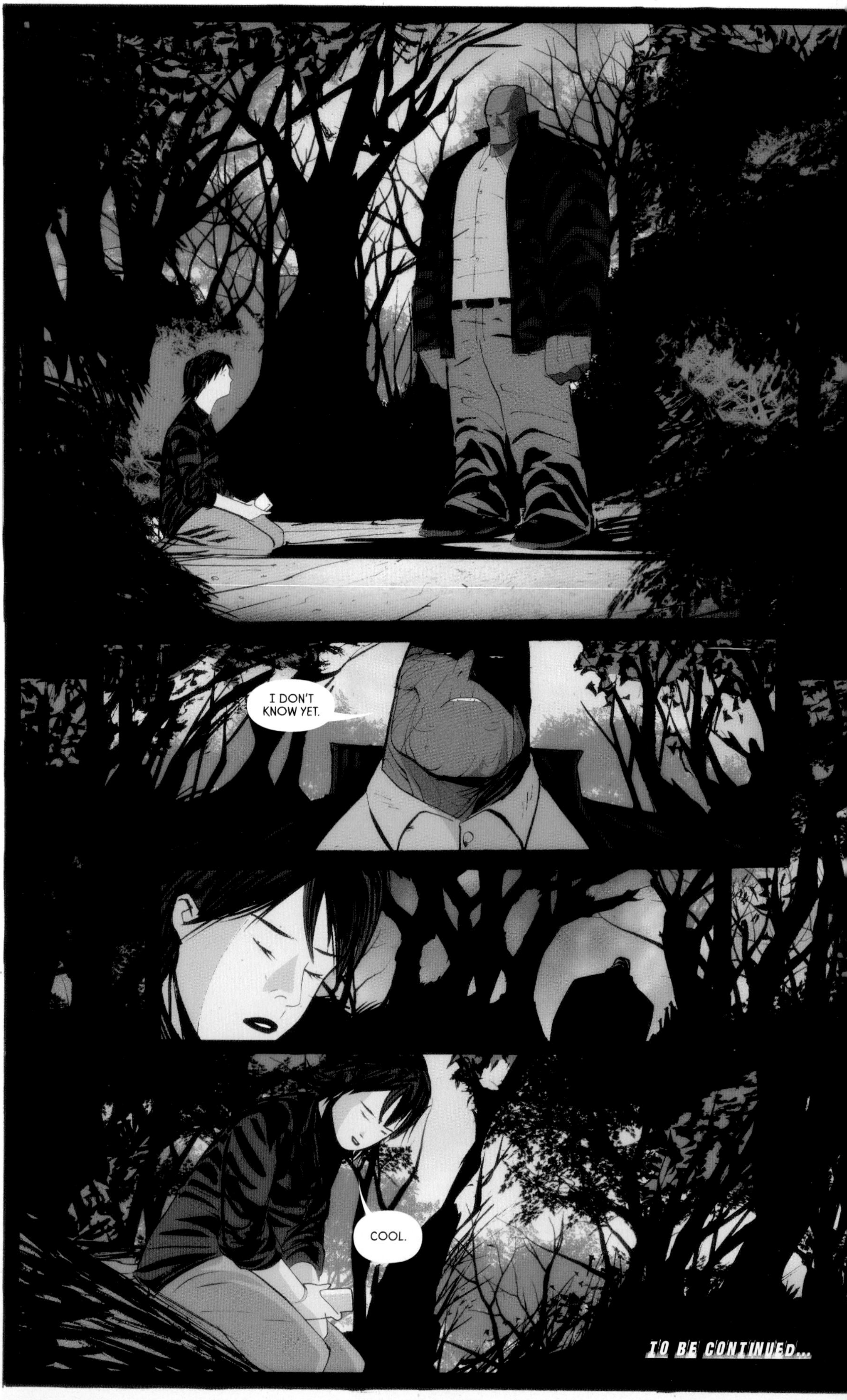
I DON'T KNOW YET.
COOL.
TO BE CONTINUED...

4

"UNDERGOD"

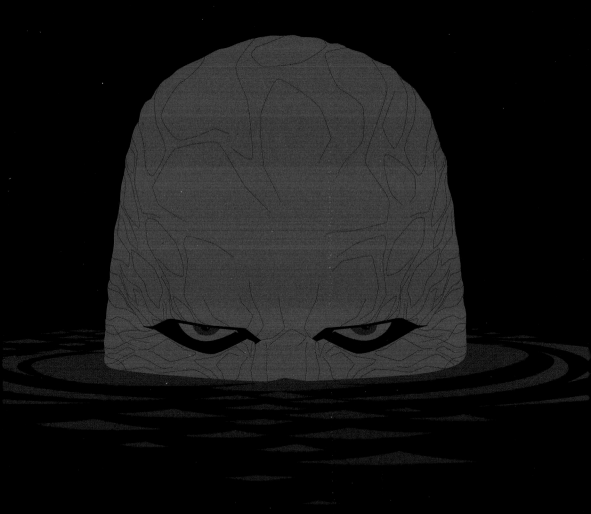

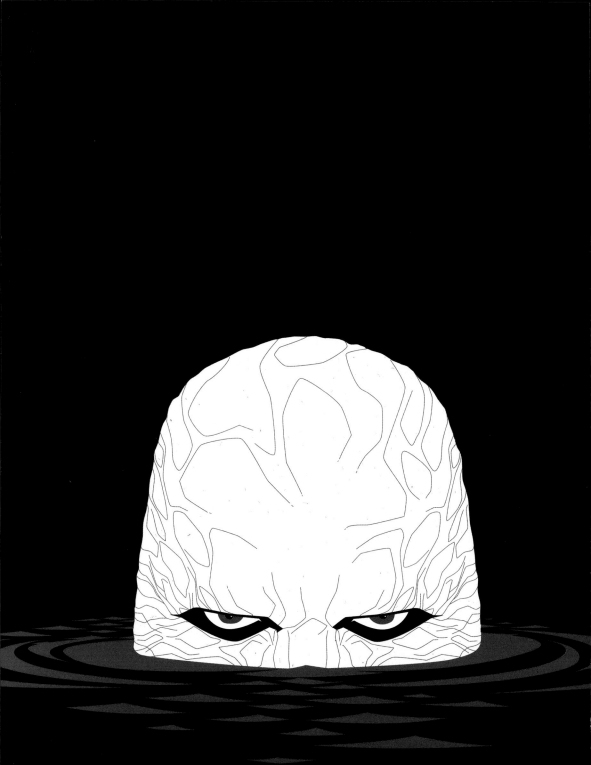

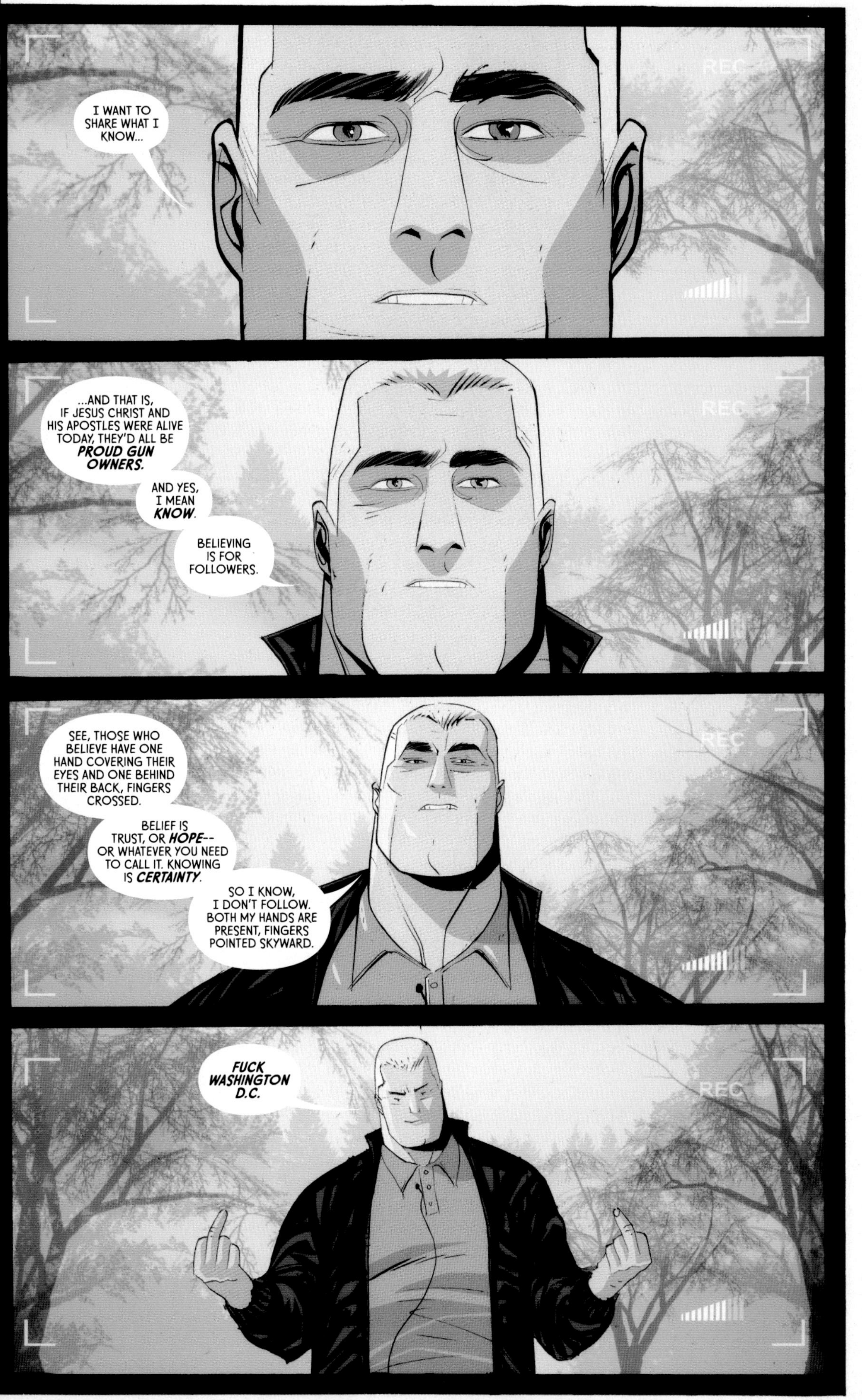

I WANT TO SHARE WHAT I KNOW...
...AND THAT IS, IF JESUS CHRIST AND HIS APOSTLES WERE ALIVE TODAY, THEY'D ALL BE ***PROUD GUN OWNERS.***
AND YES, I MEAN ***KNOW***.
BELIEVING IS FOR FOLLOWERS.
REC
SEE, THOSE WHO BELIEVE HAVE ONE HAND COVERING THEIR EYES AND ONE BEHIND THEIR BACK, FINGERS CROSSED.
BELIEF IS TRUST, OR ***HOPE***-- OR WHATEVER YOU NEED TO CALL IT. KNOWING IS ***CERTAINTY***.
SO I KNOW, I DON'T FOLLOW. BOTH MY HANDS ARE PRESENT, FINGERS POINTED SKYWARD.
REC
FUCK WASHINGTON D.C.
REC

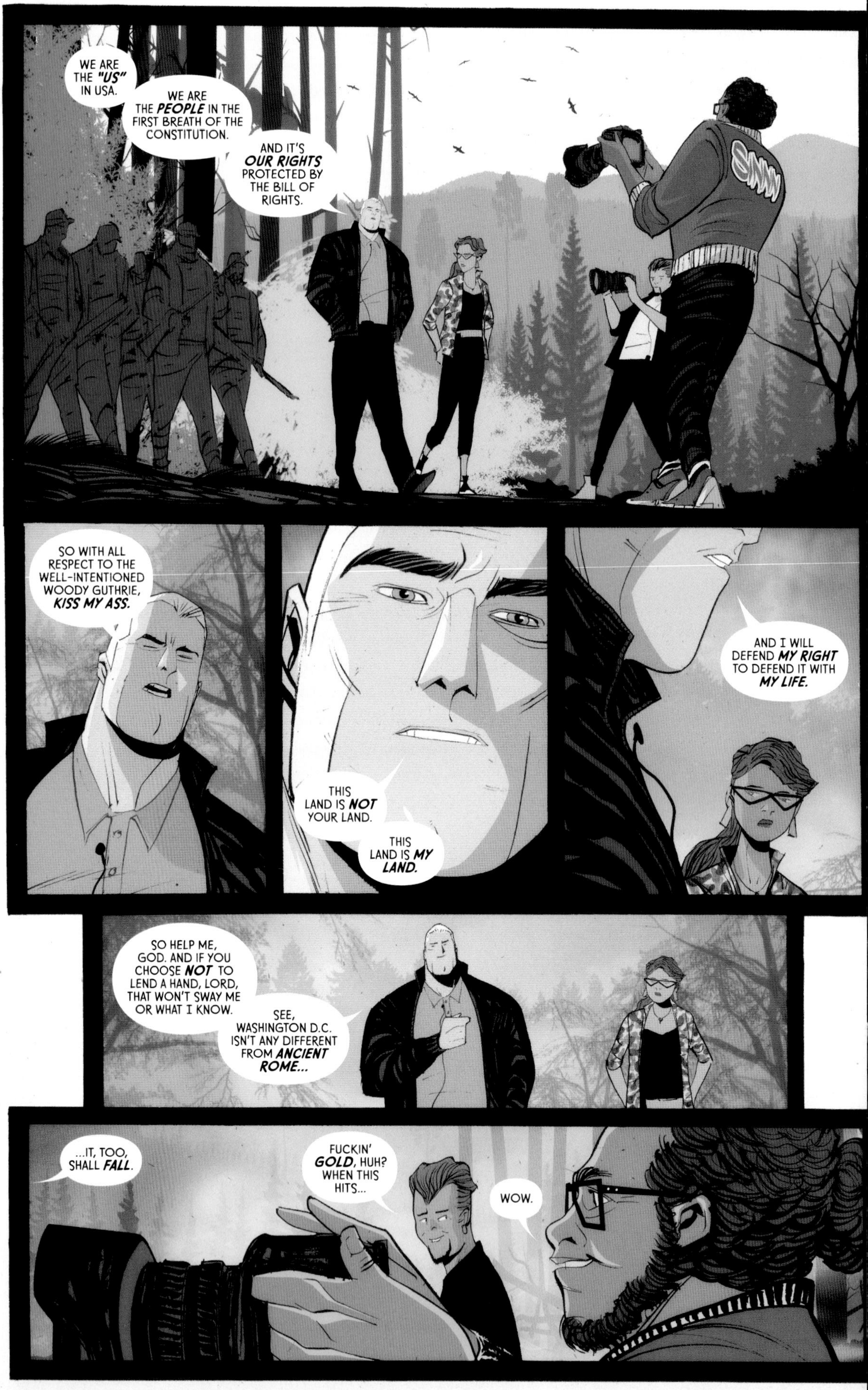
WE ARE THE "US" IN USA.
WE ARE THE PEOPLE IN THE FIRST BREATH OF THE CONSTITUTION.
AND IT'S OUR RIGHTS PROTECTED BY THE BILL OF RIGHTS.
SO WITH ALL RESPECT TO THE WELL-INTENTIONED WOODY GUTHRIE, KISS MY ASS.
THIS LAND IS NOT YOUR LAND.
THIS LAND IS MY LAND.
AND I WILL DEFEND MY RIGHT TO DEFEND IT WITH MY LIFE.
SO HELP ME, GOD. AND IF YOU CHOOSE NOT TO LEND A HAND, LORD, THAT WON'T SWAY ME OR WHAT I KNOW.
SEE, WASHINGTON D.C. ISN'T ANY DIFFERENT FROM ANCIENT ROME...
...IT, TOO, SHALL FALL.
FUCKIN' GOLD, HUH? WHEN THIS HITS...
WOW.

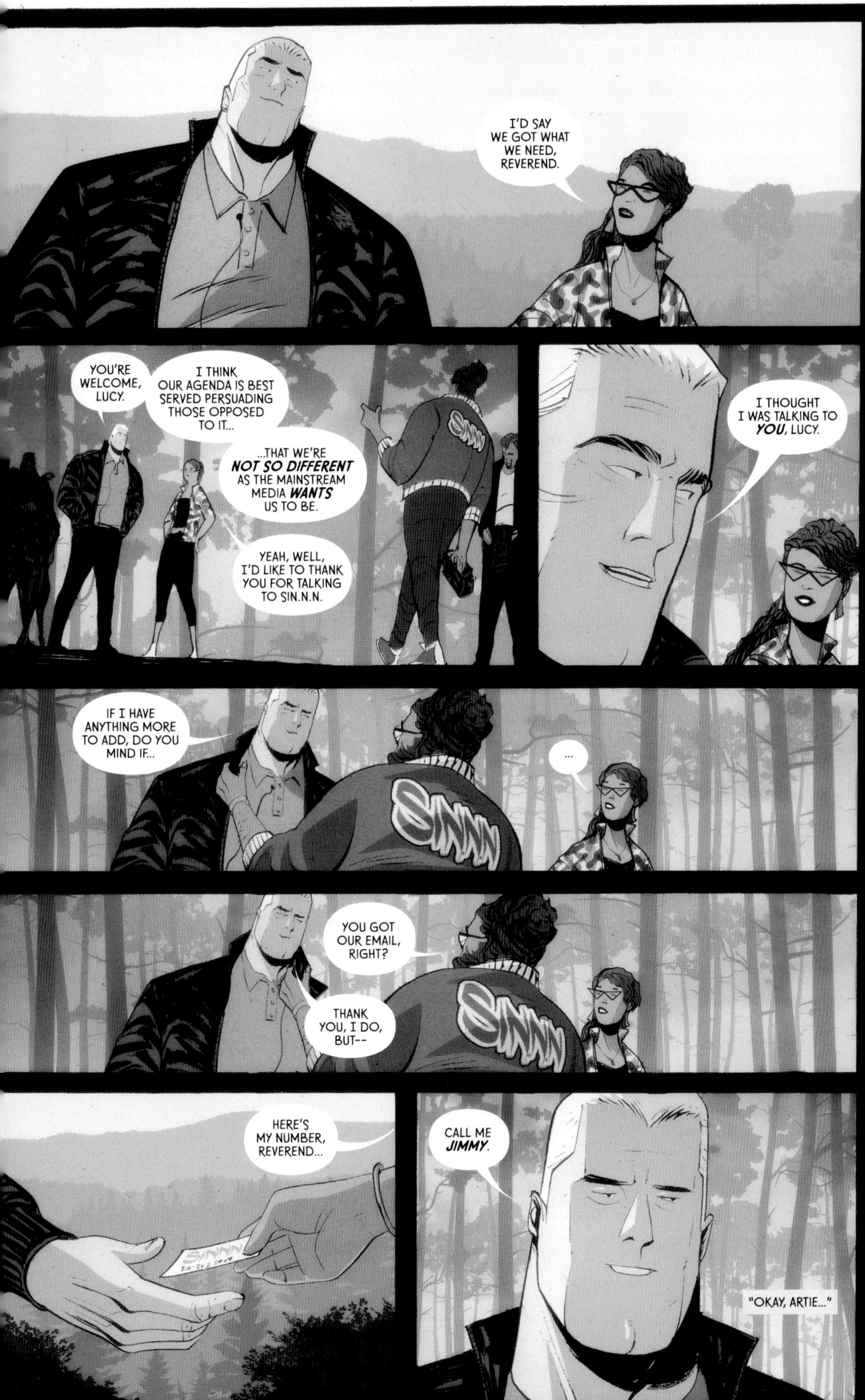
I'D SAY WE GOT WHAT WE NEED, REVEREND.
YOU'RE WELCOME, LUCY.
I THINK OUR AGENDA IS BEST SERVED PERSUADING THOSE OPPOSED TO IT...
...THAT WE'RE **NOT SO DIFFERENT** AS THE MAINSTREAM MEDIA **WANTS** US TO BE.
YEAH, WELL, I'D LIKE TO THANK YOU FOR TALKING TO SIN.N.N.
SINNN
I THOUGHT I WAS TALKING TO **YOU**, LUCY.
IF I HAVE ANYTHING MORE TO ADD, DO YOU MIND IF...
...
SINNN
YOU GOT OUR EMAIL, RIGHT?
THANK YOU, I DO, BUT--
SINNN
HERE'S MY NUMBER, REVEREND...
SINNN
CALL ME **JIMMY**.
"OKAY, ARTIE..."

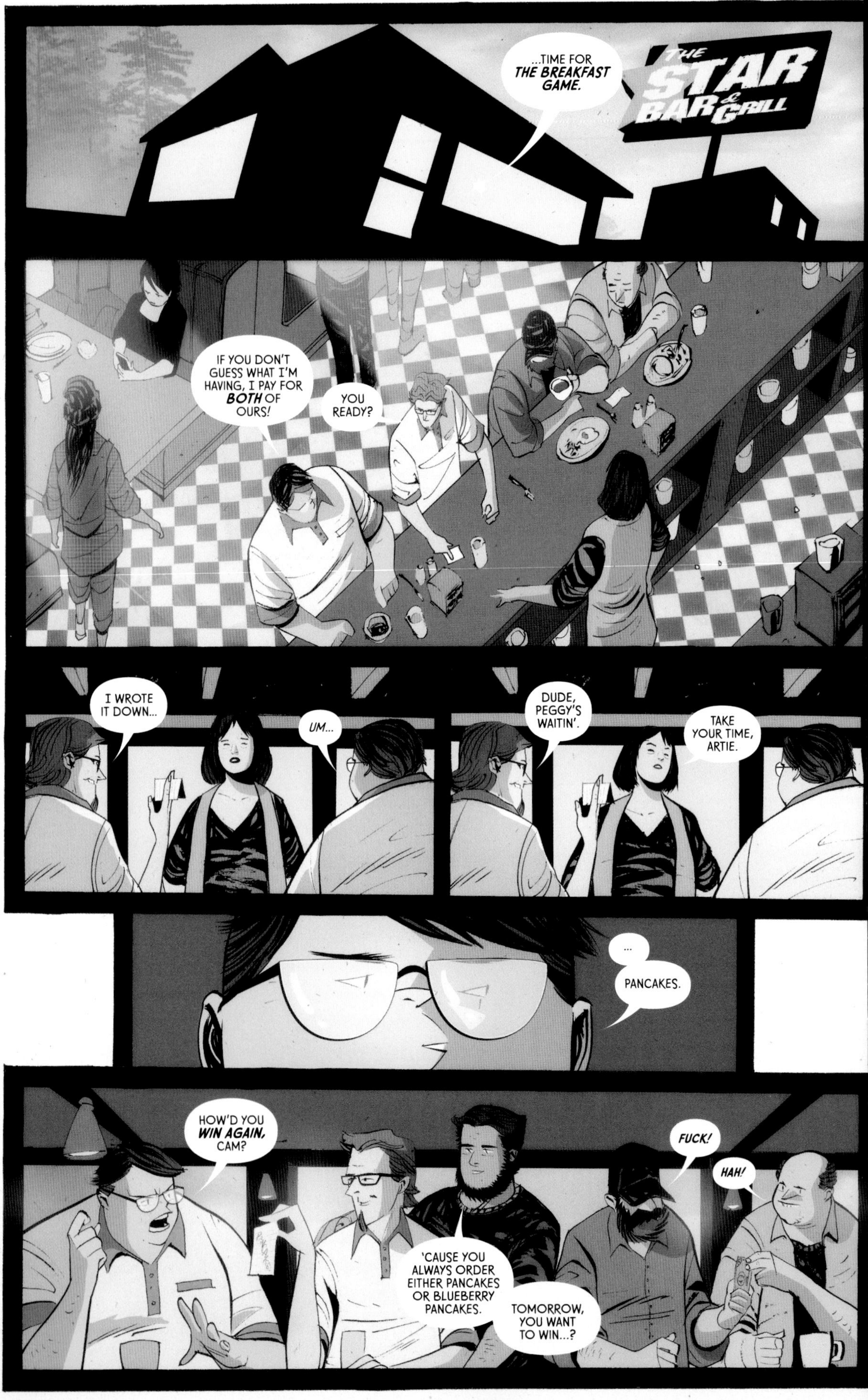
...TIME FOR *THE BREAKFAST GAME.*
THE STAR BAR & GRILL
IF YOU DON'T GUESS WHAT I'M HAVING, I PAY FOR *BOTH* OF OURS!
YOU READY?
I WROTE IT DOWN...
UM...
DUDE, PEGGY'S WAITIN'.
TAKE YOUR TIME, ARTIE.
...
PANCAKES.
HOW'D YOU *WIN AGAIN,* CAM?
'CAUSE YOU ALWAYS ORDER EITHER PANCAKES OR BLUEBERRY PANCAKES.
TOMORROW, YOU WANT TO WIN...?
FUCK!
HAH!

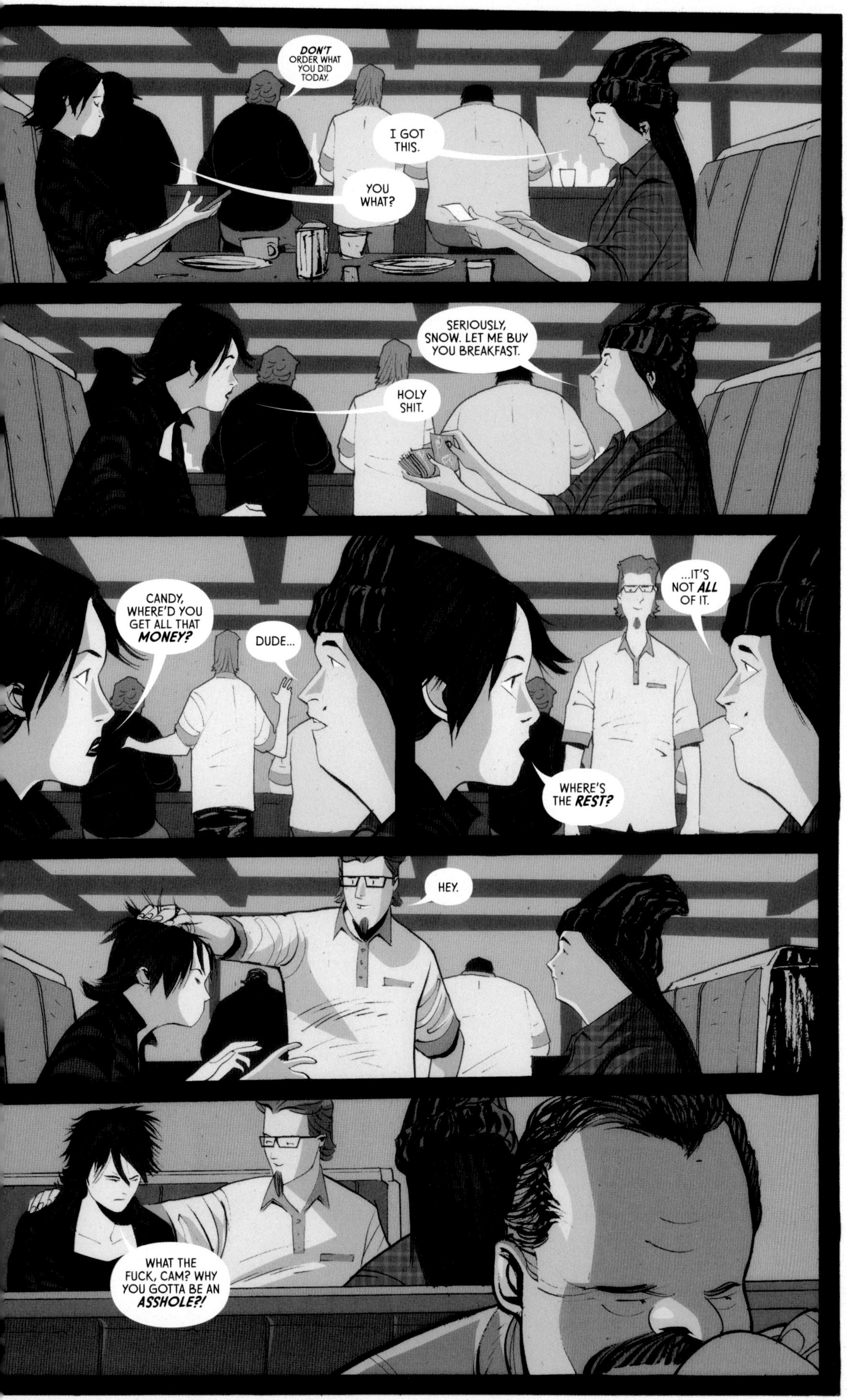

DON'T ORDER WHAT YOU DID TODAY.
I GOT THIS.
YOU WHAT?
SERIOUSLY, SNOW. LET ME BUY YOU BREAKFAST.
HOLY SHIT.
CANDY, WHERE'D YOU GET ALL THAT MONEY?
DUDE...
...IT'S NOT ALL OF IT.
WHERE'S THE REST?
HEY.
WHAT THE FUCK, CAM? WHY YOU GOTTA BE AN ASSHOLE?!

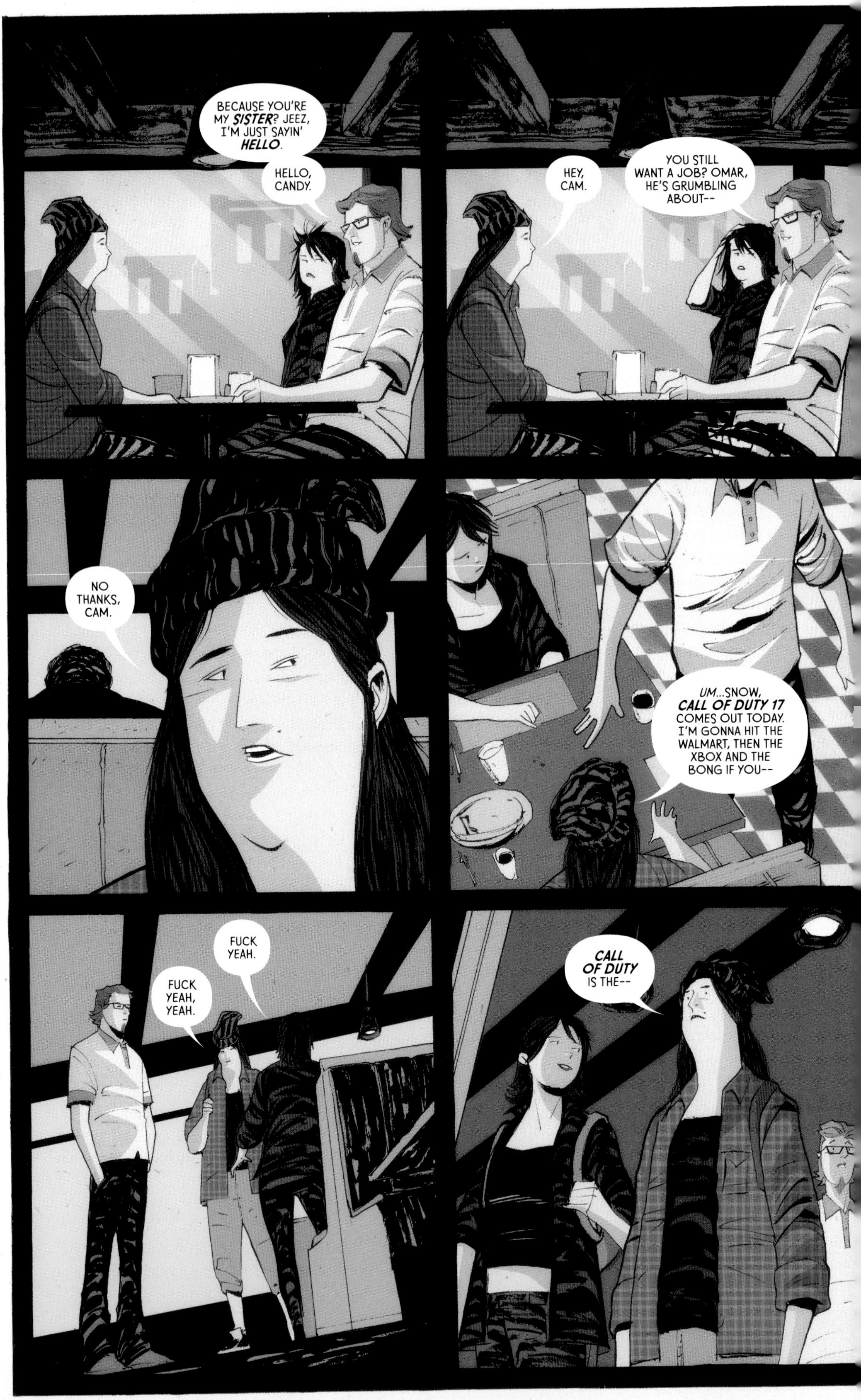
BECAUSE YOU'RE MY SISTER? JEEZ, I'M JUST SAYIN' HELLO.
HELLO, CANDY.
HEY, CAM.
YOU STILL WANT A JOB? OMAR, HE'S GRUMBLING ABOUT--
NO THANKS, CAM.
UM...SNOW, CALL OF DUTY 17 COMES OUT TODAY. I'M GONNA HIT THE WALMART, THEN THE XBOX AND THE BONG IF YOU--
FUCK YEAH.
FUCK YEAH, YEAH.
CALL OF DUTY IS THE--

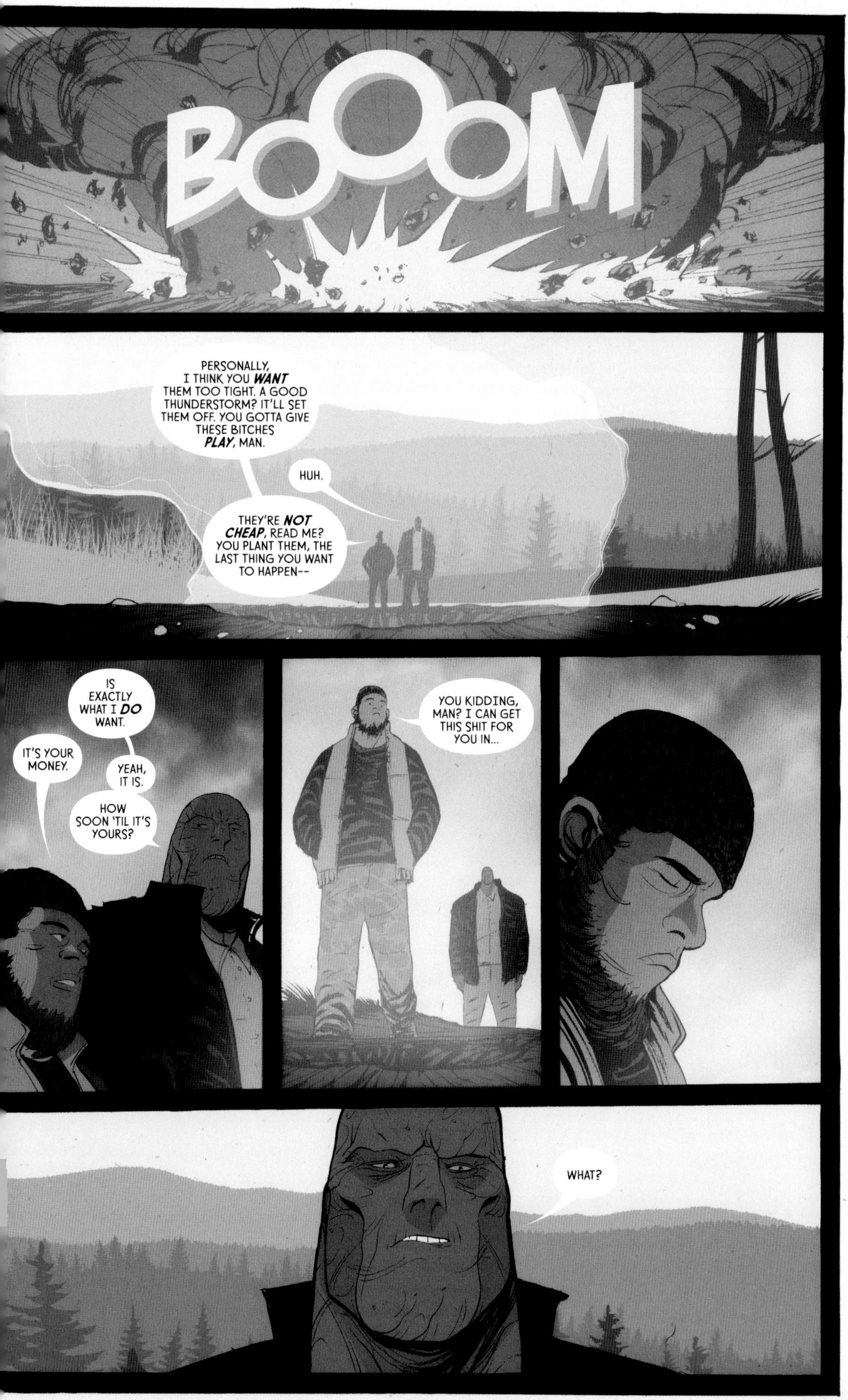
BOOOM
PERSONALLY, I THINK YOU WANT THEM TOO TIGHT. A GOOD THUNDERSTORM? IT'LL SET THEM OFF. YOU GOTTA GIVE THESE BITCHES PLAY, MAN.
HUH.
THEY'RE NOT CHEAP, READ ME? YOU PLANT THEM, THE LAST THING YOU WANT TO HAPPEN--
IS EXACTLY WHAT I DO WANT.
IT'S YOUR MONEY.
YEAH, IT IS.
HOW SOON 'TIL IT'S YOURS?
YOU KIDDING, MAN? I CAN GET THIS SHIT FOR YOU IN...
WHAT?

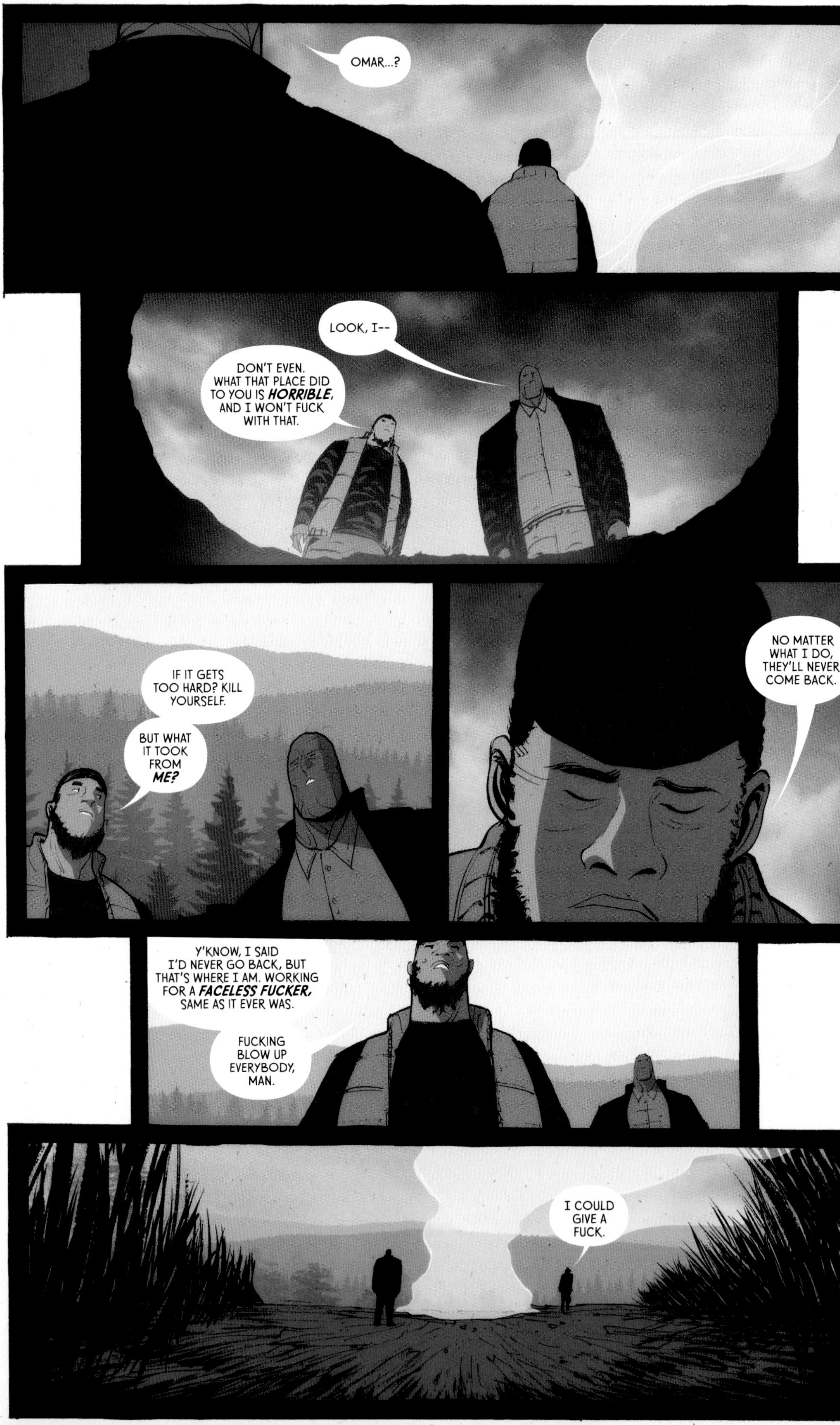
OMAR...?
LOOK, I--
DON'T EVEN. WHAT THAT PLACE DID TO YOU IS ***HORRIBLE***, AND I WON'T FUCK WITH THAT.
IF IT GETS TOO HARD? KILL YOURSELF.
BUT WHAT IT TOOK FROM ***ME?***
NO MATTER WHAT I DO, THEY'LL NEVER COME BACK.
Y'KNOW, I SAID I'D NEVER GO BACK, BUT THAT'S WHERE I AM. WORKING FOR A ***FACELESS FUCKER,*** SAME AS IT EVER WAS.
FUCKING BLOW UP EVERYBODY, MAN.
I COULD GIVE A FUCK.

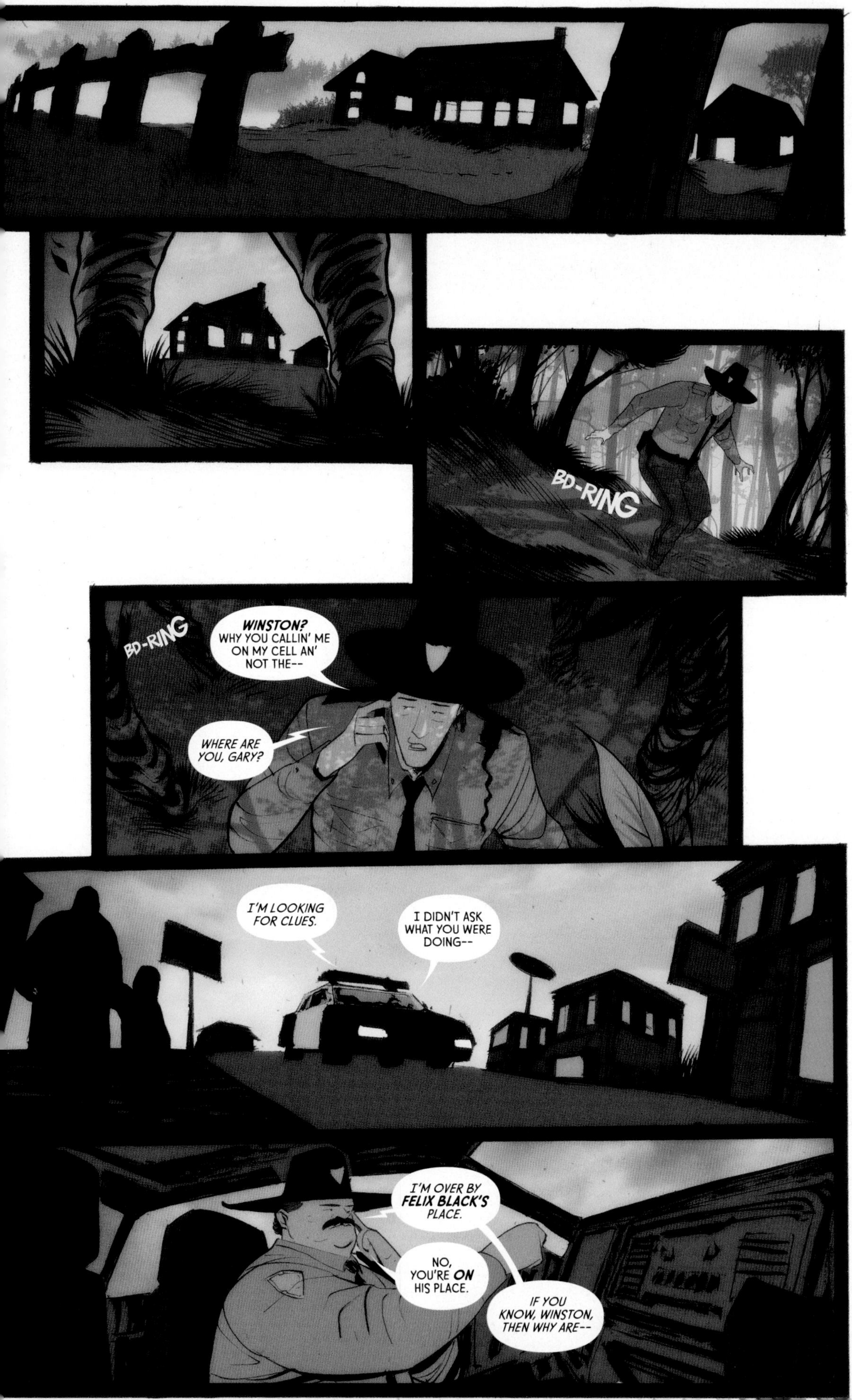

BD-RING
BD-RING
WINSTON? WHY YOU CALLIN' ME ON MY CELL AN' NOT THE--
WHERE ARE YOU, GARY?
I'M LOOKING FOR CLUES.
I DIDN'T ASK WHAT YOU WERE DOING--
I'M OVER BY **FELIX BLACK'S** PLACE.
NO, YOU'RE **ON** HIS PLACE.
IF YOU KNOW, WINSTON, THEN WHY ARE--

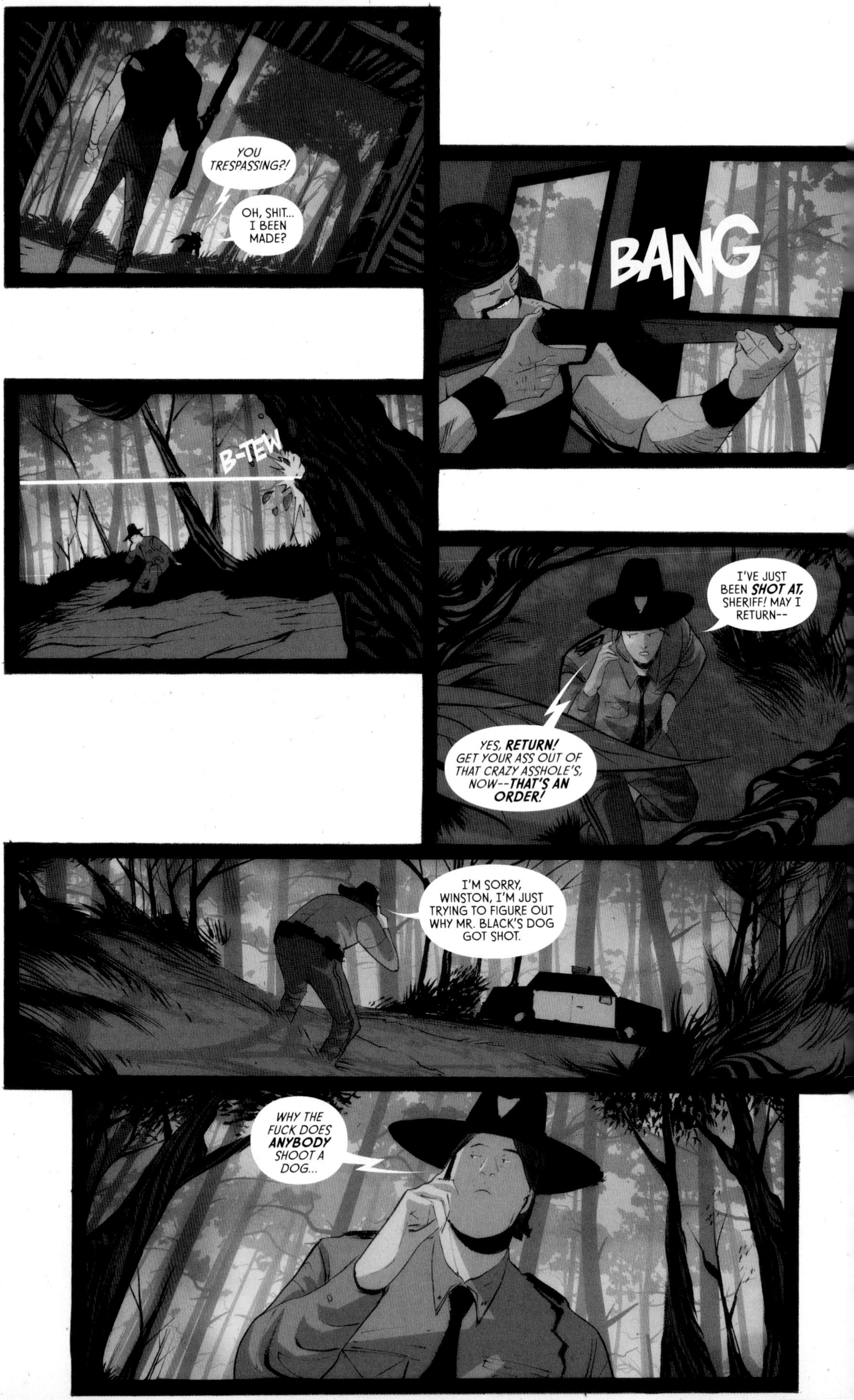
YOU TRESPASSING?!
OH, SHIT... I BEEN MADE?
BANG
B-TEW
I'VE JUST BEEN **SHOT AT,** SHERIFF! MAY I RETURN--
YES, ***RETURN!*** *GET YOUR ASS OUT OF THAT CRAZY ASSHOLE'S, NOW--* ***THAT'S AN ORDER!***
I'M SORRY, WINSTON, I'M JUST TRYING TO FIGURE OUT WHY MR. BLACK'S DOG GOT SHOT.
WHY THE FUCK DOES ***ANYBODY*** *SHOOT A DOG...*

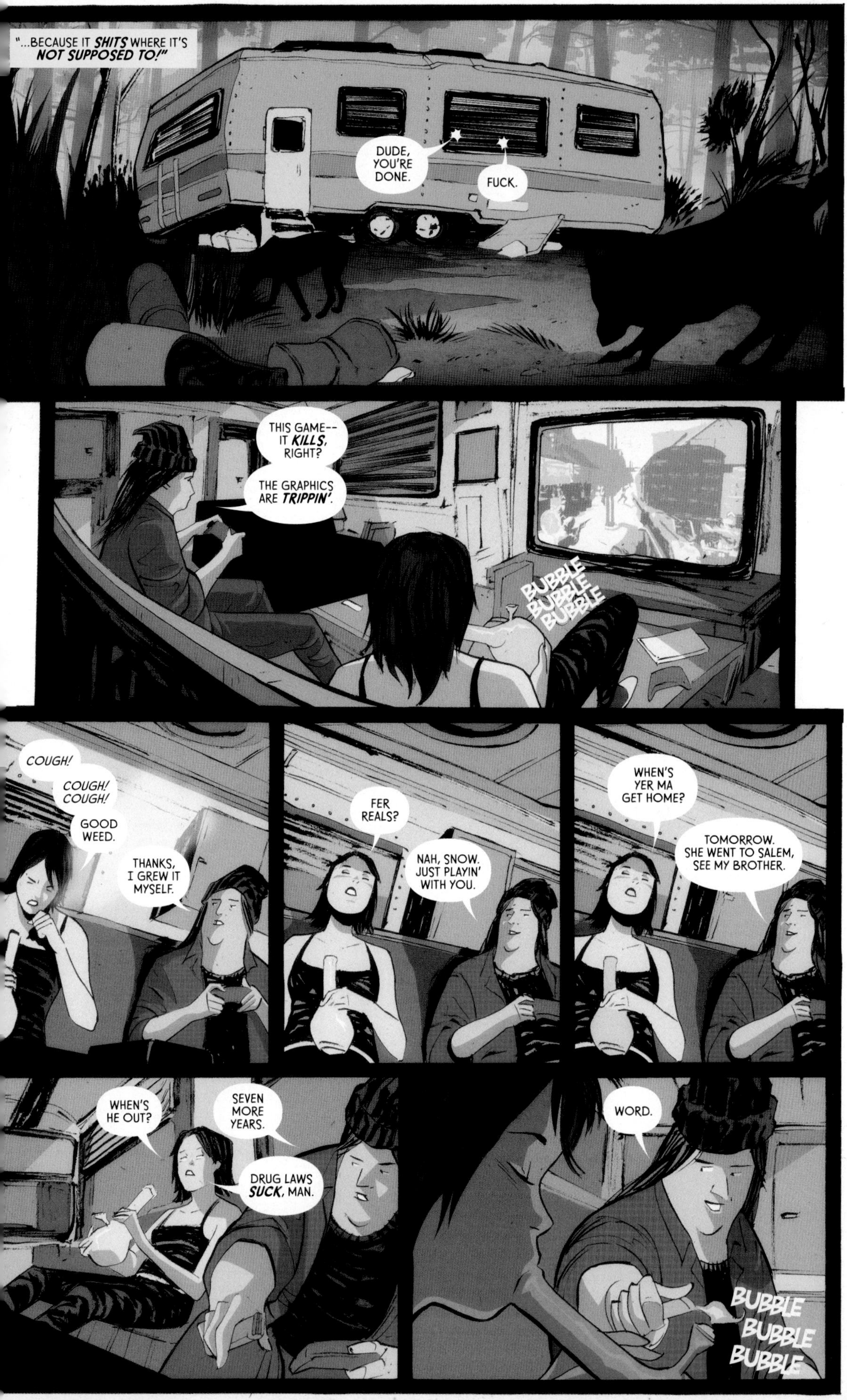
"...BECAUSE IT **SHITS** WHERE IT'S **NOT SUPPOSED TO!**"
DUDE, YOU'RE DONE.
FUCK.
THIS GAME-- IT **KILLS**, RIGHT?
THE GRAPHICS ARE **TRIPPIN'**.
BUBBLE BUBBLE BUBBLE
COUGH!
COUGH! COUGH!
GOOD WEED.
THANKS, I GREW IT MYSELF.
FER REALS?
NAH, SNOW. JUST PLAYIN' WITH YOU.
WHEN'S YER MA GET HOME?
TOMORROW. SHE WENT TO SALEM, SEE MY BROTHER.
WHEN'S HE OUT?
SEVEN MORE YEARS.
DRUG LAWS **SUCK**, MAN.
WORD.
BUBBLE BUBBLE BUBBLE

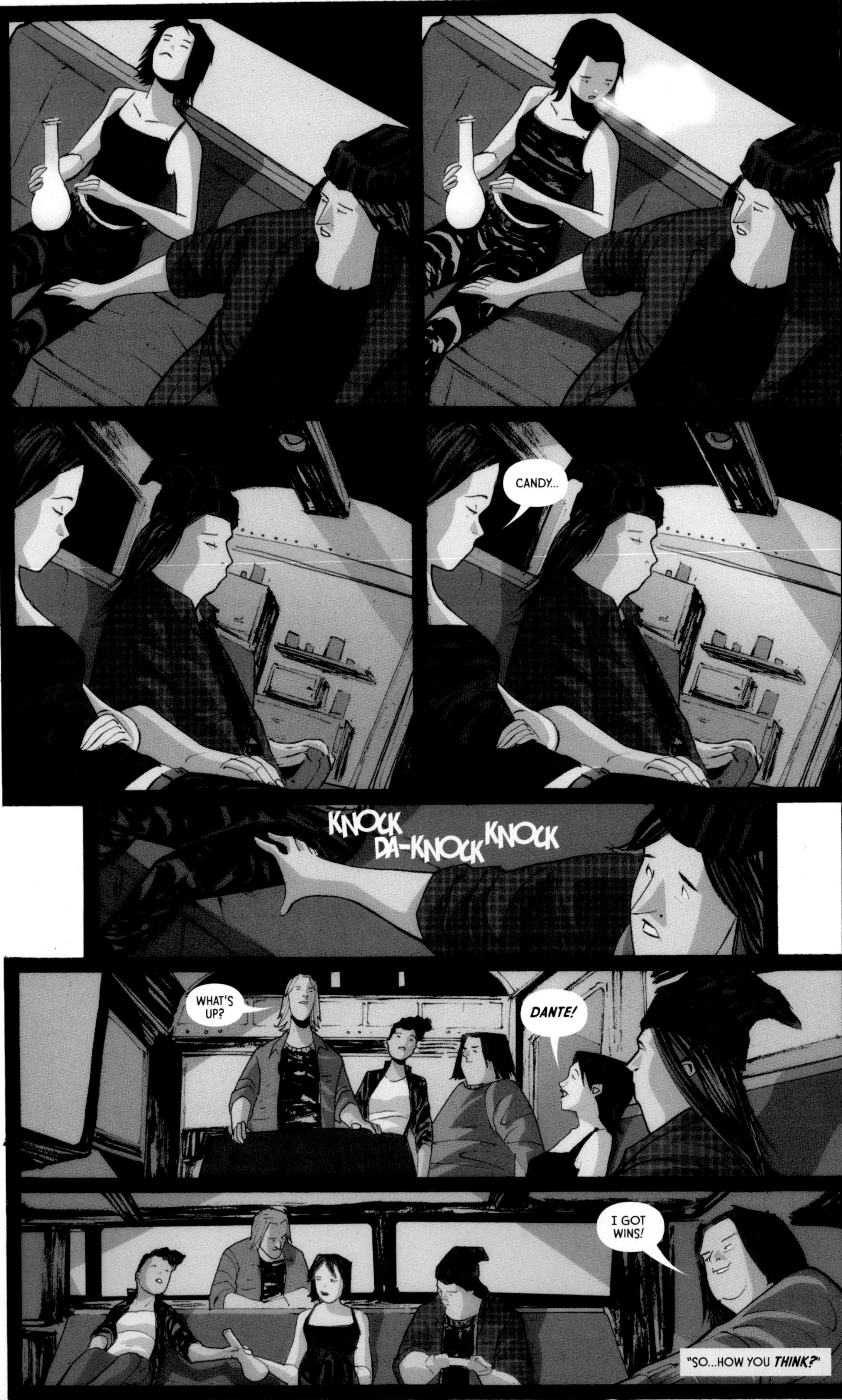
CANDY...
KNOCK DA-KNOCK KNOCK
WHAT'S UP?
DANTE!
I GOT WINS!
"SO...HOW YOU THINK?"

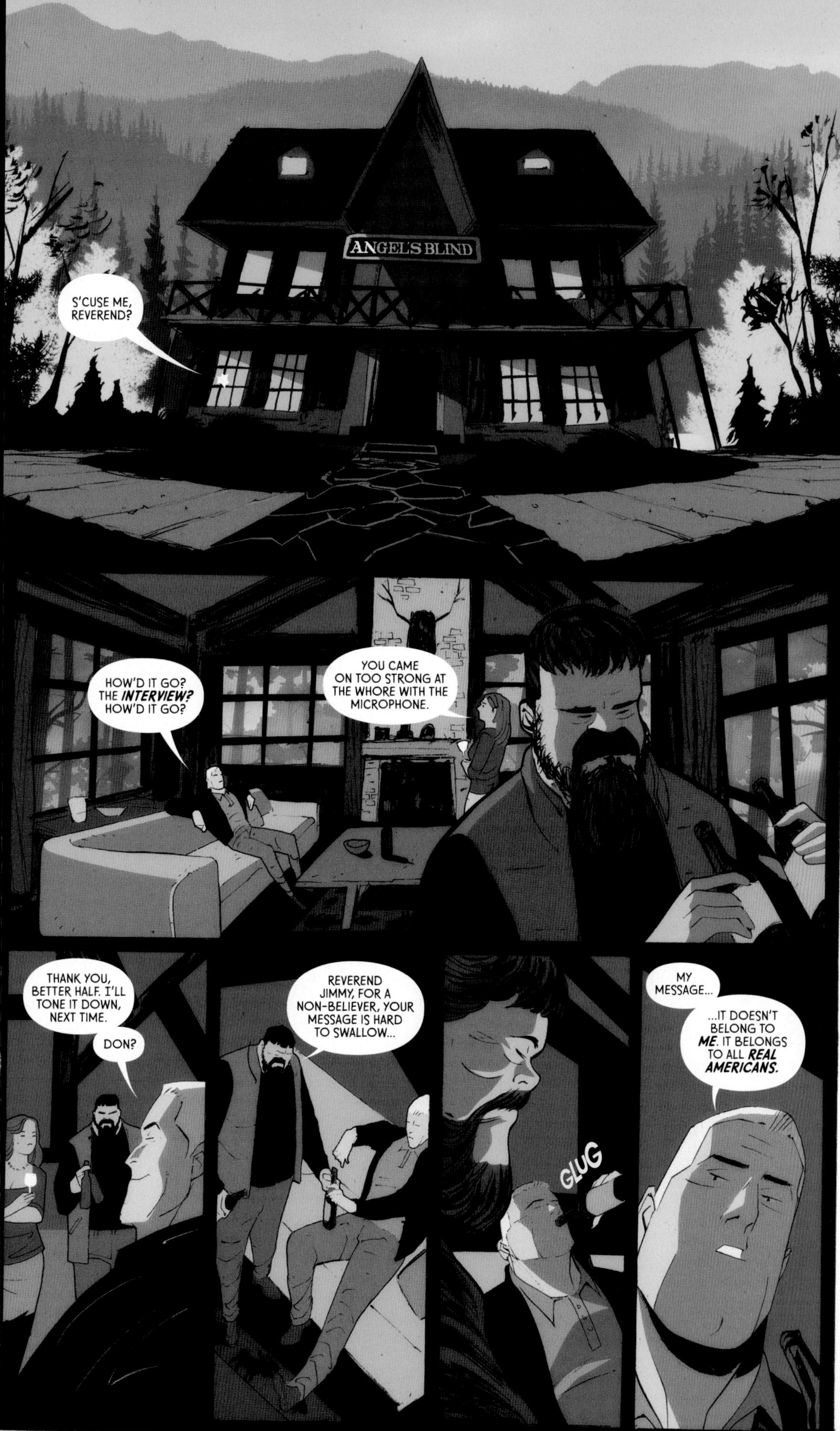
ANGEL'S BLIND
S'CUSE ME, REVEREND?
HOW'D IT GO? THE INTERVIEW? HOW'D IT GO?
YOU CAME ON TOO STRONG AT THE WHORE WITH THE MICROPHONE.
THANK YOU, BETTER HALF. I'LL TONE IT DOWN, NEXT TIME.
DON?
REVEREND JIMMY, FOR A NON-BELIEVER, YOUR MESSAGE IS HARD TO SWALLOW...
GLUG
MY MESSAGE...
...IT DOESN'T BELONG TO ME. IT BELONGS TO ALL REAL AMERICANS.

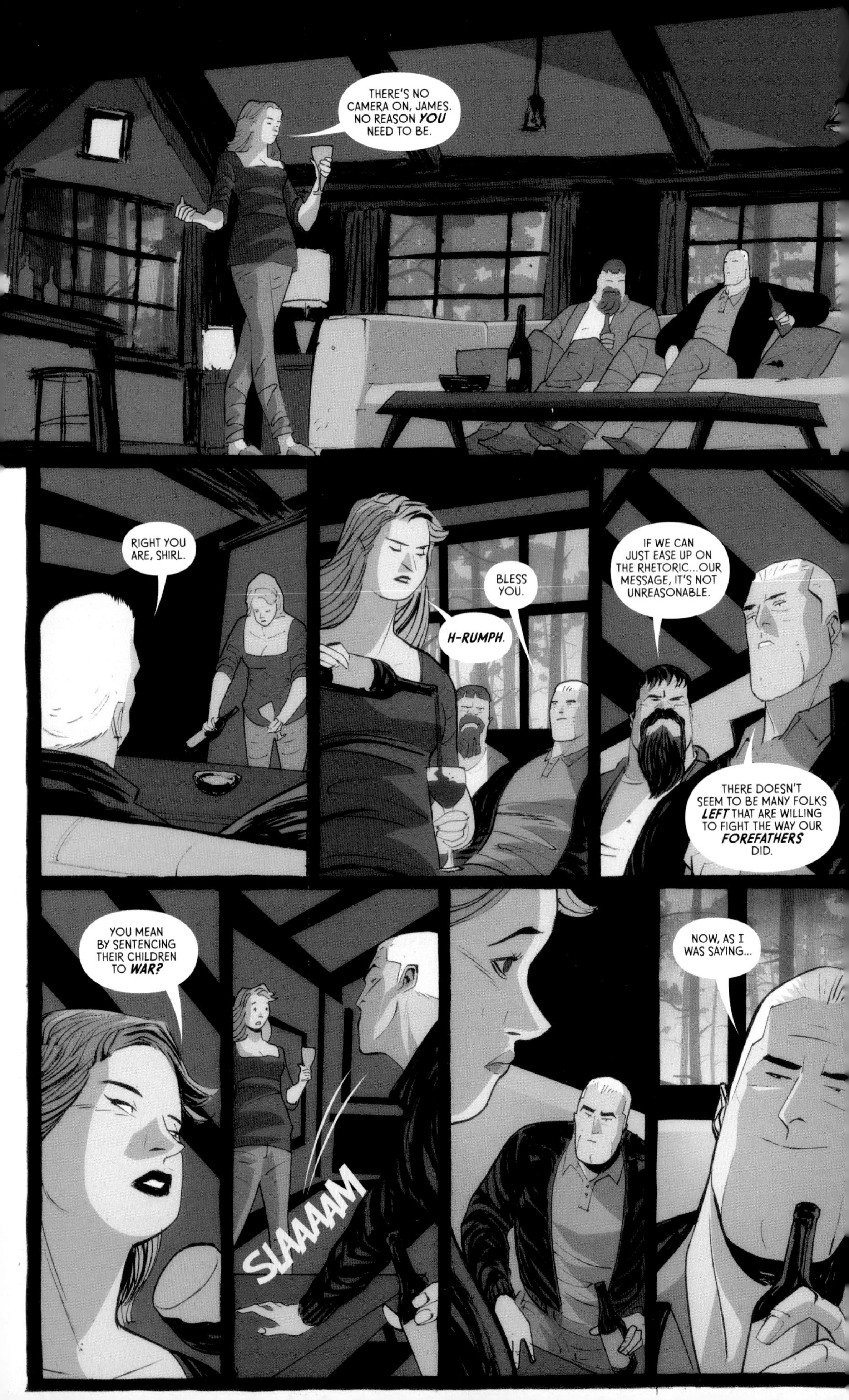
THERE'S NO CAMERA ON, JAMES. NO REASON *YOU* NEED TO BE.
RIGHT YOU ARE, SHIRL.
H-RUMPH.
BLESS YOU.
IF WE CAN JUST EASE UP ON THE RHETORIC...OUR MESSAGE, IT'S NOT UNREASONABLE.
THERE DOESN'T SEEM TO BE MANY FOLKS *LEFT* THAT ARE WILLING TO FIGHT THE WAY OUR *FOREFATHERS* DID.
YOU MEAN BY SENTENCING THEIR CHILDREN TO *WAR?*
SLAAAAM
NOW, AS I WAS SAYING...

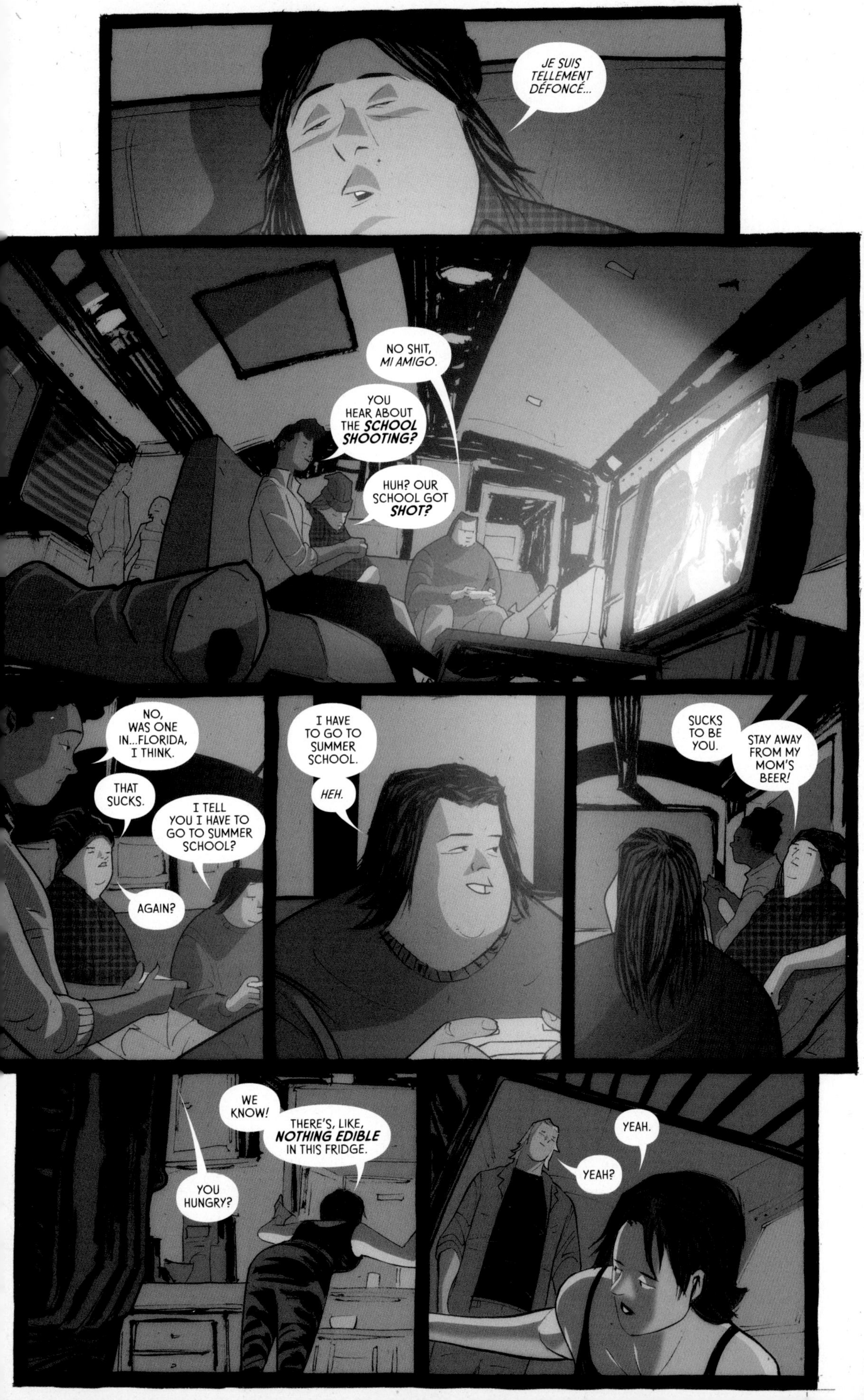
JE SUIS TELLEMENT DÉFONCÉ...
NO SHIT, MI AMIGO.
YOU HEAR ABOUT THE SCHOOL SHOOTING?
HUH? OUR SCHOOL GOT SHOT?
NO, WAS ONE IN...FLORIDA, I THINK.
THAT SUCKS.
I TELL YOU I HAVE TO GO TO SUMMER SCHOOL?
AGAIN?
I HAVE TO GO TO SUMMER SCHOOL.
HEH.
SUCKS TO BE YOU.
STAY AWAY FROM MY MOM'S BEER!
WE KNOW!
THERE'S, LIKE, NOTHING EDIBLE IN THIS FRIDGE.
YOU HUNGRY?
YEAH?
YEAH.

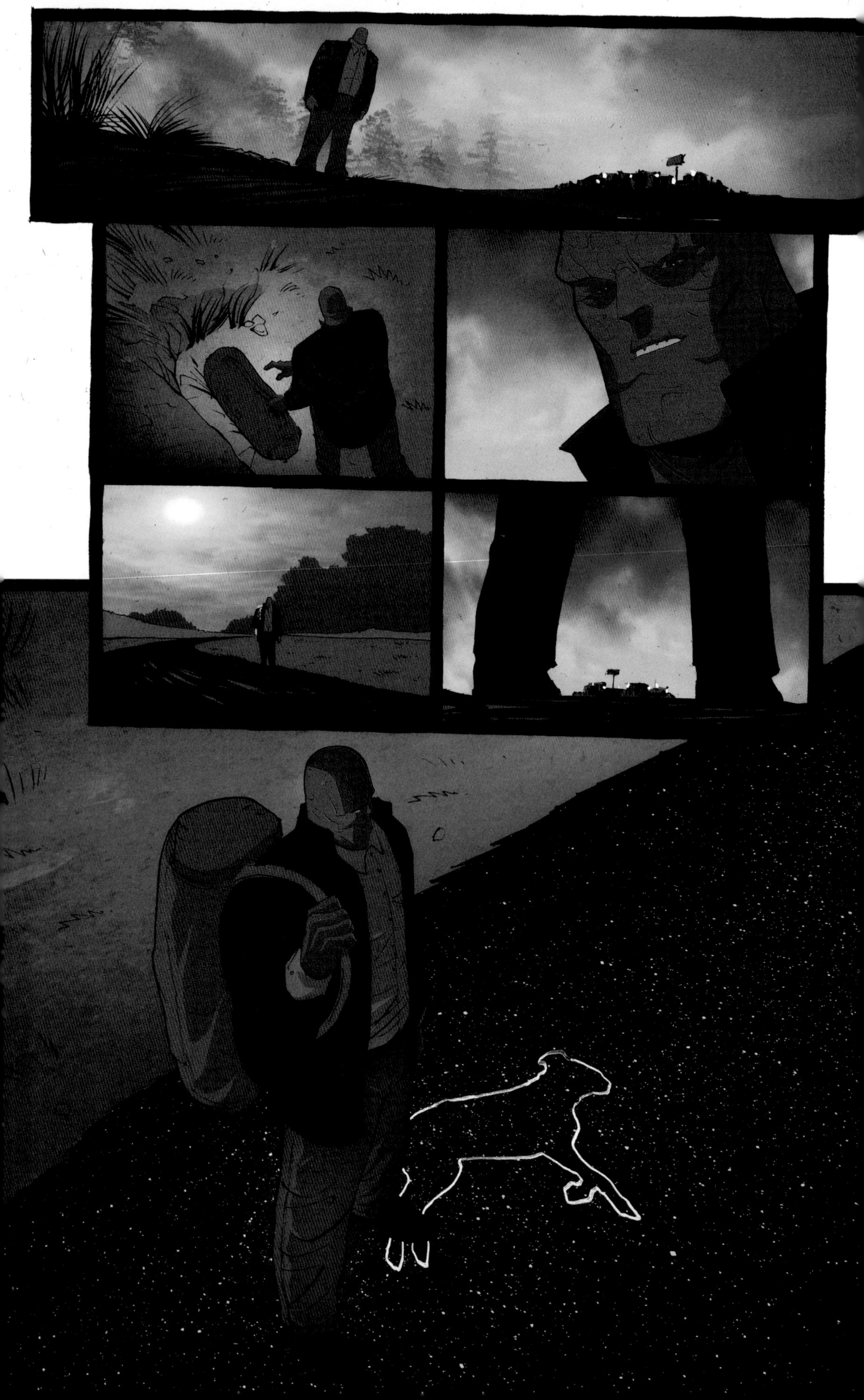

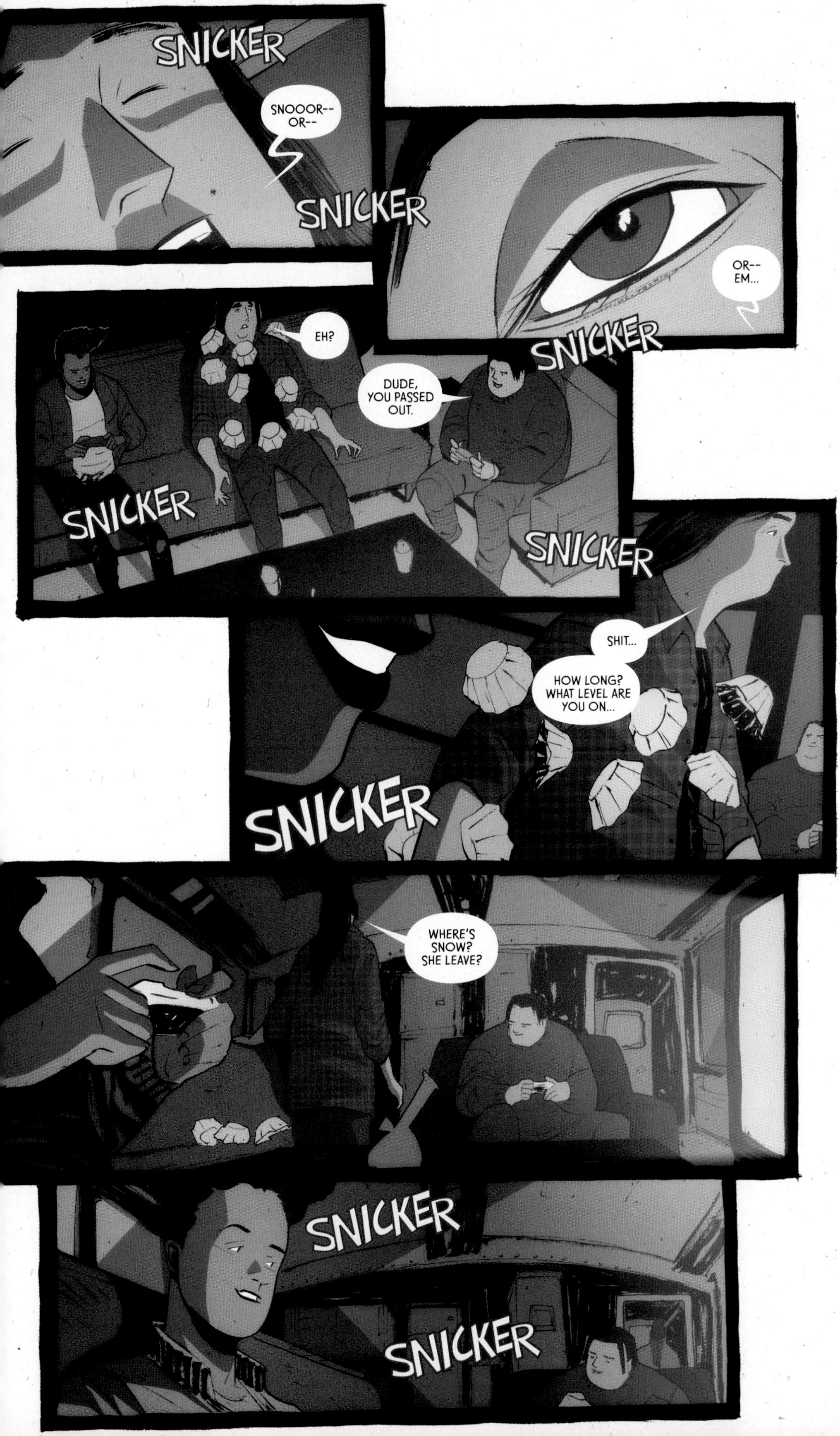
SNICKER
SNOOOR-- OR--
SNICKER
OR-- EM...
SNICKER
EH?
DUDE, YOU PASSED OUT.
SNICKER
SNICKER
SHIT...
HOW LONG? WHAT LEVEL ARE YOU ON...
SNICKER
WHERE'S SNOW? SHE LEAVE?
SNICKER
SNICKER

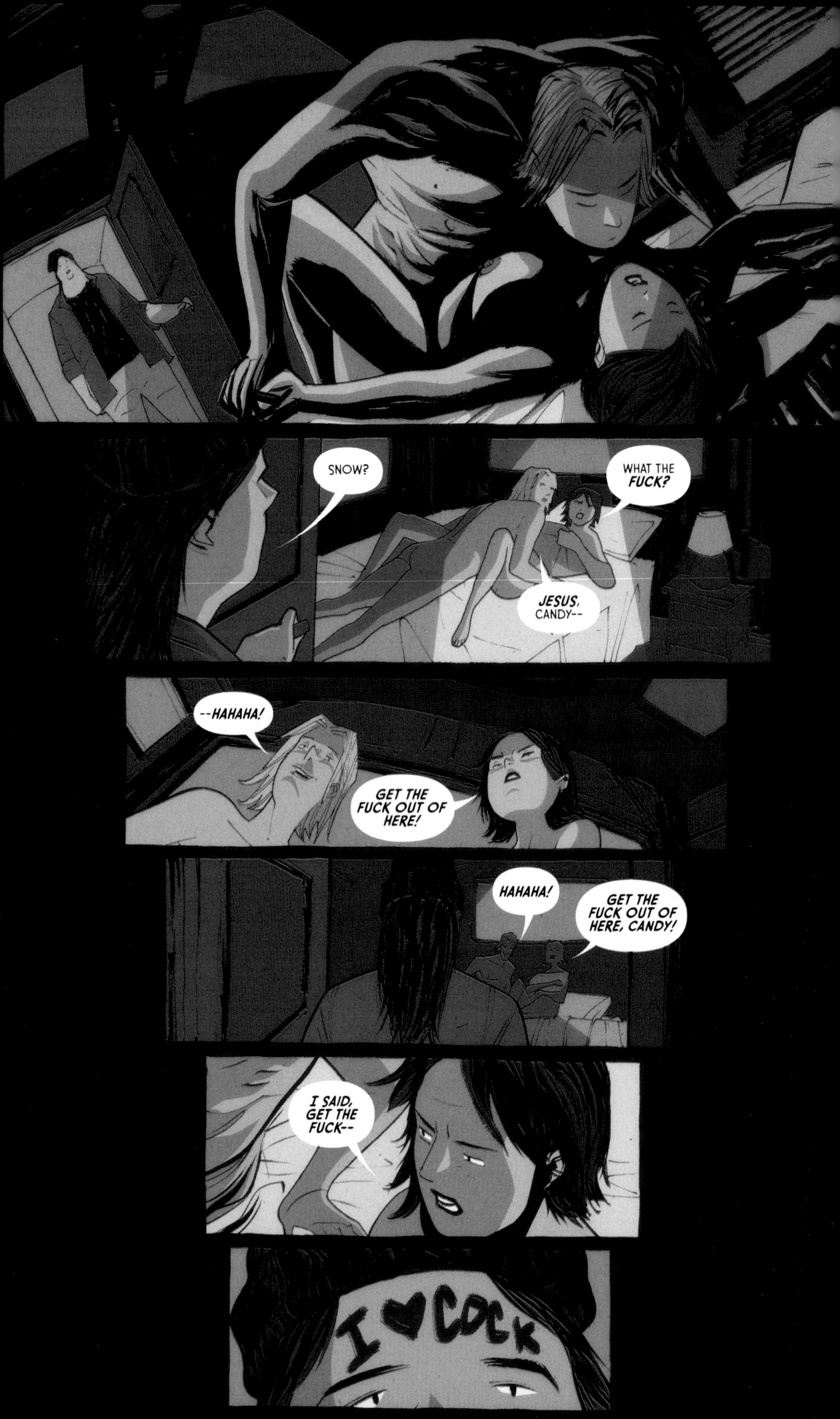
SNOW?
WHAT THE *FUCK?*
JESUS, CANDY--
--HAHAHA!
GET THE FUCK OUT OF HERE!
HAHAHA!
GET THE FUCK OUT OF HERE, CANDY!
I SAID, GET THE FUCK--
I ♥ COCK

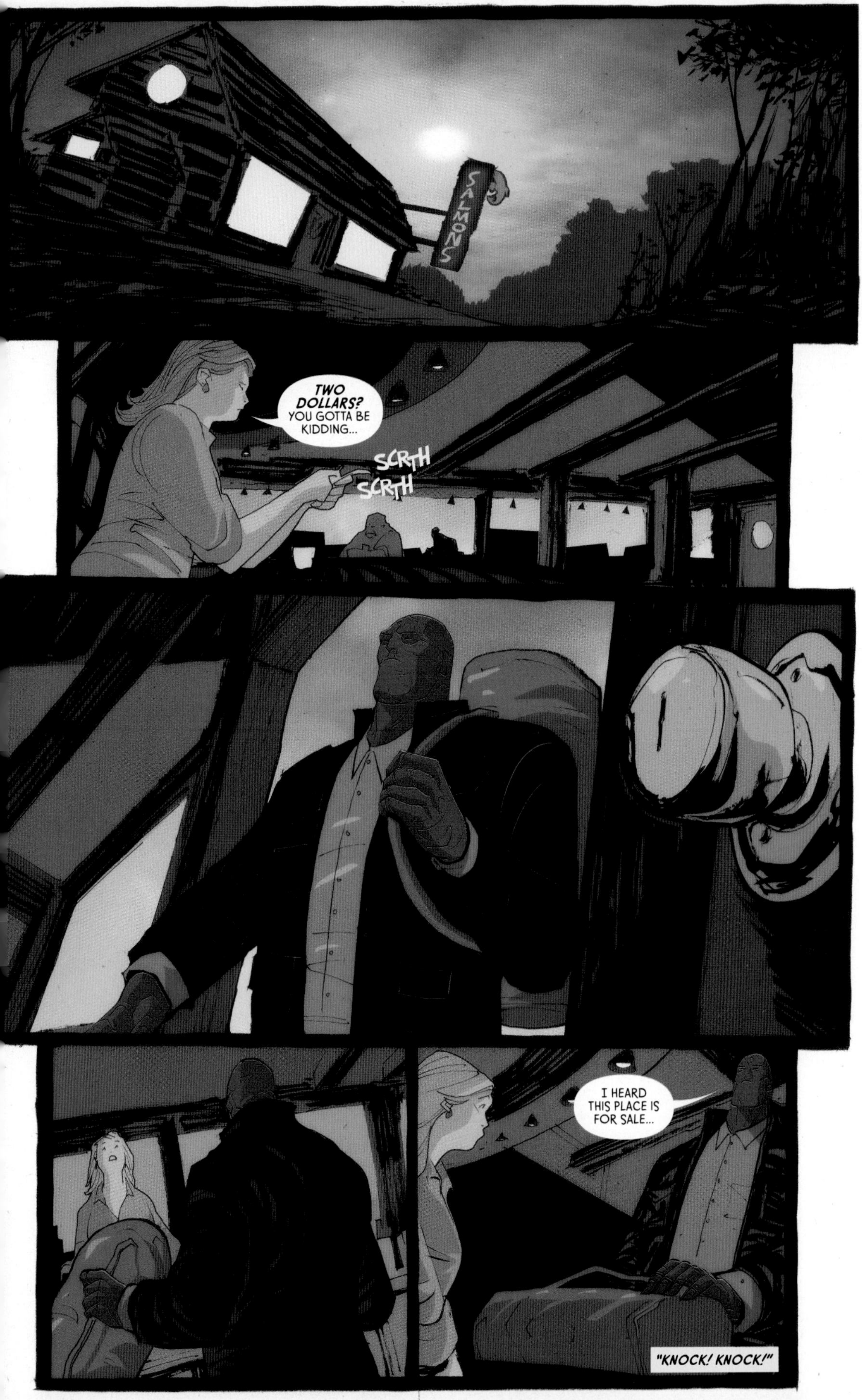
SALMONS
TWO DOLLARS? YOU GOTTA BE KIDDING...
SCRTH
SCRTH
I HEARD THIS PLACE IS FOR SALE...
"KNOCK! KNOCK!"

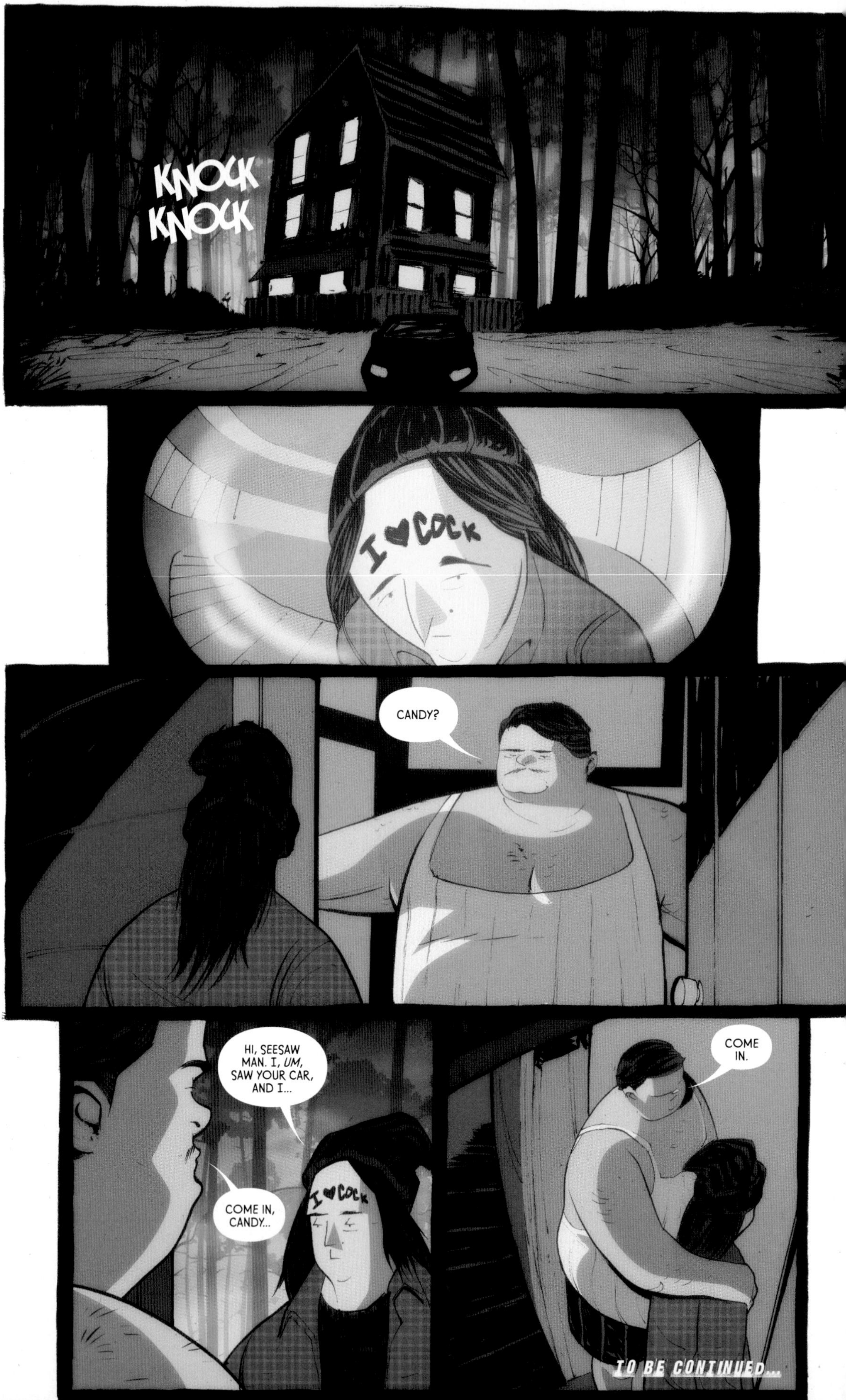
KNOCK KNOCK
I ♥ COCK
CANDY?
HI, SEESAW MAN. I, *UM*, SAW YOUR CAR, AND I...
COME IN, CANDY...
I ♥ COCK
COME IN.
TO BE CONTINUED...

5

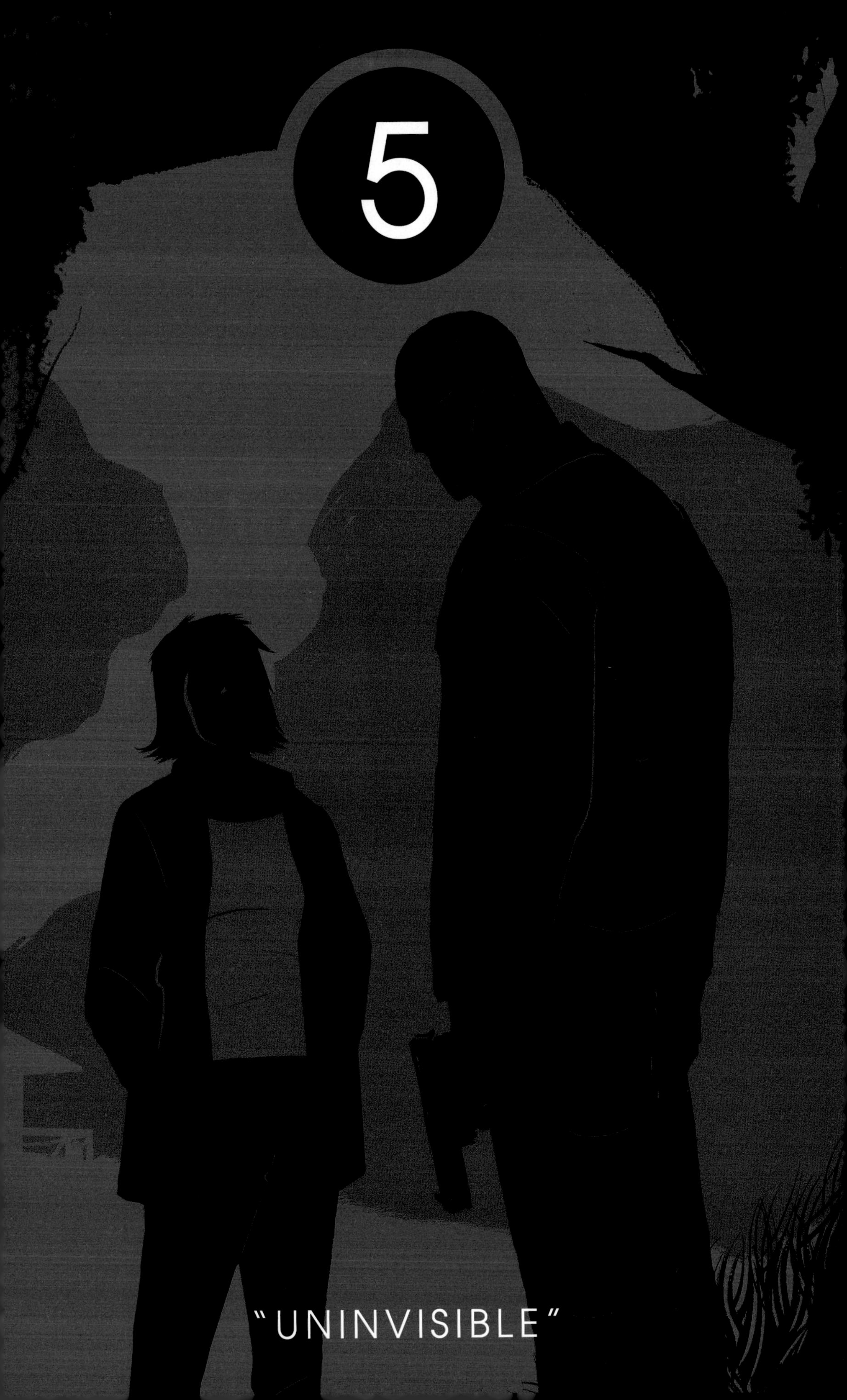

"UNINVISIBLE"

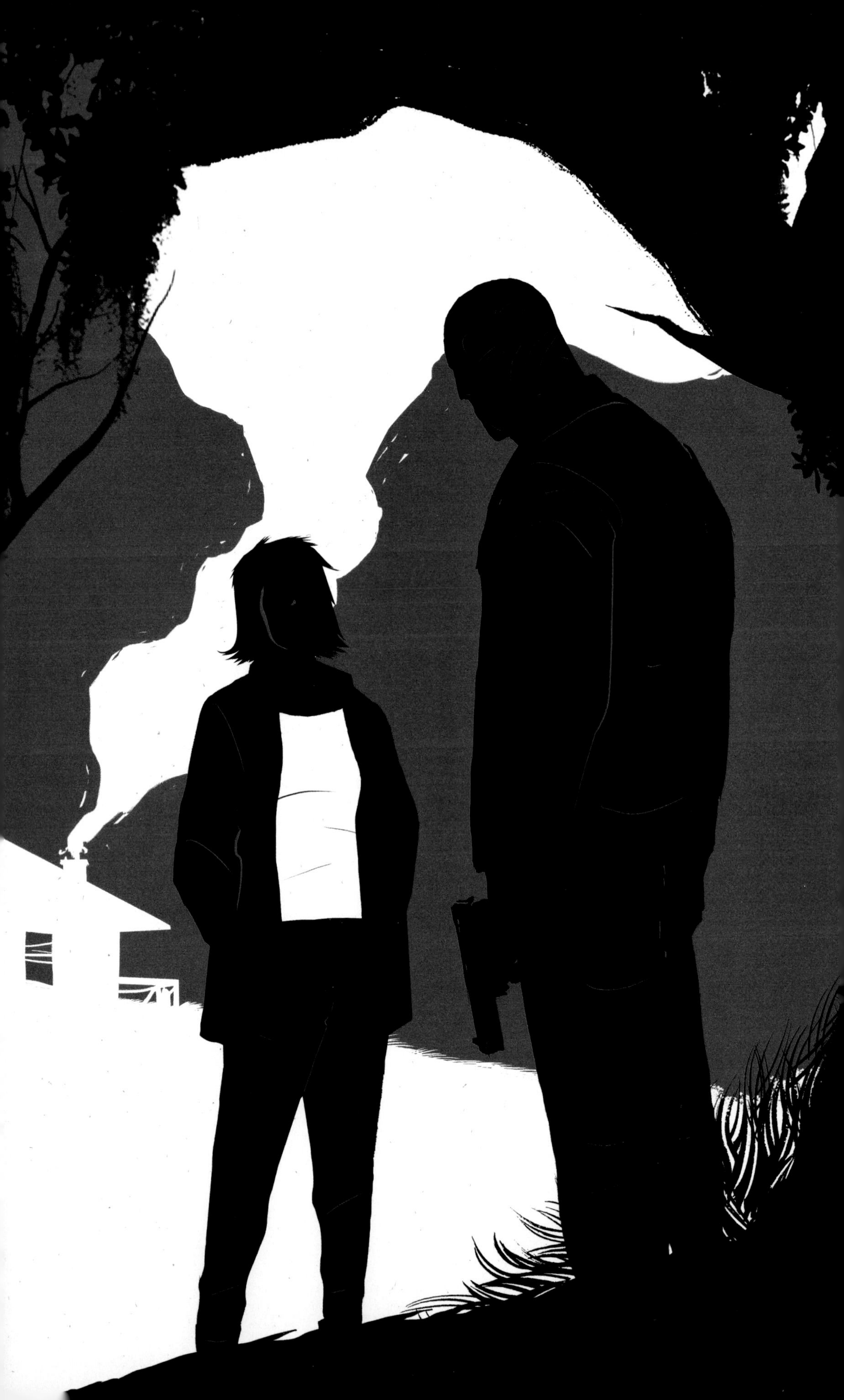

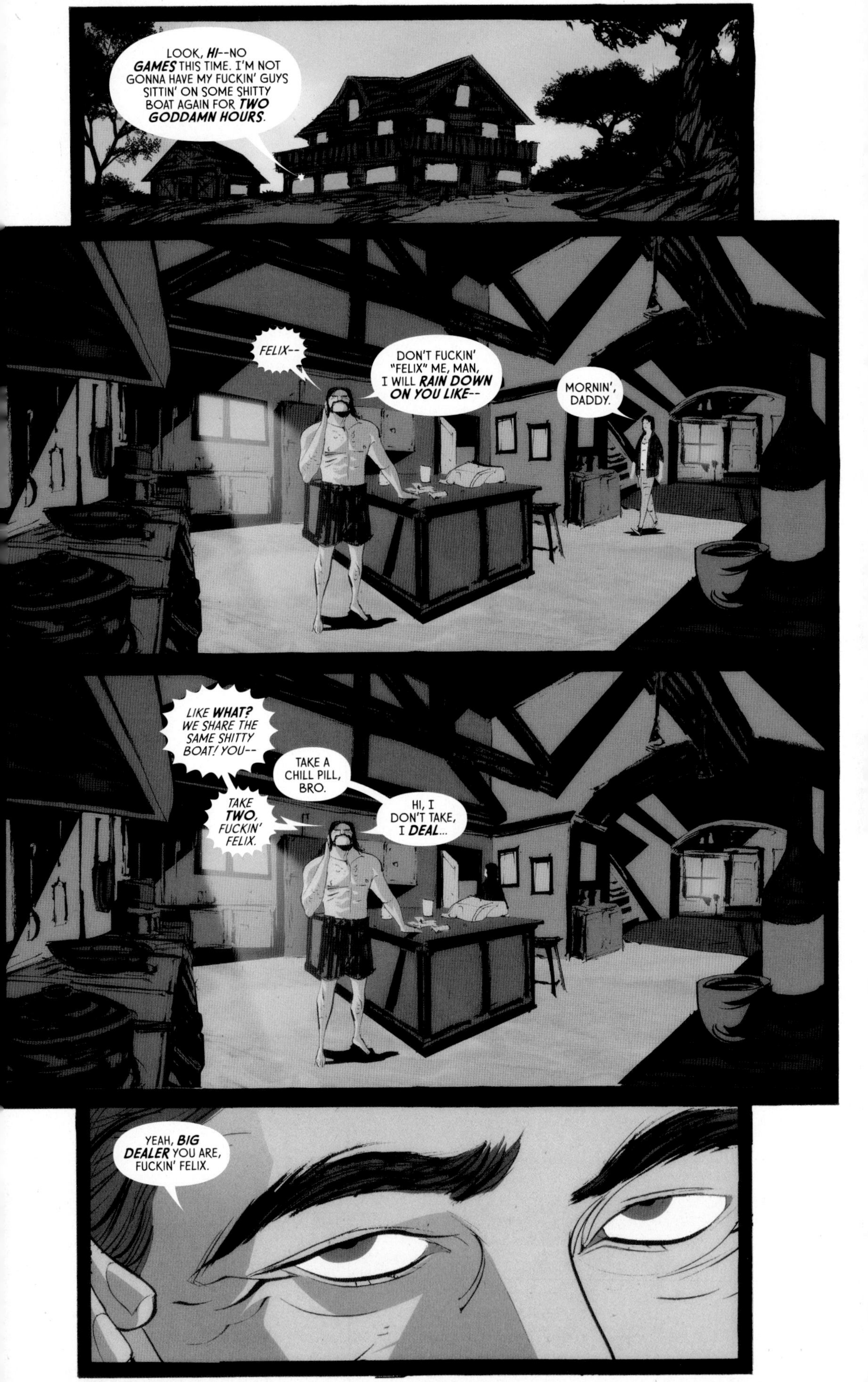
LOOK, HI--NO GAMES THIS TIME. I'M NOT GONNA HAVE MY FUCKIN' GUYS SITTIN' ON SOME SHITTY BOAT AGAIN FOR TWO GODDAMN HOURS.
FELIX--
DON'T FUCKIN' "FELIX" ME, MAN, I WILL RAIN DOWN ON YOU LIKE--
MORNIN', DADDY.
LIKE WHAT? WE SHARE THE SAME SHITTY BOAT! YOU--
TAKE A CHILL PILL, BRO.
TAKE TWO, FUCKIN' FELIX.
HI, I DON'T TAKE, I DEAL...
YEAH, BIG DEALER YOU ARE, FUCKIN' FELIX.

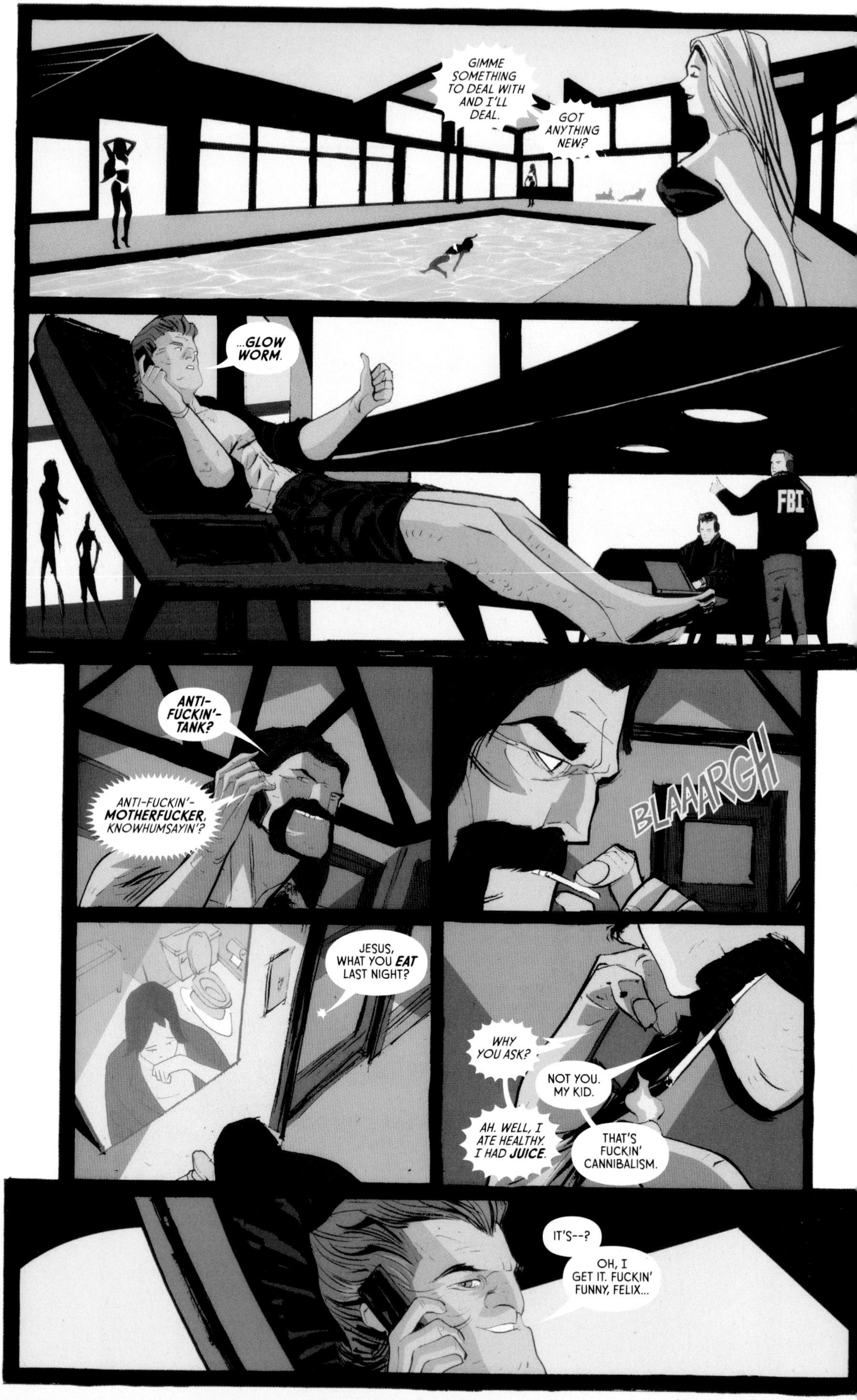
GIMME SOMETHING TO DEAL WITH AND I'LL DEAL.
GOT ANYTHING NEW?
...GLOW WORM.
FBI
ANTI-FUCKIN'-TANK?
ANTI-FUCKIN'-MOTHERFUCKER, KNOWHUMSAYIN'?
BLAAARGH
JESUS, WHAT YOU EAT LAST NIGHT?
WHY YOU ASK?
NOT YOU. MY KID.
AH. WELL, I ATE HEALTHY. I HAD JUICE.
THAT'S FUCKIN' CANNIBALISM.
IT'S--?
OH, I GET IT. FUCKIN' FUNNY, FELIX...

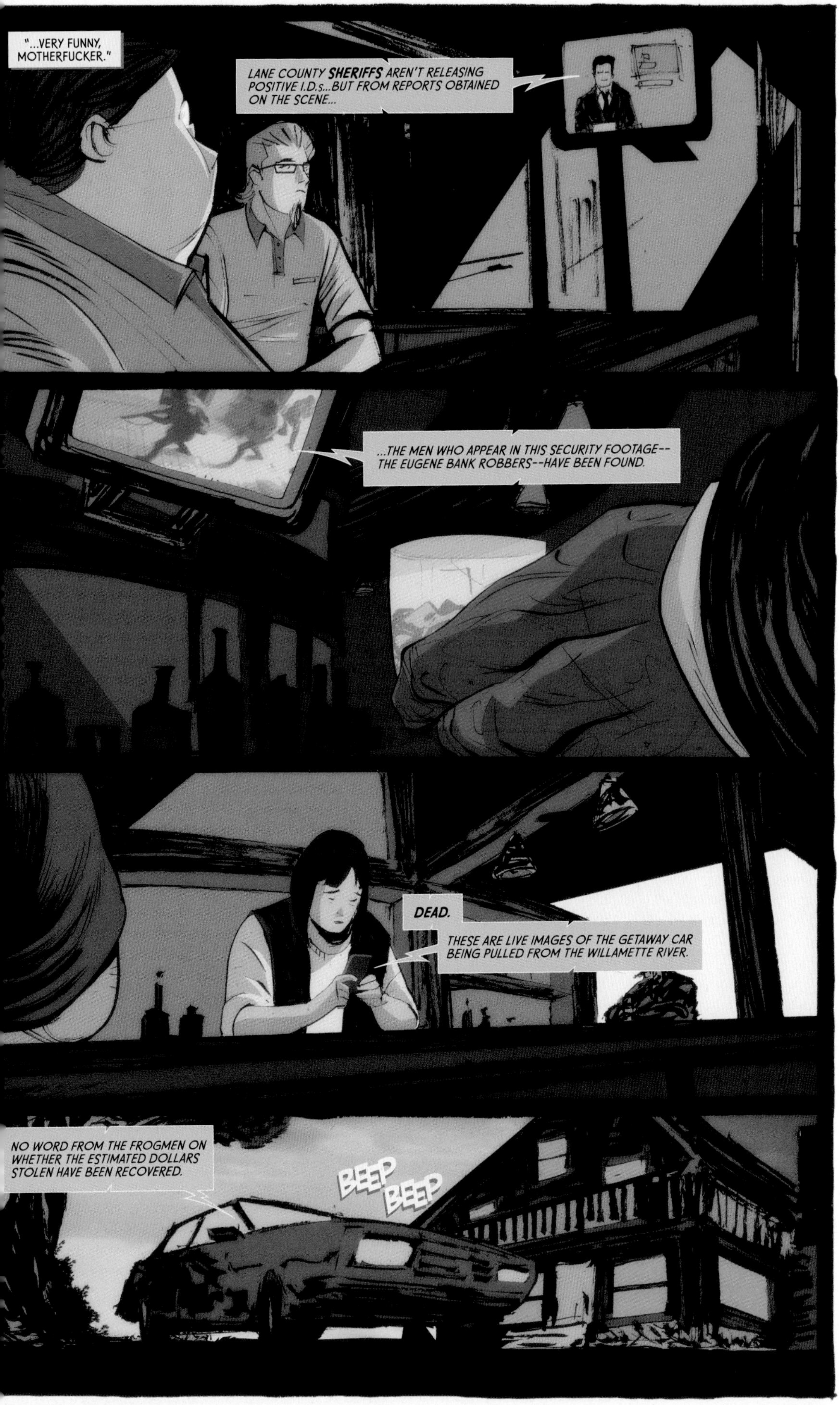
"...VERY FUNNY, MOTHERFUCKER."
LANE COUNTY SHERIFFS AREN'T RELEASING POSITIVE I.D.s...BUT FROM REPORTS OBTAINED ON THE SCENE...
...THE MEN WHO APPEAR IN THIS SECURITY FOOTAGE-- THE EUGENE BANK ROBBERS--HAVE BEEN FOUND.
DEAD.
THESE ARE LIVE IMAGES OF THE GETAWAY CAR BEING PULLED FROM THE WILLAMETTE RIVER.
NO WORD FROM THE FROGMEN ON WHETHER THE ESTIMATED DOLLARS STOLEN HAVE BEEN RECOVERED.
BEEP BEEP

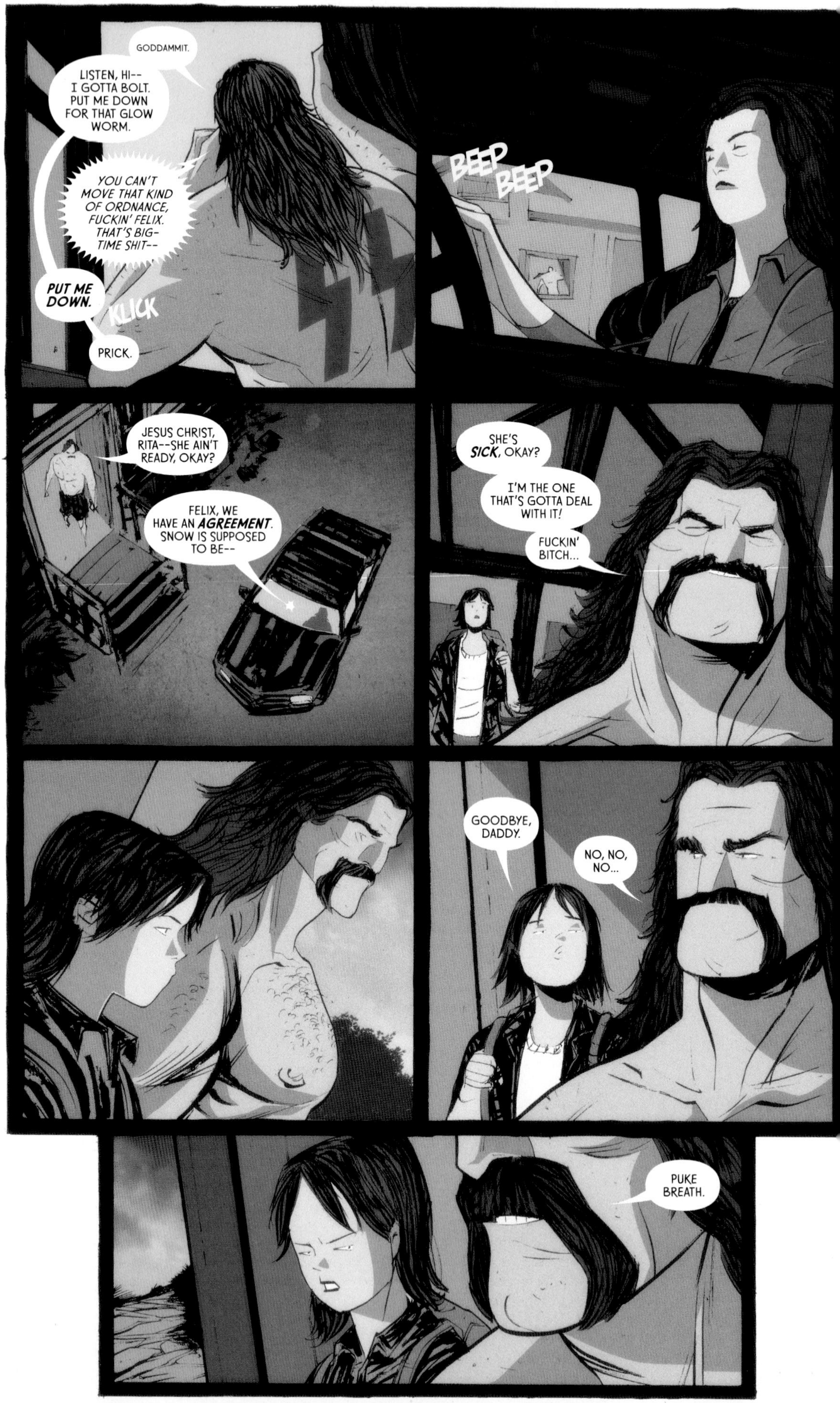
GODDAMMIT.
LISTEN, HI-- I GOTTA BOLT. PUT ME DOWN FOR THAT GLOW WORM.
YOU CAN'T MOVE THAT KIND OF ORDNANCE, FUCKIN' FELIX. THAT'S BIG-TIME SHIT--
PUT ME DOWN.
KLICK
PRICK.
BEEP BEEP
JESUS CHRIST, RITA--SHE AIN'T READY, OKAY?
FELIX, WE HAVE AN AGREEMENT. SNOW IS SUPPOSED TO BE--
SHE'S SICK, OKAY?
I'M THE ONE THAT'S GOTTA DEAL WITH IT!
FUCKIN' BITCH...
GOODBYE, DADDY.
NO, NO, NO...
PUKE BREATH.

HEY, MOM, CAN I ASK YOU SOMETHING?

I DON'T WANT A SANDWICH FOR BREAKFAST, GARY.

IT'S LUNCHTIME.

DO YOU REMEMBER *ARTHUR THE PARROT?* I MUSTA BEEN IN FIRST GRADE... WE GOT HIM WHEN UNCLE DAVE DIED--

OH, DID HE *GO!*

YEAH, UNCLE DAVE WENT TAKE-NO-PRISONERS, THAT'S FOR SURE.

DAVE? NO, I MEANT ARTHUR.

THAT BIRD *CRAPPED* OVER EVERYTHING. IT'S WHY I LEFT THE BACK DOOR OPEN AND SHOO'D HIM OUT.

YOU TOLD ME YOU GAVE HIM TO A *PIRATE*.

I DID?

I DON'T REMEMBER EVER SAYING...

I DON'T REMEMBER...

IT'S OKAY, MOM...

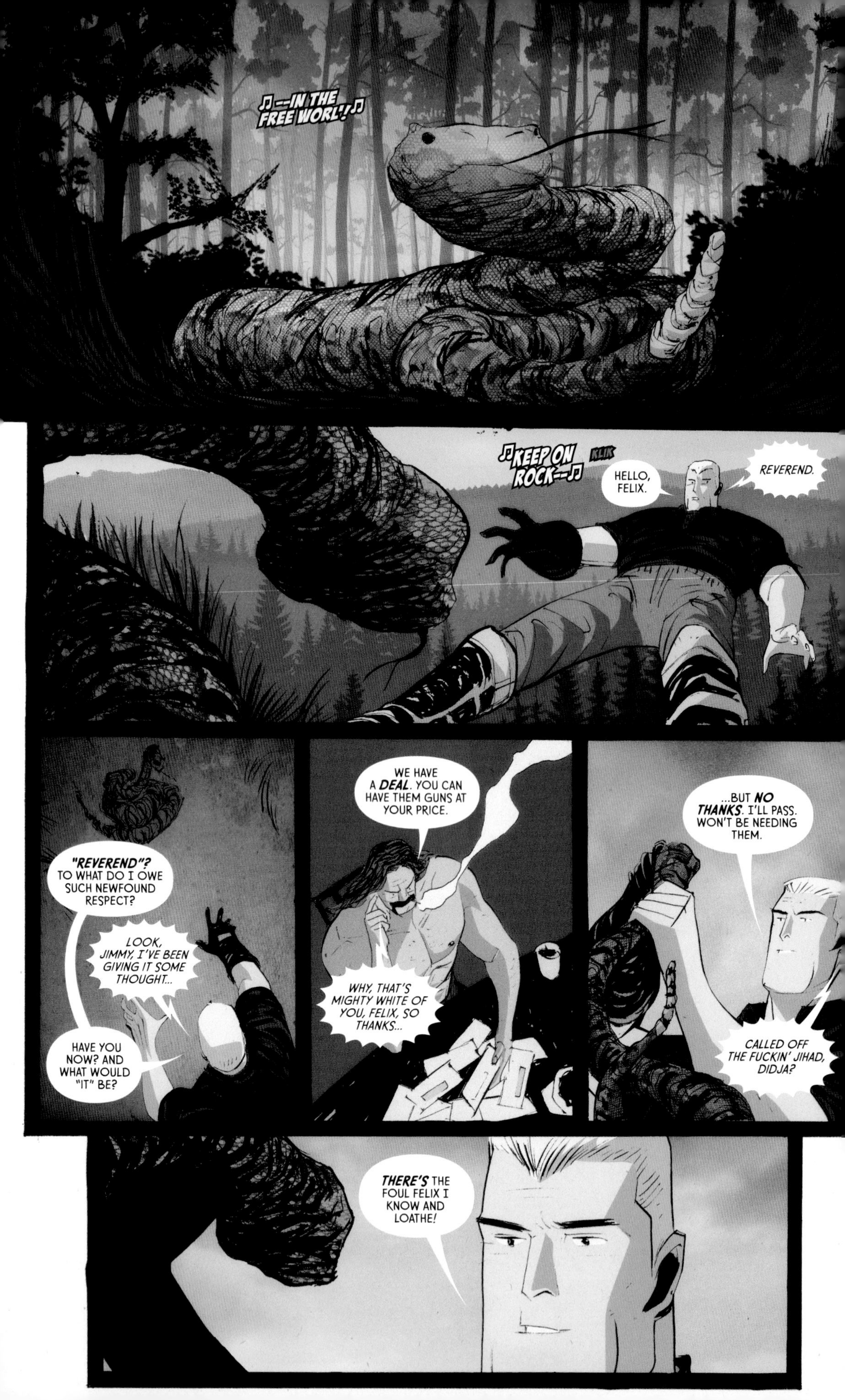

♫ --IN THE FREE WORL'! ♫
♫ KEEP ON ROCK-- ♫
KLIK
HELLO, FELIX.
REVEREND.
"REVEREND"? TO WHAT DO I OWE SUCH NEWFOUND RESPECT?
LOOK, JIMMY, I'VE BEEN GIVING IT SOME THOUGHT...
HAVE YOU NOW? AND WHAT WOULD "IT" BE?
WE HAVE A DEAL. YOU CAN HAVE THEM GUNS AT YOUR PRICE.
WHY, THAT'S MIGHTY WHITE OF YOU, FELIX, SO THANKS...
...BUT NO THANKS. I'LL PASS. WON'T BE NEEDING THEM.
CALLED OFF THE FUCKIN' JIHAD, DIDJA?
THERE'S THE FOUL FELIX I KNOW AND LOATHE!

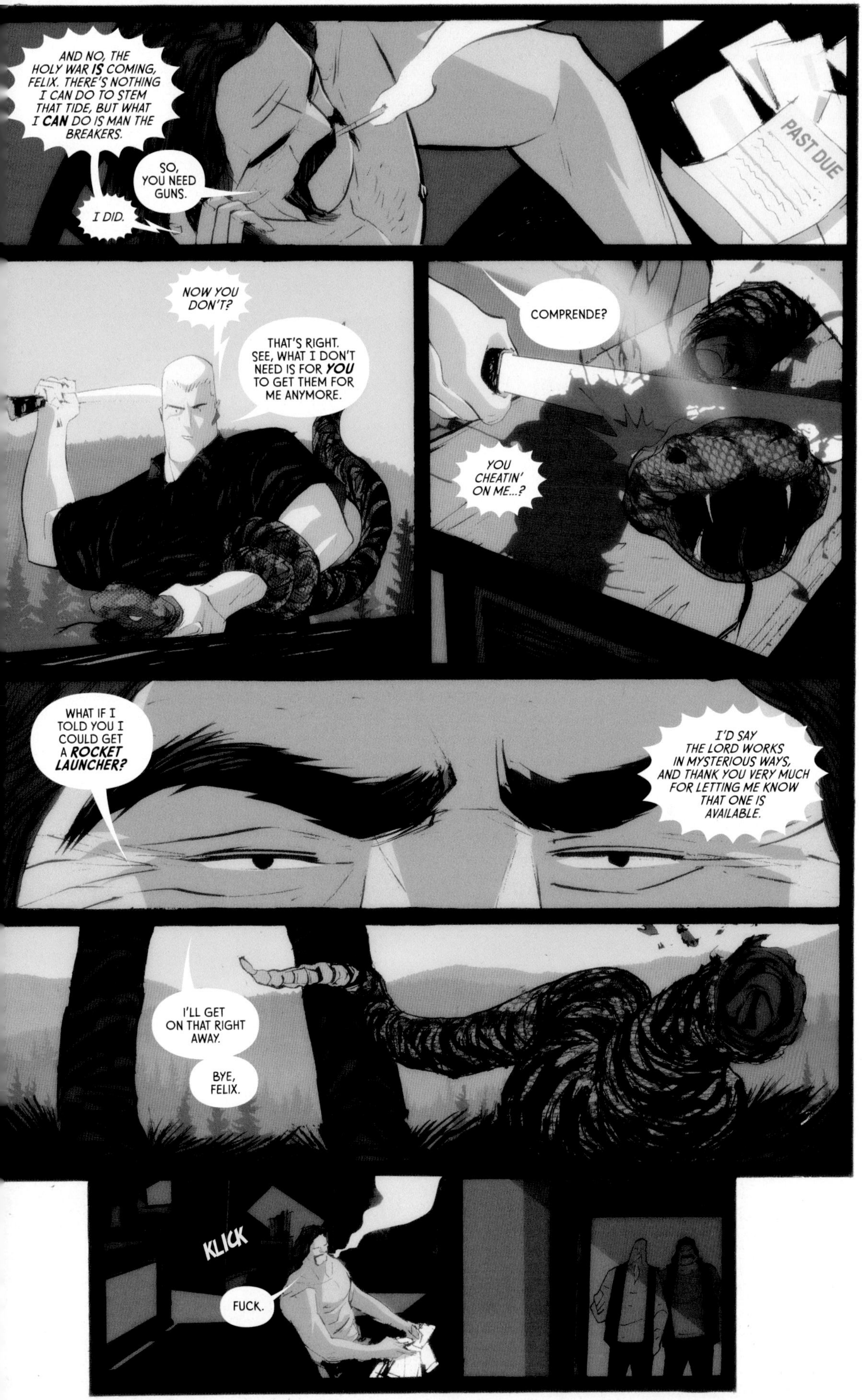
AND NO, THE HOLY WAR **IS** COMING, FELIX. THERE'S NOTHING I CAN DO TO STEM THAT TIDE, BUT WHAT I **CAN** DO IS MAN THE BREAKERS.
SO, YOU NEED GUNS.
I DID.
PAST DUE
NOW YOU DON'T?
THAT'S RIGHT. SEE, WHAT I DON'T NEED IS FOR **YOU** TO GET THEM FOR ME ANYMORE.
COMPRENDE?
YOU CHEATIN' ON ME...?
WHAT IF I TOLD YOU I COULD GET A **ROCKET LAUNCHER?**
I'D SAY THE LORD WORKS IN MYSTERIOUS WAYS, AND THANK YOU VERY MUCH FOR LETTING ME KNOW THAT ONE IS AVAILABLE.
I'LL GET ON THAT RIGHT AWAY.
BYE, FELIX.
KLICK
FUCK.

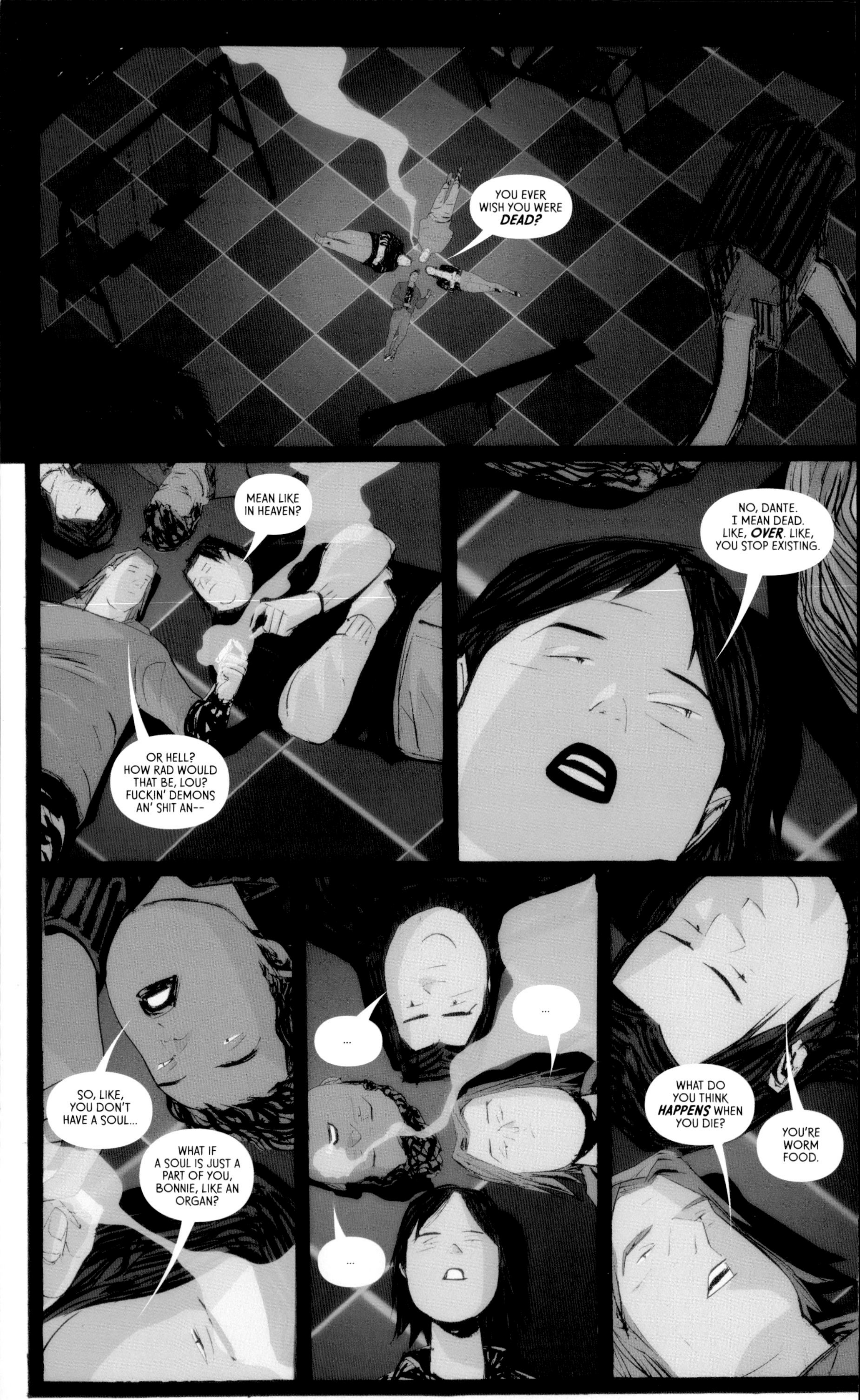
YOU EVER WISH YOU WERE *DEAD?*
MEAN LIKE IN HEAVEN?
OR HELL? HOW RAD WOULD THAT BE, LOU? FUCKIN' DEMONS AN' SHIT AN--
NO, DANTE. I MEAN DEAD. LIKE, *OVER*. LIKE, YOU STOP EXISTING.
SO, LIKE, YOU DON'T HAVE A SOUL...
WHAT IF A SOUL IS JUST A PART OF YOU, BONNIE, LIKE AN ORGAN?
...
...
...
WHAT DO YOU THINK *HAPPENS* WHEN YOU DIE?
YOU'RE WORM FOOD.

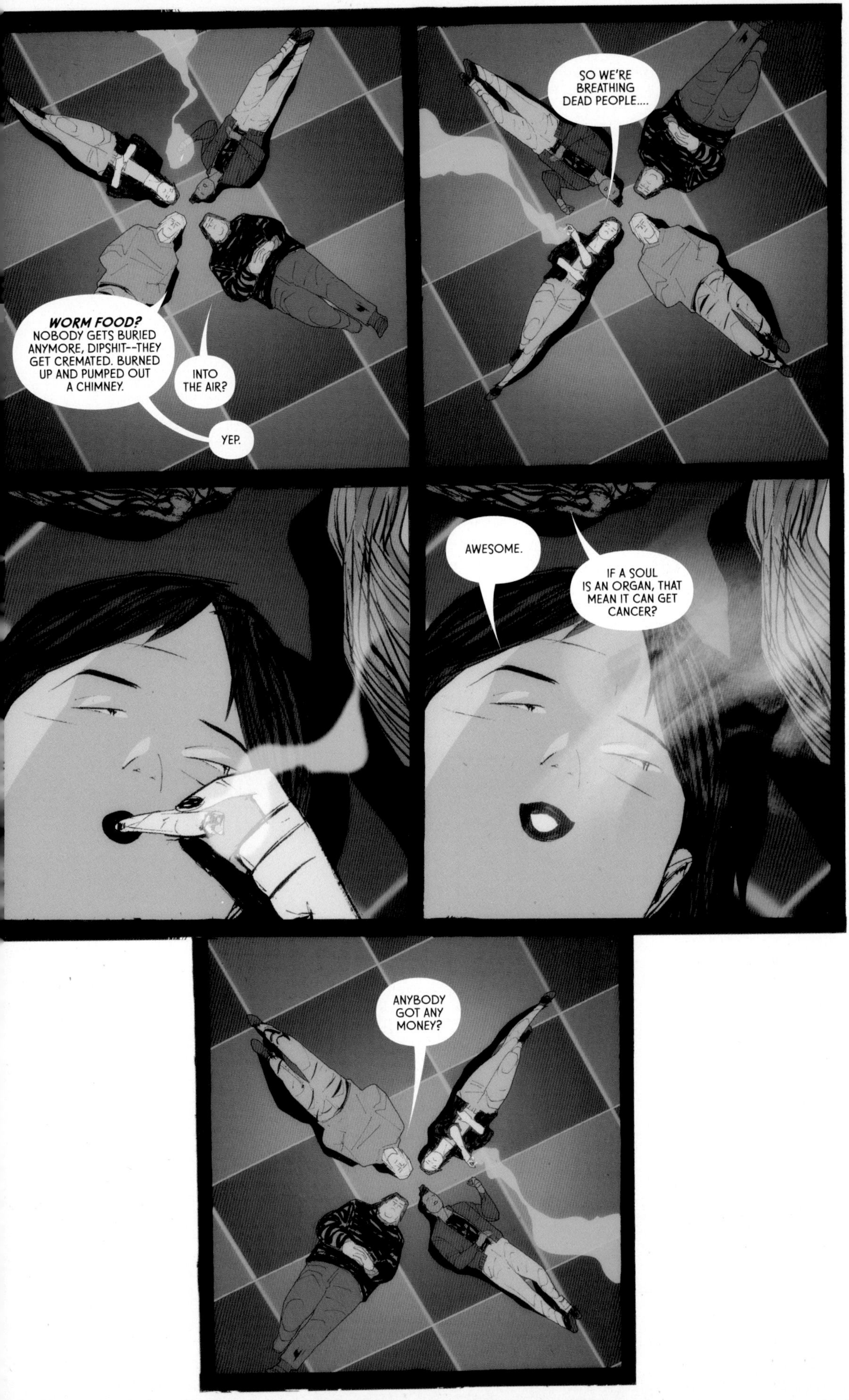
WORM FOOD? NOBODY GETS BURIED ANYMORE, DIPSHIT--THEY GET CREMATED. BURNED UP AND PUMPED OUT A CHIMNEY.
INTO THE AIR?
YEP.
SO WE'RE BREATHING DEAD PEOPLE....
AWESOME.
IF A SOUL IS AN ORGAN, THAT MEAN IT CAN GET CANCER?
ANYBODY GOT ANY MONEY?

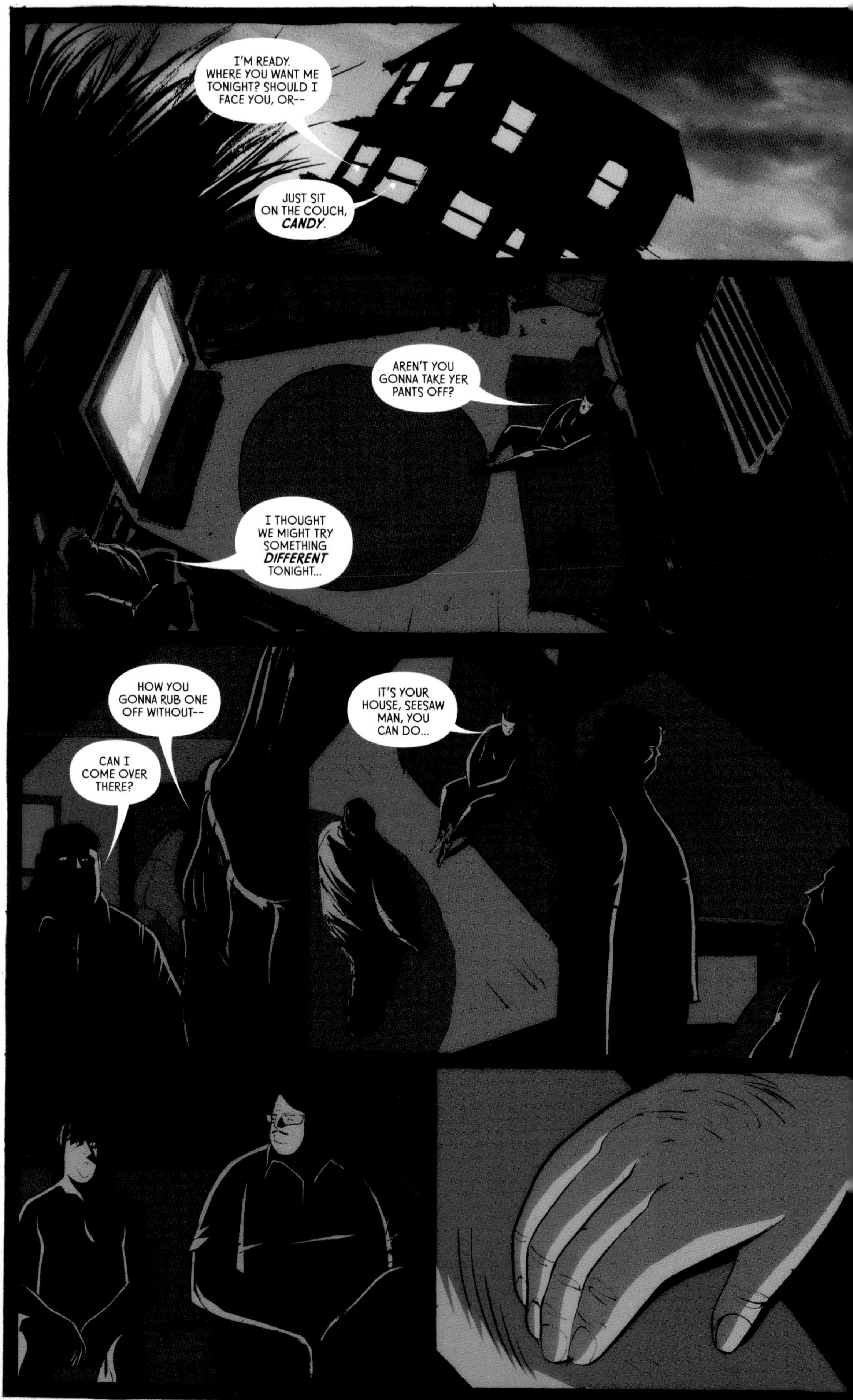
I'M READY. WHERE YOU WANT ME TONIGHT? SHOULD I FACE YOU, OR--
JUST SIT ON THE COUCH, *CANDY*.
AREN'T YOU GONNA TAKE YER PANTS OFF?
I THOUGHT WE MIGHT TRY SOMETHING ***DIFFERENT*** TONIGHT...
HOW YOU GONNA RUB ONE OFF WITHOUT--
CAN I COME OVER THERE?
IT'S YOUR HOUSE, SEESAW MAN, YOU CAN DO...

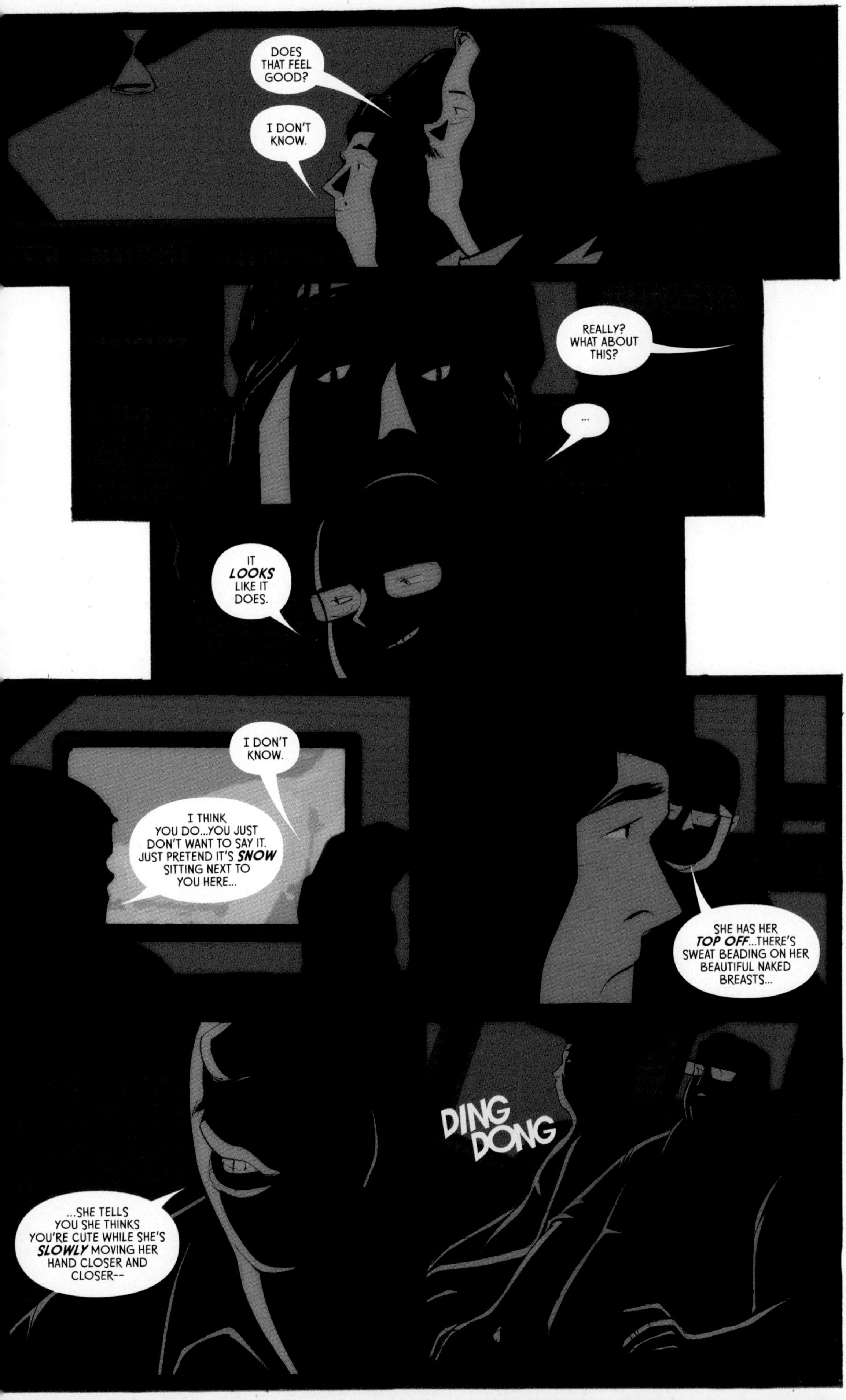

DOES THAT FEEL GOOD?
I DON'T KNOW.
REALLY? WHAT ABOUT THIS?
...
IT LOOKS LIKE IT DOES.
I DON'T KNOW.
I THINK YOU DO...YOU JUST DON'T WANT TO SAY IT. JUST PRETEND IT'S SNOW SITTING NEXT TO YOU HERE...
SHE HAS HER TOP OFF...THERE'S SWEAT BEADING ON HER BEAUTIFUL NAKED BREASTS...
...SHE TELLS YOU SHE THINKS YOU'RE CUTE WHILE SHE'S SLOWLY MOVING HER HAND CLOSER AND CLOSER--
DING DONG

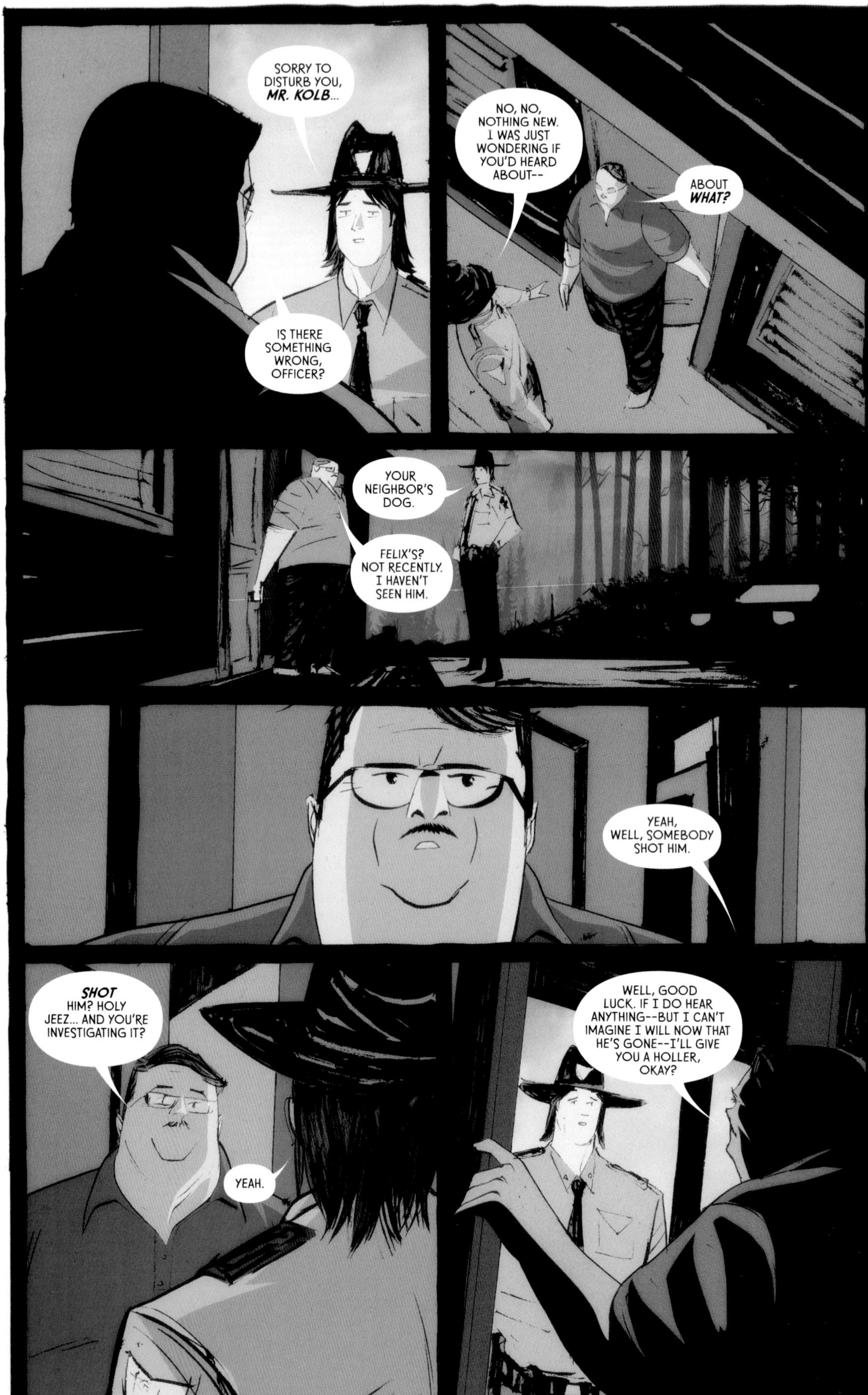
SORRY TO DISTURB YOU, MR. KOLB...
IS THERE SOMETHING WRONG, OFFICER?
NO, NO, NOTHING NEW. I WAS JUST WONDERING IF YOU'D HEARD ABOUT--
ABOUT WHAT?
YOUR NEIGHBOR'S DOG.
FELIX'S? NOT RECENTLY. I HAVEN'T SEEN HIM.
YEAH, WELL, SOMEBODY SHOT HIM.
SHOT HIM? HOLY JEEZ... AND YOU'RE INVESTIGATING IT?
YEAH.
WELL, GOOD LUCK. IF I DO HEAR ANYTHING--BUT I CAN'T IMAGINE I WILL NOW THAT HE'S GONE--I'LL GIVE YOU A HOLLER, OKAY?

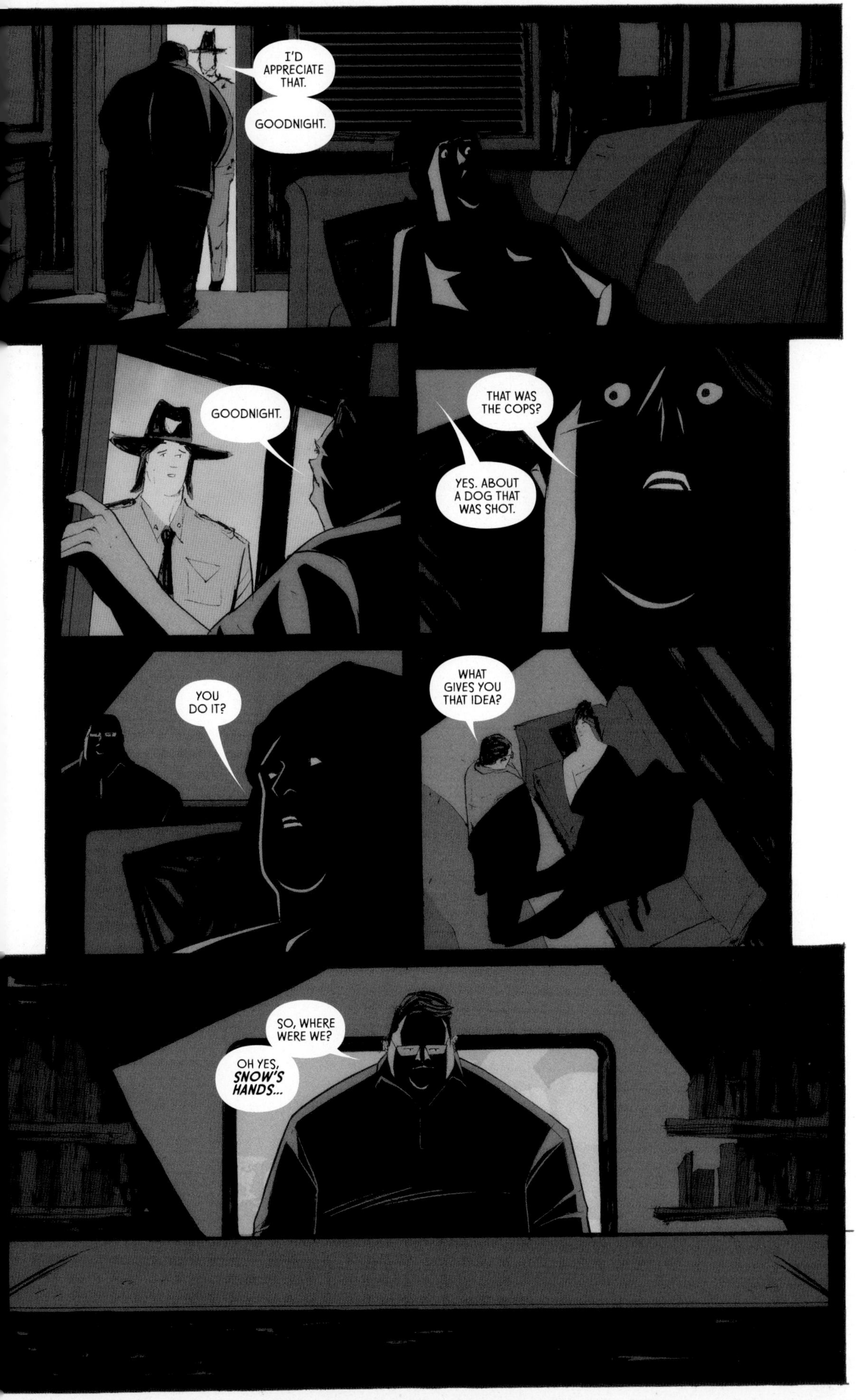
I'D APPRECIATE THAT.
GOODNIGHT.
GOODNIGHT.
THAT WAS THE COPS?
YES. ABOUT A DOG THAT WAS SHOT.
YOU DO IT?
WHAT GIVES YOU THAT IDEA?
SO, WHERE WERE WE?
OH YES, ***SNOW'S HANDS...***

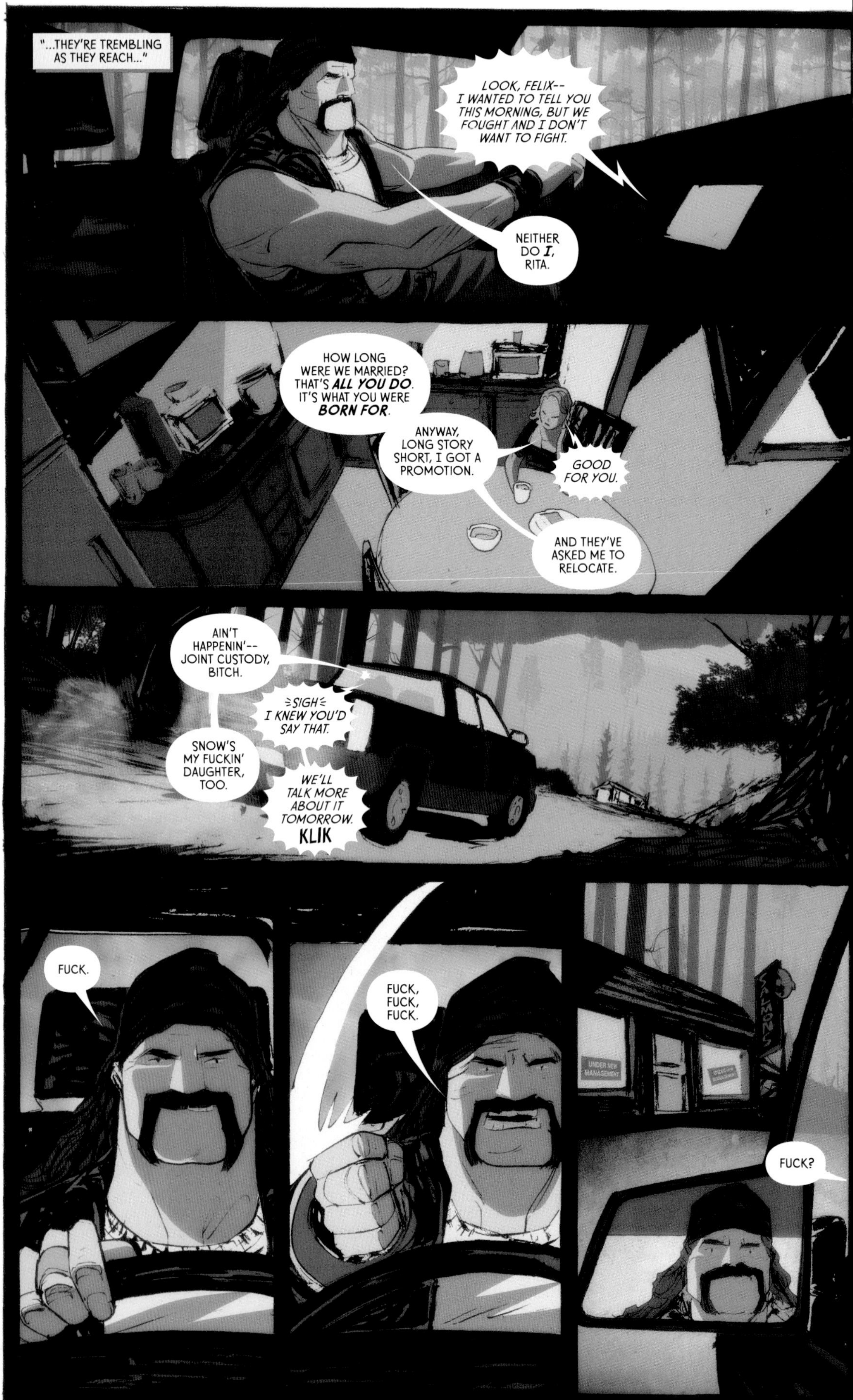
"...THEY'RE TREMBLING AS THEY REACH..."
LOOK, FELIX-- I WANTED TO TELL YOU THIS MORNING, BUT WE FOUGHT AND I DON'T WANT TO FIGHT.
NEITHER DO *I*, RITA.
HOW LONG WERE WE MARRIED? THAT'S **ALL YOU DO**. IT'S WHAT YOU WERE **BORN FOR**.
ANYWAY, LONG STORY SHORT, I GOT A PROMOTION.
GOOD FOR YOU.
AND THEY'VE ASKED ME TO RELOCATE.
AIN'T HAPPENIN'-- JOINT CUSTODY, BITCH.
SIGH I KNEW YOU'D SAY THAT.
SNOW'S MY FUCKIN' DAUGHTER, TOO.
WE'LL TALK MORE ABOUT IT TOMORROW.
KLIK
FUCK.
FUCK, FUCK, FUCK.
UNDER NEW MANAGEMENT
FUCK?

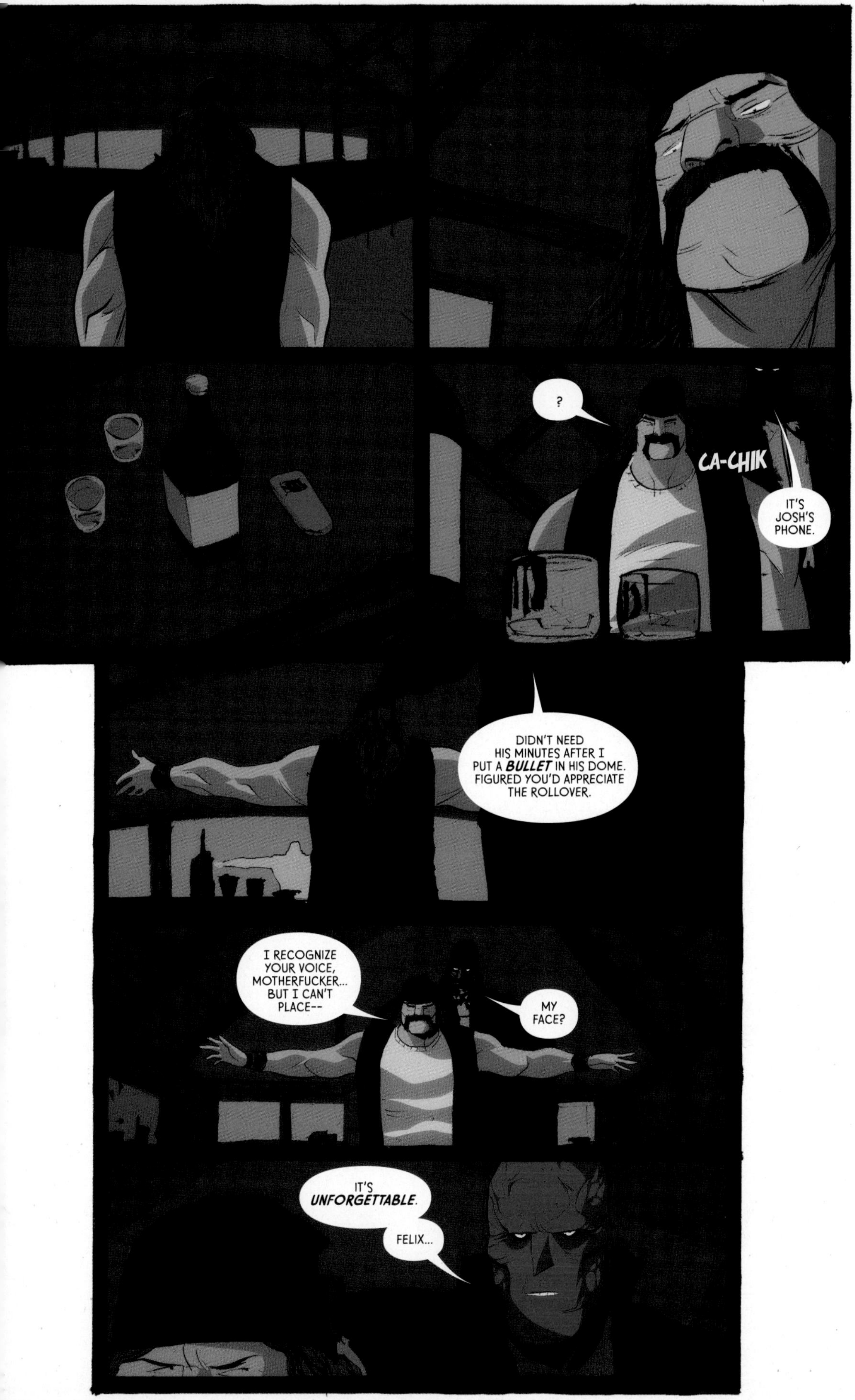
?
CA-CHIK
IT'S JOSH'S PHONE.
DIDN'T NEED HIS MINUTES AFTER I PUT A ***BULLET*** IN HIS DOME. FIGURED YOU'D APPRECIATE THE ROLLOVER.
I RECOGNIZE YOUR VOICE, MOTHERFUCKER... BUT I CAN'T PLACE--
MY FACE?
IT'S ***UNFORGETTABLE***.
FELIX...

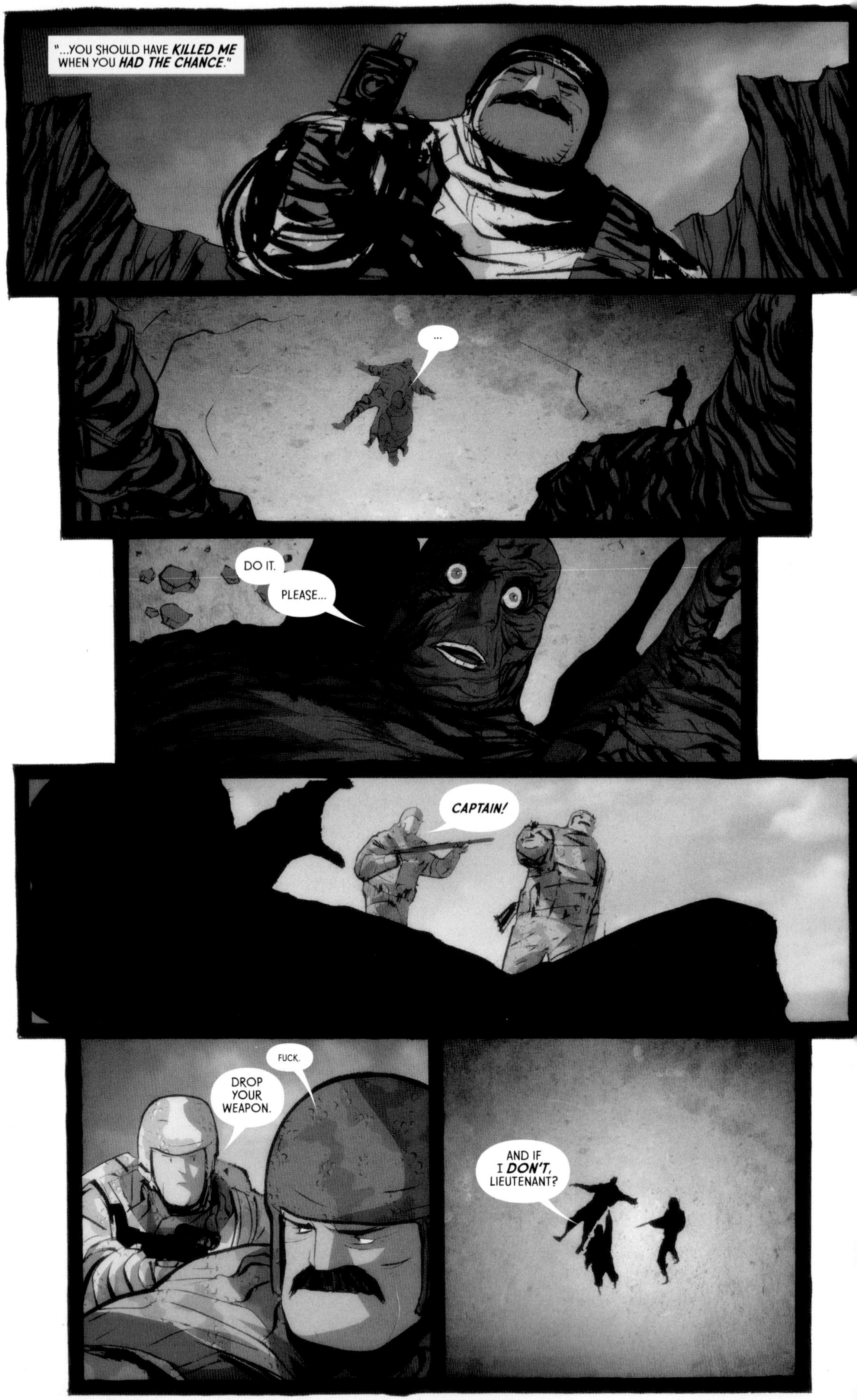
"...YOU SHOULD HAVE KILLED ME WHEN YOU HAD THE CHANCE."
...
DO IT.
PLEASE...
CAPTAIN!
FUCK.
DROP YOUR WEAPON.
AND IF I DON'T, LIEUTENANT?

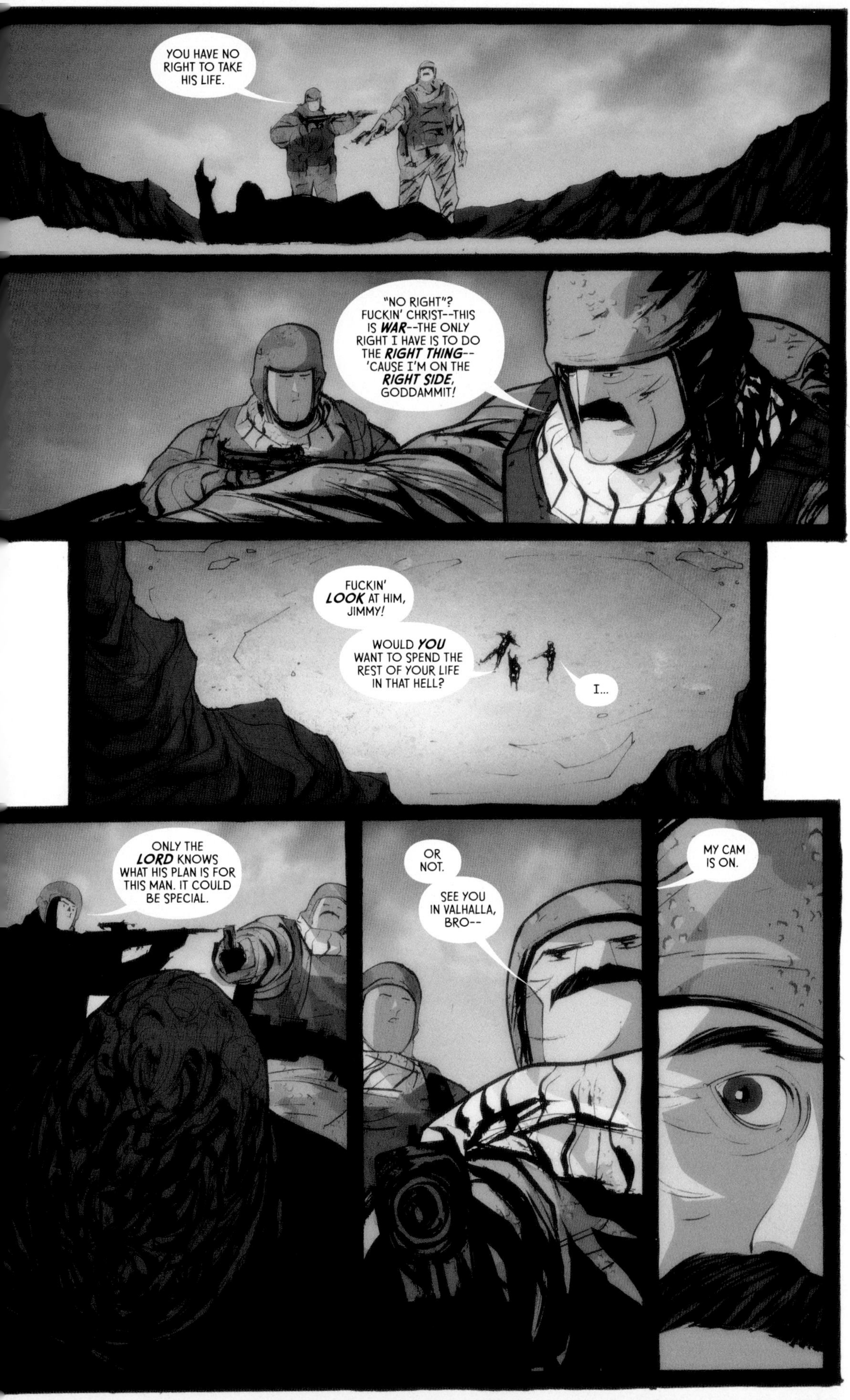
YOU HAVE NO RIGHT TO TAKE HIS LIFE.
"NO RIGHT"? FUCKIN' CHRIST--THIS IS *WAR*--THE ONLY RIGHT I HAVE IS TO DO THE *RIGHT THING*--'CAUSE I'M ON THE *RIGHT SIDE*, GODDAMMIT!
FUCKIN' *LOOK* AT HIM, JIMMY!
WOULD *YOU* WANT TO SPEND THE REST OF YOUR LIFE IN THAT HELL?
I...
ONLY THE *LORD* KNOWS WHAT HIS PLAN IS FOR THIS MAN. IT COULD BE SPECIAL.
OR NOT.
SEE YOU IN VALHALLA, BRO--
MY CAM IS ON.

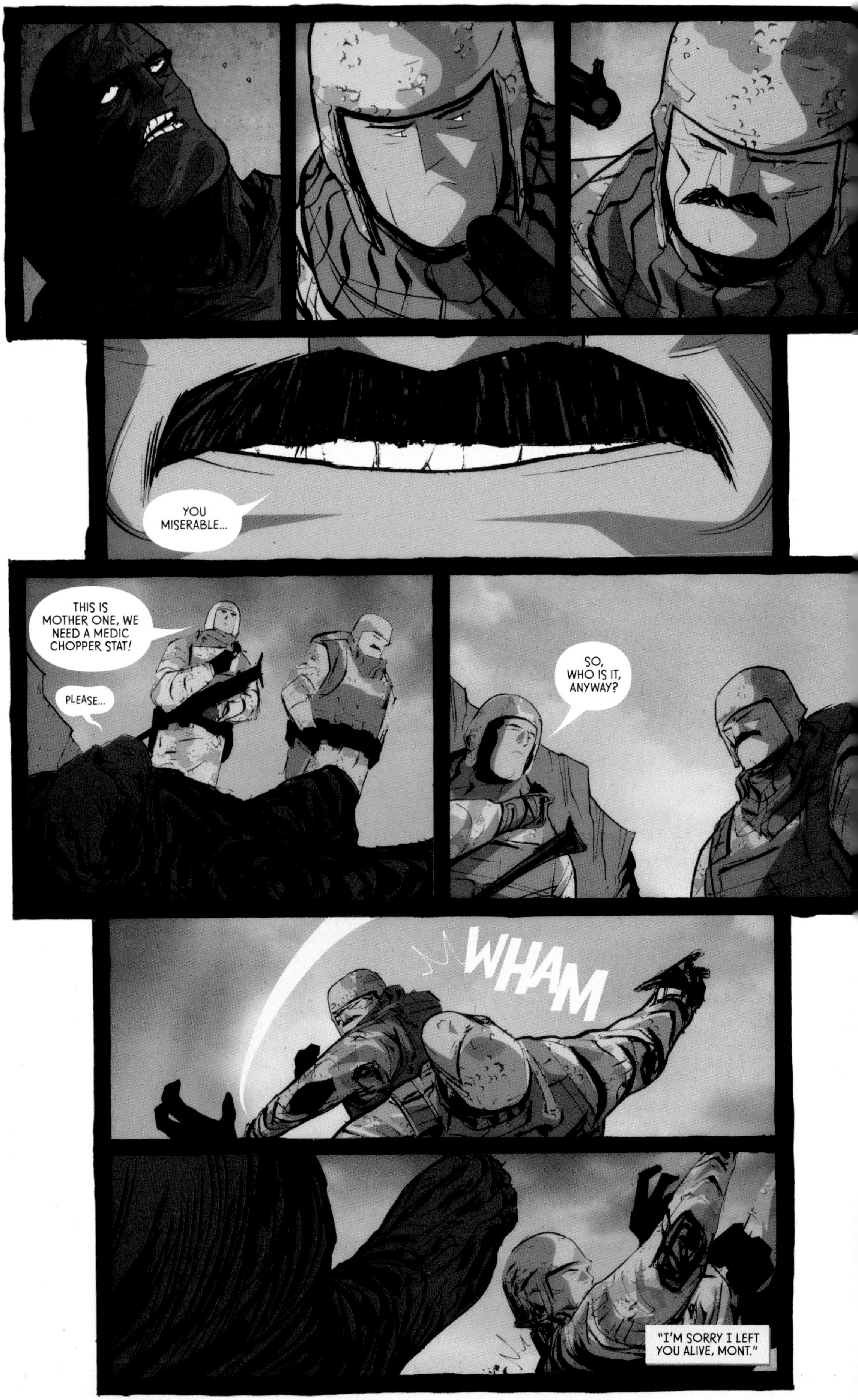
YOU MISERABLE...
THIS IS MOTHER ONE, WE NEED A MEDIC CHOPPER STAT!
PLEASE...
SO, WHO IS IT, ANYWAY?
WHAM
"I'M SORRY I LEFT YOU ALIVE, MONT."

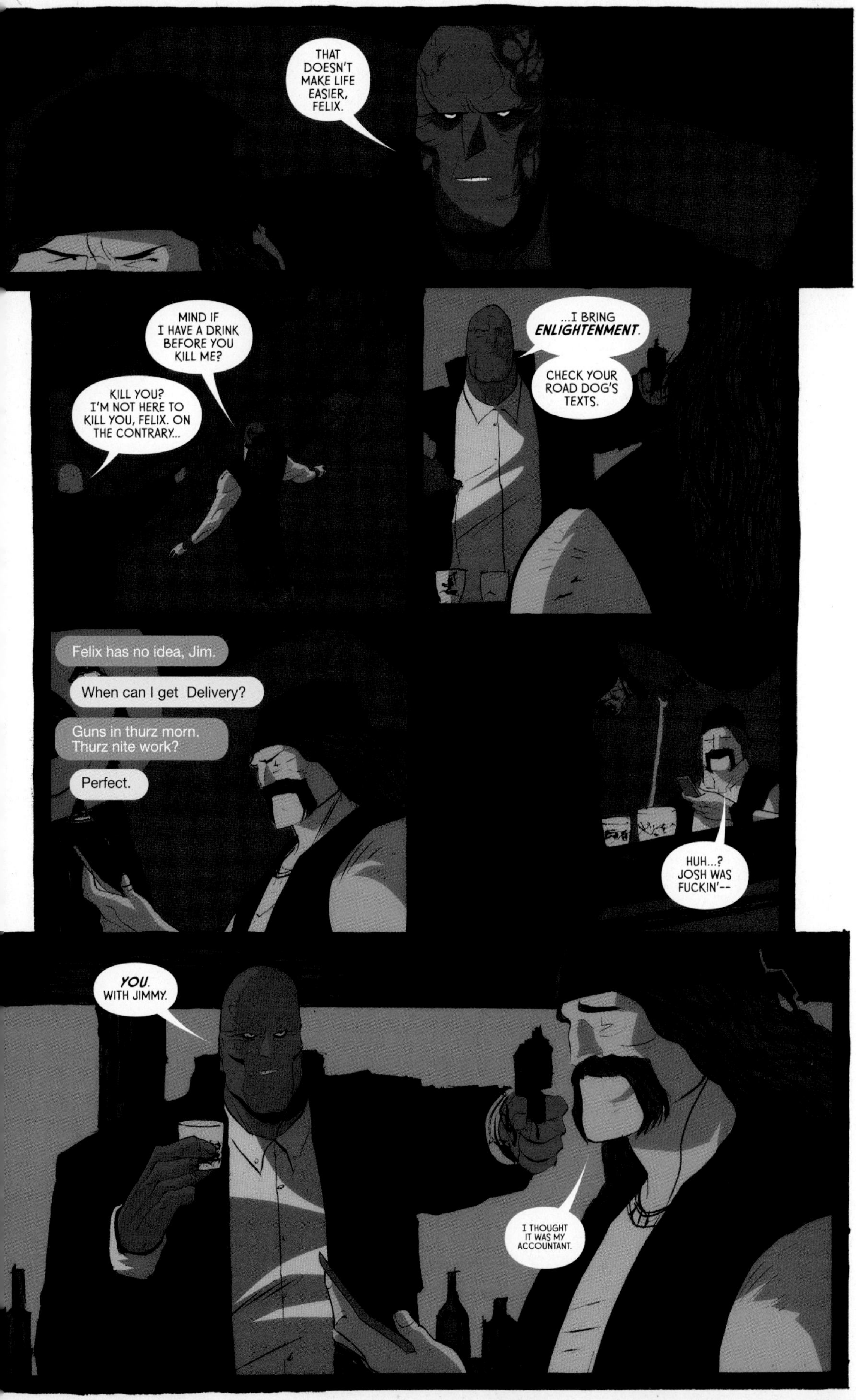
THAT DOESN'T MAKE LIFE EASIER, FELIX.
MIND IF I HAVE A DRINK BEFORE YOU KILL ME?
KILL YOU? I'M NOT HERE TO KILL YOU, FELIX. ON THE CONTRARY...
...I BRING ENLIGHTENMENT.
CHECK YOUR ROAD DOG'S TEXTS.
Felix has no idea, Jim.
When can I get Delivery?
Guns in thurz morn. Thurz nite work?
Perfect.
HUH...? JOSH WAS FUCKIN'--
YOU. WITH JIMMY.
I THOUGHT IT WAS MY ACCOUNTANT.

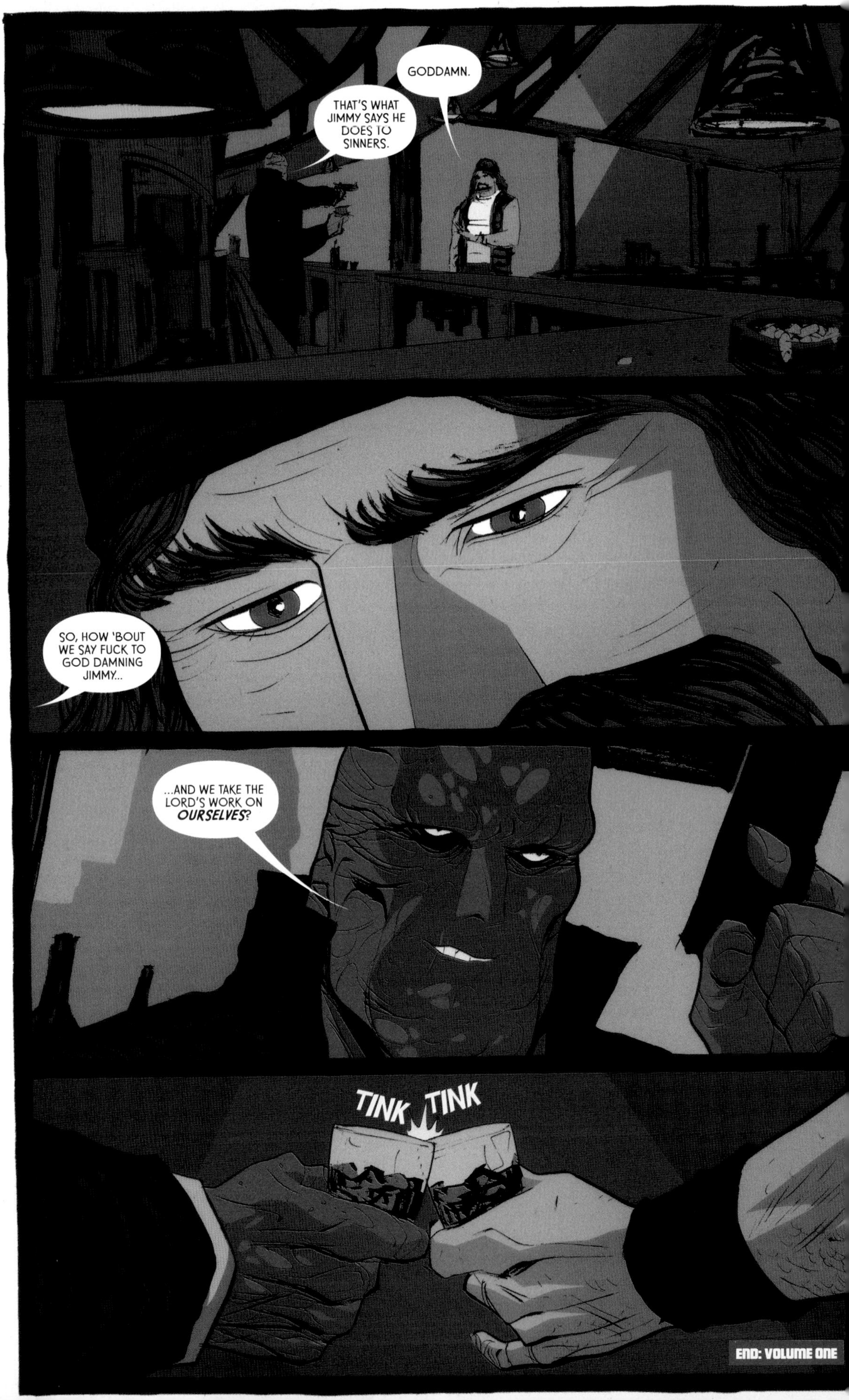
THAT'S WHAT JIMMY SAYS HE DOES TO SINNERS.
GODDAMN.
SO, HOW 'BOUT WE SAY FUCK TO GOD DAMNING JIMMY...
...AND WE TAKE THE LORD'S WORK ON *OURSELVES*?
TINK TINK
END: VOLUME ONE

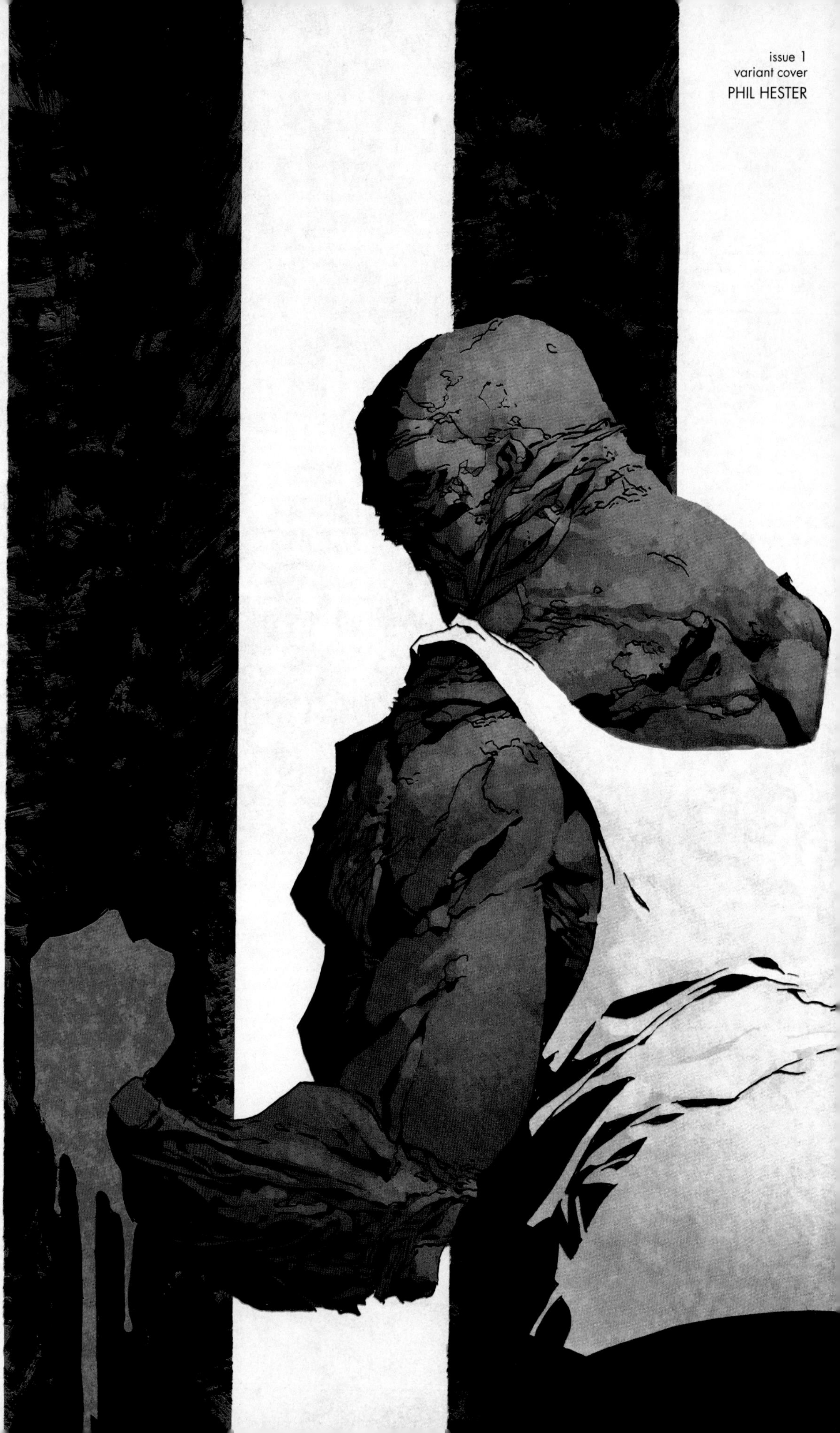

issue 1
variant cover
PHIL HESTER

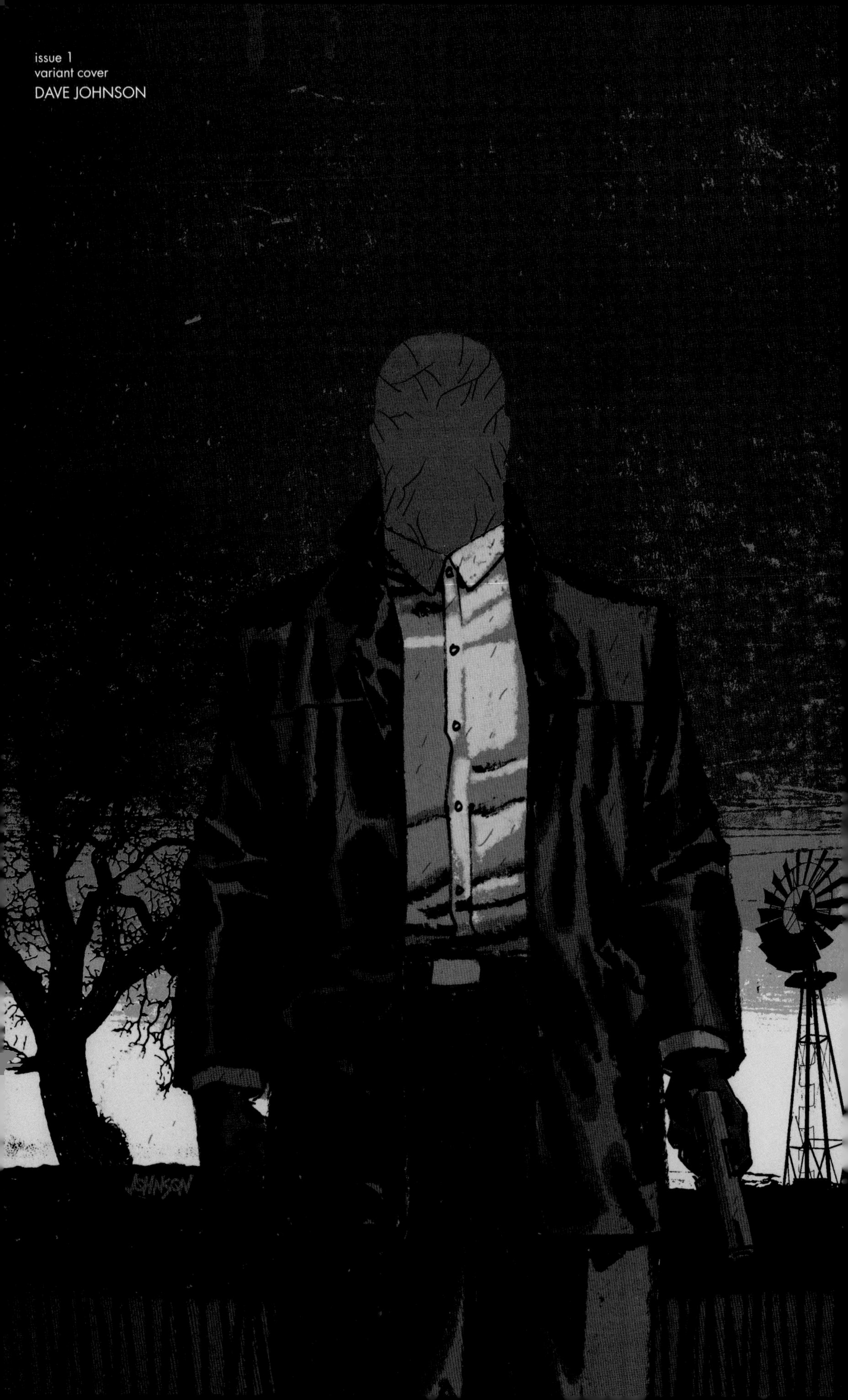
JOHNSON

issue 1
variant cover
DAVE JOHNSON

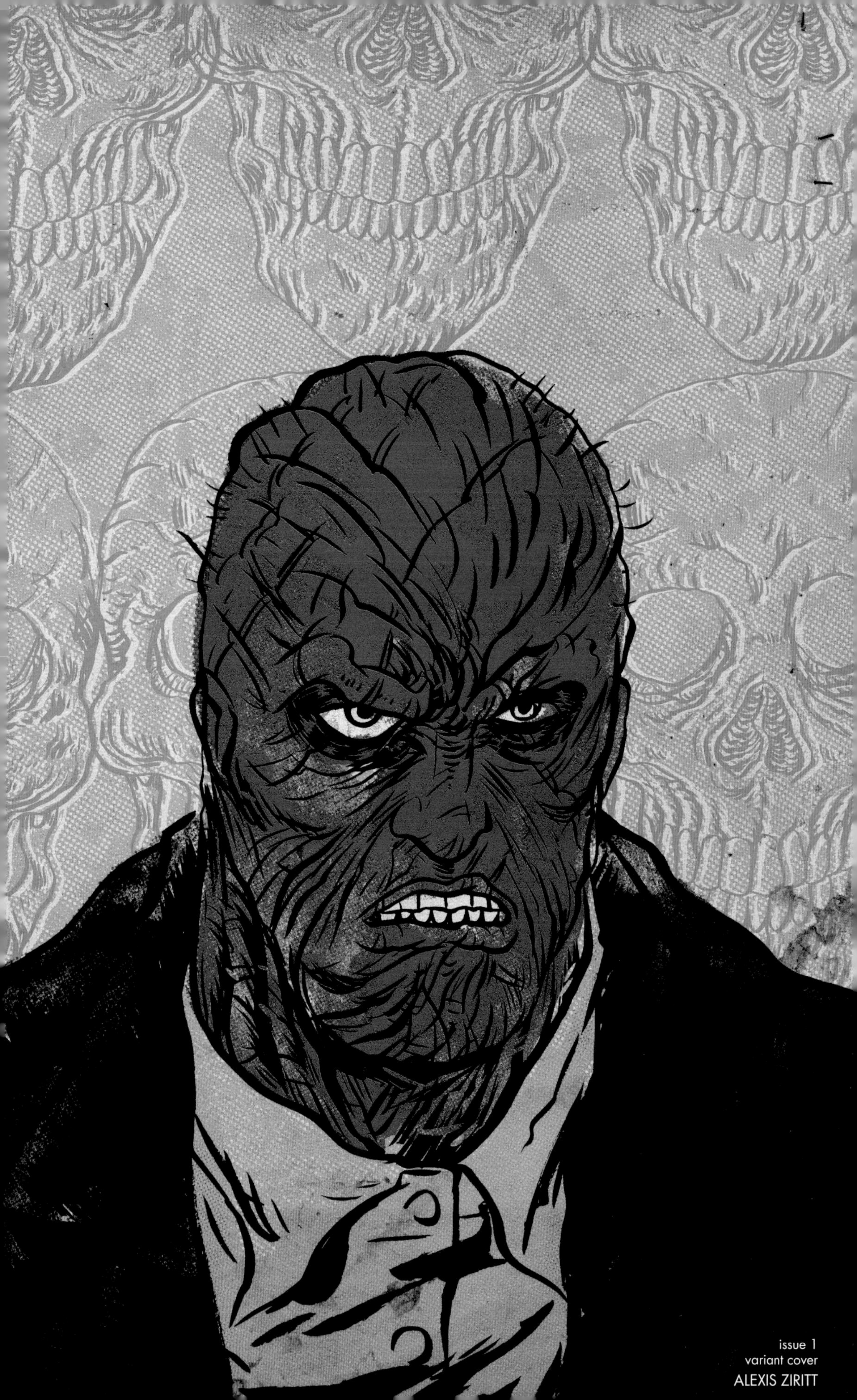
issue 1
variant cover
ALEXIS ZIRITT

BRIAN AZZARELLO
writer
🐦 @brianazzarello

Considered one of the top writers in comics and a six-time Eisner Award winner, Brian Azzarello came to prominence with his multi-Eisner and Harvey Award-winning Vertigo/DC Comics title *100 Bullets*, along with Argentine artist Eduardo Risso. His recently completed reboot of DC's *Wonder Woman* has been considered the "definitive *Wonder Woman* run" according to pastemagazine.com.

In addition, Azzarello has written *Batman*, *Sgt. Rock*, *Cage* and *Superman*. He also enjoyed a long, controversial run on Vertigo's *Hellblazer* series, and with his *Hellblazer* collaborator artist Marcelo Frusin, he created *Loveless*, a Civil War western. Later, Brian re-teamed with *100 Bullets* collaborator Eduardo Risso on the Image series *Moonshine*.

Recently, Azzarello garnered national media attention by joining legendary comic creator Frank Miller for the third installment of the iconic Batman series *The Dark Knight*, titled *The Master Race*.

JUAN DOE
artist
🐦 @juandoe

Juan Doe is a professional illustrator with over ten years experience in the comic book industry. He has produced over 100 covers and his sequential highlights include the *Fantastic Four in Puerto Rico* trilogy, *The Legion of Monsters* mini-series for Marvel and *Joker's Asylum: Scarecrow* for DC. He is currently the artist for AMERICAN MONSTER with writer Brian Azzarello and ANIMOSITY: THE RISE with writer Marguerite Bennett.